PAT SPRINGLE

Untangling Relationships

A Christian Perspective on Codependency

Learning Activities by Susan A. Lanford

LifeWay Press
Nashville, Tennessee

ACKNOWLEDGEMENTS

Untangling Relationships: A Christian Perspective on Codependency
Copyright © 1993 by Rapha Publishing

Codependency was originally co-published by Word, Inc. and Rapha Resources, Inc. and is available in its original version in Christian bookstores. We want to thank Rapha Hospital Treatment Centers for making this book available to the LifeWay Press for its use.

Rapha Hospital Treatment Centers is an independent, nationwide provider of adult and adolescent in-hospital psychiatric care and substance abuse treatment from a Christian perspective. For information about Rapha Hospital Treatment Centers you may contact Rapha at 1-800-383-HOPE or write to Rapha, 12700 Featherwood, Houston, Texas 77034.

LifeWay Press books are published by The Sunday School Board, 127 Ninth Avenue, North, Nashville, Tennessee 37234

For help for facilitators and leaders in carrying out LIFE Support ministries in your church, write Discipleship and Family Development, 127 Ninth Avenue North, Nashville, TN 31234-0151. Be sure to include your area code and phone number.

Item 7202-73   ISBN 0-8054-9973-3   Dewey Decimal Number 616.89
Subject Heading: CODEPENDENCY // COMPULSIVE BEHAVIOR

Sources for definitions in *Untangling Relationships: A Christian Perspective on Codependency*: *Webster's Ninth New Collegiate Dictionary* (Springfield, Mass.: Merriam-Webster Inc., Publishers, 1991); *Webster's New Twentieth Century Dictionary*, Unabridged Second Edition (New York: Prentice Hall Press, 1983); W.E. Vine, *The Expanded Vine's Expository Dictionary of New Testament Words* (Minneapolis, MN: Bethany House Publishers, 1984).

Unless otherwise indicated, biblical quotations are from the *New American Standard Bible*. © The Lockman Foundation, 1960, 1962, 1963, 1968, 1971, 1972, 1973, 1975, 1977. Used by permission. Other versions used: From the Holy Bible, *New International Version*, copyright © 1973, 1978, 1984 by International Bible Society (NIV); the *King James Version* (KJV); Scriptures quoted from the *International Children's Bible, New Century Version*, copyright © 1986, 1988 by Word Publishing, Dallas, Texas 75039. Used by permission (ICB); Verses marked TLB are taken from *The Living Bible*. Copyright © Tyndale House Publishers, Wheaton, Illinois, 1971. Used by permission; From *The Amplified New Testament* © The Lockman Foundation 1954, 1958, 1987. Used by permission; and From the *New King James Version*. Copyright © 1979, 1980, 1982, Thomas Nelson, Inc., Publishers.

Printed in the United States of America

To order additional copies of this resource: WRITE Customer Service Center, 127 Ninth Avenue North, Nashville, TN 37234-0113; FAX order to (615) 251-5933; PHONE 1-800-458-2772; EMAIL to Compuserve ID 70423,2526; or visit your local Baptist Book Store or LifeWay Christian Store.

Table of Contents

THE AUTHORS

Pat Springle is senior vice president of Rapha Resources. Rapha is a manager of inpatient psychiatric care and substance-abuse treatment from a distinctively Christian perspective in hospitals located nationwide. He served on the staff of Campus Crusade for Christ for 18 years.

Susan A. Lanford is a marriage and family-life conference leader and writer on family-related topics. She is a family enrichment specialist at the Baptist Sunday School Board. She wrote the learning activities for *Untangling Relationships: A Christian Perspective on Codependency* member's book and wrote the leader's guide.

LIFE Support Editorial Team
Kay Moore, Design Editor
Dale McCleskey, Editor
Debbie Colclough, Manuscript Assistant

Johnny Jones, LIFE Support Project Coordinator

What to Expect

DRIVEN BY THE PAST

When Sandy was 11 her parents divorced, leaving Sandy's mother a depressed, overworked woman. Sandy tried to make her mother happy by doing whatever her mother wanted. *If mother is happy,* she thought, *then I will be happy.* But Sandy felt unloveable and afraid. She tried to prove herself by doing well in school and in athletics. She excelled in almost everything she did, but she still felt lonely and empty inside.

Sandy thought Mike was wonderful because he was strong and assertive. His assurance made her feel secure.

After they were married instead of the sense of security she wanted she found that she felt dominated. She felt belittled by Mike's constant criticism and confused by his mixed messages like "you're wonderful, don't mess up again."

Sandy tries to please and manipulate Mike just like she tried to control her mother. Sandy is lonely, depressed, and hurting.

Can you identify in any way with Sandy? Many persons from difficult and painful backgrounds think that their families and their lives are normal because they don't have enough objectivity to see their own pain, or the manipulation, and neglect they have suffered. This book is designed to help you become more objective about your relationships and yourself so that you can experience growth and health in every aspect of your life.

Codependency is a word which often is used to describe persons who have been affected by difficult life circumstances. As a result of events either during childhood or later in life, many individuals—

- have difficulty seeing persons and situations realistically;
- feel that they are responsible for the thoughts and actions of others;
- are susceptible to control by others and are controlling of others;
- feel unhealthy amounts of hurt and anger;
- feel guilty for things about which they have no control;
- develop a life of loneliness without true intimacy.

Many of these persons find themselves in relationships with physically or psychologically abusive persons. They try hard to please, rescue, and serve others, but the harder they try, the less peace of mind, intimacy, and joy they receive for their efforts.

Untangling Relationships will help you to understand and begin to change the lifelong habits which professionals have come to call codependency. It will help you to identify those patterns of thinking, feeling, and acting. It will enable you better to understand your emotions and actions. It will teach you to use the three-part process *identify*, *detach*, and *decide* to bring real change in your life.

If you are in a relationship with a person who is guilt-riddled and compelled to fix and rescue others, *Untangling Relationships* will help you to understand this person better. It will help you to understand what that person will have to do to find recovery, and it will help you to be supportive in the process.

What's in a word?

Some diseases, like Hodgkin's disease, are named after the person who discovered the condition. Some, like Lou Gehrig's disease, are named after a famous person who suffered from the condition. Some diseases, like malaria—thought to be caused by bad air, are named after some idea about what caused the problem. In the 1970s a spiritual, emotional, and psychological syndrome first was identified among family members of chemical dependents. The combination of feelings, thought and behavior patterns at that time was named *codependency*. We since have discovered that a vast array of circumstances can cause the same problem, including any family difficulty which causes significant and unresolved hurt, anger, fear, or anxiety. Some of us have become comfortable with the term. It reminds us where we have been and how much the Lord has done in our lives. Others are irritated by the term because the word has been overused by some people.

However the term strikes you, remember that *codependent* is just a word. The word helps us to make sense out of our world and experience. As you read and work through *Untangling Relationships*, you will find that we have substituted several other terms for the word codependent. Some of those words include—

- persons with a compulsion to fix others;
- persons with a compulsion to please others;
- persons in tangled or enmeshed relationships;
- rescuers;
- persons who are driven to control others and are easily controlled by others.

What's in it for you?

After you complete a study of *Untangling Relationships* you will have the tools to identify the ways that past experience is damaging your present life or the life of someone you love. You will be equipped to begin a healing process from codependency which will bring you a clear sense of identity and a healthy relationship to the lordship of Christ built on a positive experience of the unconditional love of God.

To help you to accomplish this goal, *Untangling Relationships* will help you to learn—

- the nature of codependency and how understanding our past and ourselves helps to change the painful results of hurtful family behaviors;
- the perceptions and behaviors that make up the core of the problem;
- to identify the painful emotional results of codependency;
- the three-part process which leads to recovery from this compulsion to serve, please, help, fix, and control;
- that the goal of recovery is not simply relief from pain, or even emotional health, but the goal is a life that honors Christ;
- how to progress through the grief process which is part of recovery;

- how to develop new ways of relating to others which will bring a sense of wisdom and strength in your life;
- to recognize realistically the challenges involved in recovery.

Untangling Relationships is not merely designed for you to understand concepts. The purpose of this material is life change.

Untangling Relationships is part of the LIFE Support Series. The LIFE Support Series is an educational system of discovery-group and support-group resources for providing Christian ministry and emotional support to individuals in the areas of social, emotional, and physical need. These resources deal with such life issues as chemical dependency, codependency, recovery from sexual abuse, eating disorders, divorce recovery, and how to grieve the losses of life. Persons using LIFE-Support courses will be led through recovery to discipleship and ministry by using these courses.

Untangling Relationships is a discovery-group course that can be basic to any biblically-based support-group ministry. A discovery group studies dysfunctional family issues and other problem areas that individuals face. A group leader guides discussion of the topics and helps group members consider applications to life.

A wide variety of persons will profit from studying *Untangling Relationships*. All individuals will learn how to understand themselves better and how to relate to the hurting or difficult people in their lives. Likewise, people suffering from addictions and whose addictions mask underlying emotional pain will benefit from understanding the source of and solution for their pain. Persons in whom failure or rejection have produced depression, a need to achieve, or a need to control can benefit from the course to help them develop a healthy identity based on Christ's unconditional love and acceptance.

Untangling Relationships is an integrated course of study. To achieve the full benefit of the educational design, prepare your individual assignments and participate in the group sessions. The principles behind *Untangling Relationships* represent a lifelong learning process. This is not a course which you will study and then forget. It represents an opportunity to understand and change basic areas which have generated pain in your life.

For many persons participating in an *Untangling Relationships* group will be the beginning of a journey. The journey is not always easy, but it leads to a whole new world of healing and usefulness. After working through *Untangling Relationships*, some persons will choose to continue their growth. *Conquering Codependency: A Christ-Centered 12-Step Process* will provide the basis for further growth and healing. *Conquering Codependency* will help you to apply the biblical and effective 12-Step process to change the codependent patterns discovered in the present study.

Study Tips. Five days a week (which compose a unit) you will study a segment of content material. You may need from 30 to 60 minutes of study time each day. Even if you find that you can study the material in less time, spread the study out over five days. This will give you more time to apply the truths to your life. Study at your own pace. Your group may decide to take a longer time to study each unit. The leaders guide to *Untangling Relationships* will give you some helps on other formats for study. Do not become

How this course fits in

7

discouraged if you or your group members are unable to complete *Untangling Relationships* in 12 weeks. Remember that the purpose is life change, not speed reading. Take the time necessary to work the truths deeply into your life.

This book has been written as a tutorial text. Study it as if Pat Springle is sitting at your side helping you learn. When he asks you a question or gives you an assignment, you will benefit most by writing your response. Each assignment is indented and appears in **boldface type**. When you are to respond in writing, a pencil appears beside the assignment. For example, an assignment will look like this:

✎ **Read Psalm 139:13. Write what the verse tells about God's care for you.**

Of course, in an actual activity, a line would appear below each assignment or in the margin beside the assignment. You would write your response as indicated. Then, when you are asked to respond in a non-written fashion—for example, by thinking about or praying about a matter—a ◆▸ appears beside the assignment. This type of assignment will look like this:

◆▸ **Pause now to pray and thank God for unconditionally accepting you.**

In most cases your "personal tutor" will give you some feedback about your response—for example, you may see a suggestion about what you might have written. This process is designed to help you learn the material and apply the concepts more effectively. Do not deny yourself valuable learning by skipping the learning activities.

Set a definite time and select a quiet place where you can study with little interruption. Keep a Bible handy for times in which the material asks you to look up Scripture. Memorizing Scripture is an important part of your work. Set aside a portion of your study period for memory work. Make notes of problems, questions, or concerns that arise as you study. You will discuss many of these during your discovery-group sessions. Write these matters in the margins of this textbook so you can find them easily.

Discovery-Group Session. You will benefit most from *Untangling Relationships* if once each week you attend a discovery-group session. A group session is designed to help you discuss the content you studied the previous week, practice your memory work, share insights, look for answers to problems encountered, and apply the material to your life.

The discovery group adds a needed dimension to your learning. If you have started a study of *Untangling Relationships* and you are not involved in a group study, try to enlist some friends or associates who will work through this material with you. *Untangling Relationships Leader's Guide* provides guidance and learning activities for these sessions. (Send orders or inquiries to Customer Service Center; 127 Ninth Avenue, North; Nashville, TN 37234; call 1-800-458-2772; or visit your local book store. Ask for item 7203-73.)

A key decision

Untangling Relationships is written with the assumption that you already have received Jesus Christ as your Savior and Lord and that you have Him guiding you in the healing process. If you have not yet made the important decision to receive Christ, you will find guidance in unit 6. You will benefit far more from *Untangling Relationships* if you have Jesus working in your life and guiding you in the process.

Understanding Codependency

NEVER ENOUGH TO PLEASE

Scott is from a small midwestern town where his father is a prominent lawyer. His father is highly respected in the community, but at home, this model citizen becomes a bear. He often is verbally abusive and loud.

Scott's brothers and sisters helped each other grow up in that environment, but they didn't help Scott. His mother didn't help either. Even when Scott was taking a terrible tongue lashing she would look the other way. Taking cues from their father, his two older brothers began to pick on Scott when he was in junior high school. But they went beyond verbal abuse. They pushed him around and even beat him. Scott felt alone—very much alone. Though he was bright, witty, and a good athlete, Scott never could do enough to please his parents. He looked for ways to make them proud of him, but instead of approving of him, his parents criticized him. (Read more about Scott on page 11.)

What you'll learn

This week you will—

- glimpse the world of codependency in which Scott and others like him live;
- review God's plan for family life and see the consequences of not following His plan;
- understand every person's need to be loved and valued;
- learn to define codependency;
- recognize the difference between superficial and lasting solutions to the problems codependency causes.

What you'll study

Glimpses of the Problem	The Causes of Codependency	The Need to Be Loved/ The Need to Feel Valued	A Definition of Codependency	Superficial Solutions
DAY 1	DAY 2	DAY 3	DAY 4	DAY 5

Memory verse

This week's passage of Scripture to memorize

The LORD sustains all who fall, And raises up all who are bowed down. The LORD is near to all who call upon Him, To all who call upon Him in truth.
                                                                                    –Psalm 145:14,18

Glimpses of the Problem

Codependent . . . a strange word, isn't it? Although it may sound unusual, codependency is becoming a familiar term to many people. Some psychologists define **codependency** as an excessive and unhealthy compulsion to rescue and take care of people. One author said a codependent is someone "who has let another person's behavior affect him or her, and who is obsessed with controlling that person's behavior."[1]

A compulsion to rescue

A few years ago, a friend told me: "Pat, you are overly responsible. You try to help everybody and fix everything. Lighten up!" At the time, I took his statements as praise, but I've since learned those words were not so complimentary after all!

Many people I meet are like me.

They feel responsible yet they feel guilty.

- They feel responsible for almost everybody and everything, yet they also feel guilty much of the time.
- They still feel they can't measure up, no matter how much they succeed.
- They can accurately analyze everyone else's problems, but they cannot see their own.
- They often feel they are responsible for making other people both happy and successful.
- They can't say no to any request without feeling guilty for doing so.
- They are extremists: life is either wonderful or awful.
- They often feel they must be in complete control of their lives, homes, and families at all times.
- They sometimes give up on life; they become irresponsible and out of control.

Trying harder and harder

- They try harder and harder, but their increased intensity and commitment often result in more introspection, rather than more growth; more compulsion, rather than more joy and peace; and more distance in relationships, rather than more intimacy.

 Look again at the above phrases describing a codependent. Underline key words which best seem to describe codependency. Notice that some phrases seem positive and some seem negative.

You may have underlined things like try harder, responsible, and able to analyze others' problems, which are positive traits if they aren't taken to extremes. You may have also underlined guilty, can't measure up, and blind to their own problems as the negative results of codependency.

The dilemma of codependency is that seemingly positive actions, like trying harder, only produce negative feelings.

The dilemma of codependency is that seemingly positive actions, like trying harder, only produce negative feelings, like "I can't measure up." Because of this dilemma, codependents often feel caught in a trap. They're like the proverbial rat on a treadmill—running as fast as it can but getting nowhere. Codependents need to get out of the trap and off the treadmill if they ever are to live more objective and healthy lives.

✎ Codependents take some normally positive character traits to destructive extremes. In your own words describe in what ways you have seen people take to a harmful extreme one or more of the positive traits like being responsible, caring, perceptive, and capable. I have given you an example.

April felt so responsible for her husband's drinking that she was unable to allow him to face the consequences of his own irresponsibility.

Your example(s)_____

_____

_____

Scott's story

Scott is from a small midwestern town where his father is a prominent lawyer. His mother is a high school chemistry teacher. He has two brothers and two sisters—all four considerably older than he is. His father is highly respected in the community, but at home, this model citizen is a bear. He often is verbally abusive and loud.

Scott's brothers and sisters helped each other grow up in that environment, but they didn't help Scott. He was the kid brother—the "odd man out." His mother didn't help, either. Even when Scott was taking a terrible tongue-lashing from his father, his mother looked the other way—and got a drink of alcohol. Her method of coping with the anger in her family was measured in pints, fifths, and quarts.

Instead of approving of him, Scott's parents criticized him for not doing better.

His two brothers, taking cues from their father, began to pick on Scott when he was in junior high school. But they went beyond verbal abuse. They pushed him around and even beat him. Scott felt alone—very much alone. Though he was bright, witty, and a good athlete, Scott never could do enough to please his parents. He tried to make them proud of him, but instead of approving of him, his parents criticized him for not doing better.

Scott and I talked about his family. I asked him if he had any particularly painful memories. He recalled several specific incidents—like his father's screaming at him for normal childhood mistakes. He also remembered his mother's leaving him alone and defenseless before his father's wrath—no comfort from her. He remembered a particularly bad beating from his oldest brother one day after school. Then he remembered the bicycle. Scott's father always bought each of his children a new bike on their 12th birthday. When the fourth sibling turned 12, four nice bikes were lined up in the garage, and Scott knew his turn was coming. As his 12th birthday approached, he could hardly wait for his bike. Almost every day for weeks he had stopped at the bike shop. He had just the right one picked out!

On his birthday, Scott hurried down to breakfast and found a box on the breakfast table. Puzzled, he tore open the box and found a football. He looked at his father with an expression of anxiety mixed with fading hope. Was the football in addition to the bike? His father snorted, "I hope you like the ball."

"But . . . what about my bike, Dad?"

"But . . . what about my bike, Dad?" Scott asked. "Is that the thanks I get for giving you a birthday present?" his father snarled in reply. "Besides, I couldn't afford to get you a bike. I just bought a new boat yesterday. It'll be here tomorrow." The boat sat in the garage for years. Scott's father rarely used it. Every time Scott walked into the garage and saw four bicycles and that boat, he had to look the other way. It still hurt too much.

Scott had to look the other way. It still hurt too much.

Today, Scott still tries to control his parents' attitudes by doing whatever they ask him to do. No matter how hard tries to fix, rescue, and help, he considers himself a failure. He is plagued by nightmares, and he has difficulty controlling his thoughts. Though he is a tenderhearted and perceptive man, he has very few, if any, deep friendships. He feels very lonely.

Richard and Betty's story

When Richard started dating Betty, he could tell she was someone who knew how to have a good time! She was the life of the party. Sometimes she drank a little too much, but he'd excuse her by saying, "That's just Betty. She'll be all right." After they married, Betty's drinking became a problem. "It helps me relax," she explained. When she felt bad and didn't clean the house, Richard did it for her. When she was hung over and couldn't go to work, she asked Richard to call and tell her boss she was sick. The first few times, Richard made the call as he rationalized, "It surely won't happen again." But it did.

Betty's drinking progressively worsened. To cover for Betty's irresponsibility, Richard gave excuses to everyone they knew. He worked hard at his job. He worked hard at home—washing clothes, cleaning house, cooking meals. And he worked hard making excuses for Betty.

Richard thought, "Maybe a child will help Betty; maybe she will stop drinking and be OK." Ashley was born after their fifth anniversary. Instead of helping Betty stop drinking and become more responsible, Richard did even more. He was both mother and father to Ashley. He loved Betty and Ashley, but he was constantly tired and so easily angered by their demands. Then he felt guilty, especially for being angry at his little girl. Richard's life was a wreck!

Codependents usually feel "false guilt."

The problem for codependents with feeling guilty is this: they usually feel "false guilt." In fact, though they may say a certain act or thought makes them "feel guilty," what they are really expressing is, "I feel shame" or "I feel ashamed." This "shame-based identity" happens after you feel the shame of another person's behavior for a long time—for so long you accept it as your shame, too.[2]

Codependency frequently results from involvement in **dysfunctional** relationships—like Scott's with his parents and like Richard's with Betty. Read the definition of the term **dysfunctional family** in the box below:

> **dysfunctional family**–n. a family in which some behavior such as alcoholism, drug abuse, divorce, an absent father or mother, excessive anger, verbal or physical abuse interferes with the ability of the family to do its job effectively.

objectivity–n. expressing or using facts apart from self-consciousness, and without distortion by personal feelings or prejudices.

All codependents, when they are honest with themselves, have concluded that they are unworthy of love and acceptance. Interestingly, many codependents do not feel these hurts. Denial is their defense against them—"I'm OK!" "Everything's fine!" "Oh no, I'm not angry!" Gaining any **objectivity** about themselves is a long, slow process.

Codependency has six basic characteristics. The first three are perceptions and behaviors. They can be thought of as primary characteristics in the sense that they are our own responses.

Six basic characteristics

1. A lack of **objectivity**
2. A warped sense of **responsibility**
3. Being easily **controlled** and **controlling** others

The next three characteristics are the emotional results of codependent perceptions and behaviors. They could be considered the side effects, or secondary characteristics of the condition.

4. Being hurt and angry
5. Feeling guilty
6. Loneliness

The course map summarizes the origin, nature, and cure for codependency.

✎ As you study *Untangling Relationships* you will become familiar with the course map on the inside back cover. The course map is a single picture which summarizes the origin, nature, and cure for codependency. The first portion of the map, showing the characteristics of codependency, is reproduced below. Underline the three perceptions and behaviors and circle the three emotional results of the disease.

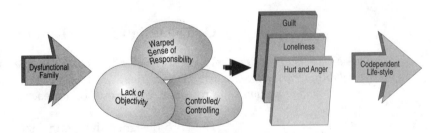

Don't misunderstand! Every person who feels angry or guilty is not necessarily codependent, but a person who experiences the three primary characteristics of codependency will experience hurt and anger, guilt, and loneliness as well.

Earlier you read the stories of Scott and Richard. In the margin box identify the characteristics of codependency these two main characters show.

Are you codependent? Do you have a family member or a friend who is codependent? How do codependents get help? Can a codependent change? *Untangling Relationships* is designed to help "turn on the lights" in your life. It enables you to understand yourself—to say, "That's why I feel this way! That's why I act this way!"

Your answers to the margin activity could include all of the characteristics. Both Scott and Richard displayed a lack of objectivity and a warped sense of responsibility. Both became controlling and felt the three painful results of codependency in their tangled relationships.

✎ **Find this unit's Scripture passage in your Bible. Mark it. Read it five times. Pray that you will persist this week in memorizing it.**

List the codependent characteristics

of Scott: _____

_____

_____

of Richard: _____

_____

_____

DAY 2

The Causes of Codependency

Codependency makes more sense as we grow in our understanding of families—healthy ones and dysfunctional ones. First we'll look at God's plan for the family. Since He first imagined the idea of family, created the first family, and filled His Word with images of family, He is the best place to start when we study about families.

God's Design for the Family

God has a plan that provides stability, security, love and protection.

The best news today's families need to hear is this: God has a plan! His plan for all families, and for your family, provides stability, security, love, protection, and provision for each family member.

The Lord designed the family as the first place where we experience His love and strength. God intends for husband-wife relationships and parent-child relationships to reflect and model our relationship with Him. The health of these relationships shapes our view of God and our self-concept.

Husbands

<u>Husbands</u>: The Bible instructs a husband to cherish his wife, to take time to understand her, to provide for her, enjoy her, and love her in the same way Christ loves His people (Read about this in Ephesians 5:25-33; 1 Peter 3:7; Colossians 3:19; Proverbs 5:15-19).

Wives

<u>Wives</u>: In response to this strong and tender love, the Bible tells the wife to respect her husband, enjoy her relationship with him, and develop her own identity and skills as she helps to provide for the family's needs (Read about this in Ephesians 5:22-33; 1 Peter 3:1-6; Colossians 3:18; Proverbs 31:10-31). God intends for the husband and wife to form an intimate unit with a common purpose, but to keep distinct, individual identities.

discipline–n. Everything a parent does to guide and teach children to direct their own lives and to take responsibility for what they do. It involves supervision, love, correction, and teaching.[4]

<u>Parents</u>: Loving **discipline** of a child prevents many difficulties in relationships throughout life. Both parents provide this caring and careful discipline. Some people think mothers are supposed to be tender and fathers are supposed to be tough, but in God's design, both are to be tender and compassionate (Learn more by reading Luke 15:4-24; Psalm 103:13; Genesis 25:28; Exodus 2; 1 Thessalonians 2:7,11), and both are to be strong (Learn more by reading Proverbs 13:24; 31:10-31; Ephesians 6:4).

✎ From the previous page choose one of the Scriptures from the paragraph about husbands, one from the paragraph about wives, and one from the paragraph about parents. Find the passages in your Bible and read them. Then fill in the following chart. In column 1, record the Scripture reference; in column 2, list key thoughts the Scripture contains about the healthy traits adult family members need to show; in column 3, record an example of that trait from your family or a family you know.

Healthy traits in families

	Scripture reference	Key thoughts	Examples of this trait
Husband			
Wife			
Parent			

A committed marriage

As I filled in this chart, I read Proverbs 5:15-19 about husbands. I was reminded of how important lifelong commitment to marriage is, and I thought about a couple celebrating their 40th wedding anniversary this year.

I read Proverbs 31:10-31 about a wife who worked hard all her life for the benefit of family and community. I thought of two grandmothers; both were single, working mothers, committed Christians, and involved church members as they reared their families.

I read in Psalm 103:13 how God's compassion is the model for parents and was reminded of the parent in our church who keeps his family active and committed to Christ while his spouse struggles with chronic illness. The Scriptures remind me that the burden of family health must be borne by caring, forgiving, responsible, and mature adults.

The burden of family health must be borne by caring, forgiving, responsible, and mature adults.

affirmation–n. a positive statement or action intended to confirm another's worth and value.[5]

self-discipline–n. the ability to take control of and responsibility for one's life[6]

Children: God intends for children to experience the consistent, loving discipline that is so important to their development. Without discipline, they have no boundaries, no clear sense of right and wrong, and no concept of the consequences of behavior. Healthy discipline requires **affirmation**, warmth, comfort, time, and attention so children come to believe they are valuable, special people. Children need a balance of both love and limits. When they have healthy, loving discipline, children develop their own inner convictions and values—**self-discipline**. Parental boundaries help children mature so that they may be weaned from external discipline.

When I learned...

_____

_____

_____

_____

How old were you at that time?

_____

Can you recall an experience from your childhood when you realized that your parents' limits or expectations had a positive influence on you? In the box in the margin describe that experience.

Signs of Functional Families

Functional, or healthy, families provide their members some of these positive qualities listed below. In dysfunctional families, one finds an absence of, or at least too little of, these qualities people need to become healthy and secure.

- unconditional love
- unconditional acceptance
- forgiveness
- laughter
- time to work and play together
- attention
- fun
- freedom to express emotions appropriately
- sense of personal worth

- compassion
- comfort
- honesty
- freedom to have your own opinion and your own identity
- objectivity
- affirmation
- friendship
- appropriate responsibility
- loving correction

Favorite family member

 Identify two of your favorite family members, past or present. Beside their names, write one or two qualities from the list above they contributed to you or your family.

1. _____

2. _____

Review the signs of a functional family in the above list. Rank their importance by placing a 1 by the quality you consider most important, a 2 by the quality you consider next in importance, and so on. Try to decide on at least your top 5!

Why did you select those particular characteristics?

_____

_____

To the degree that development of these healthy characteristics is hindered, family members are hindered in their spiritual, emotional, and relational well-being. Among the many problems in dysfunctional families is the compulsion to rescue, fix, and control people and situations, to fill in the emotional void they feel from so many unmet needs. We call this problem _codependency_.

We call the compulsion to rescue and to be in control codependency.

Dysfunctional Families

Strong, loving families seem rare in our culture. Our thirst for personal success and self-indulgent pleasures distorts God's design for the family. Selfishness replaces unconditional love in both husband-wife and parent-child relationships. We value positions, possessions, and pleasure above people and relationships. Spouses and children who interfere with our pursuits are considered nuisances, so much so that divorce has grown to epidemic proportions. Between 1960 and 1980, the divorce rate jumped from nine out of every 1,000 women to 23 per 1,000—a 255% increase in only 20 years! Divorce statistics provide only one of many examples that people and families are dysfunctional—that they are not functioning the ways God intended.

 What other trends have you noticed in our society today that are harming the family? Describe the dysfunctional behaviors you have seen in—

A dysfunctional society

. . . politics _____

_____

. . . education _____

_____

. . . the church _____

_____

You may have noted that our entire society is affected by dysfunctional behaviors. The institutions of government, education, and the church are often like a dysfunctional family. Dysfunctional families do not provide the security, love, and acceptance all their members so desperately need. They contain some painful characteristics with the corresponding absence of some needed, positive characteristics.

Use the box in the margin to describe how one or more dysfunctional behaviors has affected your life. For instance you might have a healthy home background and yet have experienced dysfunction in another area.

> ### How dysfunction has affected me—
>
> _____
>
> _____
>
> _____
>
> _____
>
> _____

Signs of Dysfunctional Families

- alcoholism
- drug addiction
- workaholism
- divorce
- eating disorders
- sexual disorders
- absent father
- absent mother
- neglect
- verbal abuse
- emotional abuse
- physical abuse
- sexual abuse
- domineering father/passive mother
- domineering mother/passive father

 As you read the list, one or more family members may come to mind. Reread the list and circle traits describing those family members.

Review the signs of a dysfunctional family. Rank their negative impact on families by placing a 1 by the quality you consider most hurtful, a 2 by the quality you consider next most hurtful, and so on. Try again to decide on at least your top five.

Why do you believe the signs which you selected are most hurtful?

_____

_____

Real, genuine, and honest relationships are far better than perfect relationships.

Obviously no family is perfect, but perfection is not the goal of family relationships. Real, genuine, and honest relationships are far better than perfect relationships. We all suffer from the devastating effects of sin. Families are created to provide some of the stability, security, love, protection, and provision each member so desperately needs. The painful proofs of dysfunctional families are many and varied. Consider these examples.

Examples of dysfunction

- The wife of a drug addict tries desperately to help him by making excuses for him. She finds a job because he wastes so much money on pills. Inside she is furious, but outwardly she smiles and denies that a problem exists.

- A business executive pours his life into his job while he neglects his family. He receives promotion after promotion, as he hopes to prove to his parents that he is worthy of their respect.

- An elderly widow, whose husband was addicted to prescription drugs and committed suicide, expects her children to provide for her every need. They do, but she still nags them constantly. None of them is happy.

She continues to feel repulsive and dirty.

- A college student is called "spacey" because she never seems to pay attention. No one realizes she was sexually abused as a child. Her drive to fix her parents' crumbling marriage is coupled with an overpowering fear of her father. She continues to feel repulsive and dirty and has withdrawn from everyone around her in an attempt to block her pain.

Secretly he wonders if his mother was right when she said—"You won't amount to anything!"

- A youth pastor is very disciplined in his personal life and expects—actually demands—the high school students involved at his church to be just as committed and disciplined as he is. He is often disappointed by their lack of maturity, or rebellion, or failure to do all he asked them to do. He appears to be the epitome of confidence and security, but secretly he wonders if his mother was right when she said—it seemed at least a hundred times—"You won't amount to anything!"

✏️ **Do you know individuals who are like these people?** ❏ Yes ❏ No

If you do, write their names in the margin beside "their" story.

Tragically, the painful consequences dysfunctional families create do not end with the children. The law of sowing and reaping in family life means the consequences will be duplicated generation after generation until the impact is diluted over time, or until someone has the insight and courage necessary to change the course of a family's history.

I, the LORD your God, am a jealous God, visiting the iniquity of the fathers on the children, and on the third and fourth generations of those who hate Me, but showing lovingkindness to thousands, to those who love Me and keep My commandments.

–Deuteronomy 5:9-10

✏️ **Read Deuteronomy 5:9-10 printed in the margin. Choose one of the five examples of dysfunction described above. Imagine that you are a child from the family in the example you have chosen. How might the family problems from the previous generation affect you as a member of the next generation?**

_____

The passage you just read from Deuteronomy seems harsh. We do not understand and want to explain away the idea of God "visiting the iniquity of the fathers on the children." Note what the passage clearly states—that our behavior radically affects our children just as our parents' behavior has radically affected our lives. Our loving God expects us to give a Christ-honoring heritage that will be a blessing to our children rather than a legacy of dysfunction. Could any language be too strong to emphasize that fact?

Review the Scripture passage again. In the margin box describe the great promise the passage gives parents who honestly seek to change their family history of dysfunction by loving God and keeping His commandments.

SUMMARY STATEMENTS

- God's plan is for the family to provide consistent discipline in an atmosphere of unconditional love.
- The health of husband-wife and parent-child relationships we experience shapes our view of God and our self concept.
- Real, genuine, and honest relationships are far better than perfect relationships.
- Dysfunctional families do not provide the security, love, and acceptance all their members so desperately need.

Hope for the codependent

Deuteronomy 5:9-10 gives me hope because . . .

_____

_____

_____

_____

DAY 3

All people need to be loved and to have a sense of worth or value.

The Need to Be Loved/ The Need to Feel Valued

All people are created with God-given needs to be loved and to have a sense of worth or value. God intends to meet these needs through two key resources—His grace extended through Christ and the reflection of His grace and strength in the family. The powerful influences of grace and family are not meant to function separately. People most profoundly experience God's love, forgiveness, and strength in families that model God's character for the children.

The Influence of the Family

You cannot overestimate the family's influence on a person's development. A child can grow up in a home where Christian parents are too strict, critical, or neglectful. The result will be a hurting, guilt-ridden, driven, overly responsible, or passive person—a codependent. On the other hand, a child can be nurtured and protected in a home where parents aren't believers. The warmth, affection, attention, and strength in this family will more likely produce a stable, secure child than will a codependent, Christian household.

This may sound like heresy to you, but children don't care much about theological correctness. They do care about being loved. Children need to be loved. For them, love means not just words but time, attention, and affection. They need time to relax, study, and play; to be listened to, to be comforted when they hurt, and to be praised when they do well. Parents can do these things; impersonal theology can't! Good theology is crucially important, but good theology is always lived out in loving actions.

Codependents long to be loved. They desperately want to possess a sense of worth and specialness. Those needs are God-given, but a codependent family often withholds the resources to meet those needs.

Look back at day 2 page 16, and review the signs of a functional family. In the margin box write the names of at least three persons you know who show others that they are loved and valued.

✎ **Review the signs of a dysfunctional family on page 17. Can you think of three individuals whose actions prevent people from believing they are loved and valued?** ❏ Yes ❏ No

◆ **Take a moment to pray. Thank God for the three persons you identified whose actions show people that they are loved and valued. Pray for the persons whose actions tear others down and prevent them from believing they are loved and valued.**

The Longing for Love and Value

Healthy families meet the needs for love, security, and self-worth of the members. Dysfunctional families leave these needs unmet. The following chart will help you compare how families deal with individual needs. The chart contrasts outward conditions, called *environment*, the *results* that family environment creates, and the *motivation* behind the family member's actions.

<table>
<tr><td colspan="4">Individual Needs: Love Security Worth Protection Provision</td></tr>
<tr><td></td><td>Environment</td><td>Results</td><td>Motivation</td></tr>
<tr><td>Healthy Families</td><td>Functional Family: the freedom to feel love, honesty, acceptance, safety, provision for needs, loving discipline</td><td>Spiritual, emotional, relational health: love, anger, fear, laughter, intimacy, willingness to take risks</td><td>Healthy Motives: love, thankfulness, obedience out of gratitude</td></tr>
<tr><td>Dysfunctional Families</td><td>Dysfunctional Family: (alcoholism, drug abuse, eating disorders, etc.): condemnation, rejection, destructive criticism, manipulation, neglect, abuse, unreality, denial</td><td>Codependency: lack of objectivity, warped sense of responsibility, controlled/controlling, guilt, hurt and anger, loneliness</td><td>Compulsive Motives: avoid pain, fear of rejection, fear of failure, gain a sense of worth, accomplish goals to win approval</td></tr>
</table>

Three persons I know who show people they are loved and valued

1. _____

2. _____

3. _____

How families meet needs

Your family of origin

✎ Use the chart you have just studied to think about the family in which you grew up. Carefully note the descriptions the chart gives of healthy and dysfunctional families. Place an *X* on the number on each of the following scales that describes the health or dysfunction in the family of your childhood.

Environment
Dysfunctional 0 1 2 3 4 5 6 7 8 9 10 Healthy

Results
Dysfunctional 0 1 2 3 4 5 6 7 8 9 10 Healthy

Motivation
Dysfunctional 0 1 2 3 4 5 6 7 8 9 10 Healthy

Your family today

✎ Think about the family in which you now live. Place an *X* on the spot on the scales below that describes the health or dysfunction in your present family.

Environment
Dysfunctional 0 1 2 3 4 5 6 7 8 9 10 Healthy

Results
Dysfunctional 0 1 2 3 4 5 6 7 8 9 10 Healthy

Motivation
Dysfunctional 0 1 2 3 4 5 6 7 8 9 10 Healthy

Use the margin box to describe the aspects of your family of origin and your present family that are similar. Use specific words from the chart to explain your answer. Describe the ways the two families are different. Again, use specific words from the chart to explain your answer.

Recall the Scripture at the end of yesterday's material. Is your family history more like

"visiting the iniquity of the fathers on the children, and on the third and fourth generations"?   ❏ Yes   ❏ No

or

"lovingkindness to thousands"?   ❏ Yes   ❏ No

➨ Review: Where in the Bible do you find this unit's memory verse?

_____ Find it in your Bible.

Try to memorize the first four lines.

How my present family is *like* my family of origin—

_____

_____

_____

_____

How my present family is *unlike* my family of origin—

_____

_____

_____

_____

SUMMARY STATEMENTS

- All people are created with God-given needs to be loved and to have a sense of worth.
- God intends to meet those needs through Christ and the reflection of His grace in the family.
- You cannot overestimate the family's continuing influence in a person's life, character, and personality.

A Definition of Codependency

Therapists in the 1970s treating alcoholism coined the term *codependency*. They observed that most alcoholics shared a consistent set of behaviors. As these therapists began treating families of alcoholics, they likewise observed in the family members fairly predictable patterns of behavior. The alcoholic depends on alcohol; the family members take their cues about acceptable behavior, feelings, decisions, and thoughts from the alcoholic, so they began to be called codependent. Although originally applied to people in alcoholic families, the term codependency is now used to describe families of those dependent on any kind of drug, including alcohol.

Some kinds of dysfunctions are very subtle.

Today the word is used to describe anyone in a significant relationship with a person who exhibits any kind of dependency. Some of these dependencies are more subtle than others. Here are some examples of things to which people can become addicted:

> * alcohol   * work   * perfectionism
> * drugs   * sex   * success
> * food   * gambling   * even religion(!)

Harmed and driven

Those harmed by the dependent person's behavior and driven by an out-of-balance responsibility to rescue, fix, and/or help the dependent person are codependent.

The dependent, addicted person—consciously or unconsciously—deprives the codependents of love and attention they need. This promotes codependents to obtain the affirmation they need by rescuing the dependent person. For example:

• A young man has parents who, by all appearances, seem to be stable. However, his mother is demanding and his father is passive. This young man doesn't think of his family as dysfunctional, yet his response to their behavior is a drivenness to fix their problems and those of everyone around him.

She feels it is her responsibility to make her mother happy.

• A woman from a divorced home feels it is her responsibility to rescue her mother and make her mother happy. Yet her responses to her mother's behavior only make her feel like a failure.

Notice, neither of these families is characterized by alcoholism or drug abuse, but both the young man and the adult woman are compulsive fixers and helpers. To some degree, they also are codependent because of their need to rescue others—a need born in tangled relationships with people they both love. Many such codependents marry persons with some form of addiction.

Everybody, it seems, has a personal definition for codependency. Here are some examples.

> • Codependency is a bondage to pleasing somebody.
> • It is being controlled by someone and trying to control that someone.

- It is being dependent on making someone else happy.
- Codependency is the responsibility sensed to make others happy, successful, and good.
- It is feeling guilty when everything is not done just right—and that's all the time.
- Codependency is trying to make a sick person well but ending up sick instead.

✎ **What other definitions of codependency have you heard from the media, books, speakers, or friends?**

_____

Review all of week 1's material to this point. Write your own definition of codependency.

_____

Codependency is an identity problem, a behavior problem, and a relationship problem.

You may have defined codependency from one of several points of view: 1. as an identity problem (being so tied into another's life and behavior that my responses to that person define who I am); 2. a behavioral problem (acting in ways to control others or rescue others); or 3. a relational problem (living in an absorbing, consuming relationship with a needy person).

You'll find that *Untangling Relationships: A Christian Perspective on Codependency* focuses most on the behavioral problems of codependency and tries to help you understand better the codependent's driving need to control and rescue other people. In the process, don't miss this message: the troubling behaviors come from a person's deep needs going unmet throughout life and from difficult, tangled relationships with people who should have been meeting some of those needs.

"Are all people codependent? Is it bad to be codependent?"

Some have asked, "Are all people codependent?" No, they aren't. All people have experienced the effects of sin and, to a degree, have lived with the misery of codependency's six characteristics. But codependents experience these difficulties at a much greater level. Some also have asked, "Is it 'bad' to be codependent?" No again, if bad means evil. Codependency is bad because anything victimizing a person is bad.

Destructive ways to cope

Codependents are deeply wounded people who have found less than ideal ways to cope. Sadly, at some point the codependent usually moves from being a victim to a victimizer. The cycle of dysfunction continues whether the addiction or dependency which started it continues or not. "Visiting the iniquity . . . on the third and fourth generation . . ." (Deuteronomy 5:9).

How Do You Know?

How do you know if you are codependent? First, look at your relationships. The rule of thumb is this: If you are in a close (typically family) relationship with someone who is addicted, abusive, neglectful, or condemning, and if you feel that you are responsible for making him or her happy, then you probably are codependent.

✎ **Are you in a close relationship with someone who is addicted or who is abusive, neglectful, or condemning of you?** ❑ Yes ❑ No

Explain your relationship to this person (spouse, grandchild, etc.):

_____

From what you know to this point, do you feel you might be a codependent person? ❑ **Yes** ❑ **No**

Second, study carefully the six characteristics of codependency in the next several units of this course. If you see that these characteristics—especially the first three—describe you and your life, then you probably are codependent.

You may be a second- or third-generation codependent.

Even if your parents, your spouse, or your children are not abusive or addicted, you may be a second- or third-generation codependent. Perhaps your grandparents or great-grandparents had these kinds of dependent behaviors, and the family still feels the effects. "Visiting the iniquity . . . to the third and fourth generation . . ." (Deuteronomy 5:9).

✎ **Look back at day 1 of this unit on page 13 and review the six characteristics of codependency. Which one do you feel you most need to understand?**

_____

Codependents are some of the most wonderful people on earth.

Are we saying codependents are terrible people? Certainly not! Codependents are some of the most generous, sensitive, bright, articulate, efficient, effective, and wonderful people on earth. At the same time, they are hurting, lonely people who desperately want to be loved. Consequently, they try to fix people and things. They try to make others happy without thinking of their own happiness. They allow themselves to be controlled by the praise or condemnation of others while they also try to control their own lives.

Codependents give up their own identity, their own ideas, and their own emotions. Instead, they force themselves to feel and act in ways that please other people. Why? Because they so desperately want to be loved. Ultimately, these coping behaviors don't work.

No matter how hard they try—and some try so hard they endure emotional or physical breakdowns, while others give up and escape into their own world of self-indulgence—their needs for love, worth, and significance go unmet.

✎ **Today's material described codependency. Think creatively for a moment. What does codependency—**

look like? _____

_____

feel like? _____

_____

sound like? _____

◆✦ **Review:** Try to write from memory this unit's Scripture passage. Find the passage and check your memory. Then memorize any part which you were unable to remember.

_____

_____

_____

_____

SUMMARY STATEMENTS

- The term codependent came from the field of alcoholism treatment but now is used to describe a much wider group.
- *Codependent* is not a bad word. Codependents are some of the most generous, sensitive, bright, articulate, efficient, effective, and wonderful people on earth.
- Codependents also are hurting, lonely people who desperately want to be loved.

DAY 5

Superficial Solutions

Living in families is like wearing glasses. Our experiences in family life provide the focus for seeing ourselves and our world. Some of us receive glasses that correct our vision 20/20—we see reality, both good and bad, because we are certain that we are loved; therefore, we are secure enough personally to face reality. The codependent's glasses won't clarify—they distort reality so that what is good seems bad and what is unhealthy seems normal.

Distorted reality

On the way to the airport for an out-of-town conference I once picked up a new pair of glasses. After a few hours, I realized that my head hurt, my eyes felt strained, my depth perception wasn't accurate, and my vision was out of focus. Something was terribly wrong with the glasses, but I had to endure them for a weekend until I could return home. Believe it or not, as bad as it was I could still see better with them than without them, but wearing them made me miserable.

When my optometrist examined them on Monday, he said, "Your lenses were ground according to your prescription, but the focus for your eyes is off center."

We must take the time to find out why our perception doesn't work and why it makes us sick.

My needs in that experience are much like a codependent's. We both need our glasses modified, but to alter them, we must take the time to find out why they don't work and why they make us sick. Then we can commit to the process of change, no matter how long it takes.

Begin the process by taking as long as you need to respond honestly to the following statements. Circle *Agree* or *Disagree*.[7]

Agree Disagree 1. I often feel isolated and afraid of people, especially people with authority.

Agree Disagree 2. I typically depend on and seek the approval of others while discounting my inner sense of "a job well done."

Agree Disagree 3. I am overly frightened of angry people and personal criticism.

Agree Disagree 4. I often feel like a victim in personal and other important relationships.

Agree Disagree 5. I sometimes feel I have an overdeveloped sense of responsibility, that it is easier to be more concerned with others than with myself.

Agree Disagree 6. I feel guilty when I stand up for myself instead of giving in to others.

Agree Disagree 7. I mix up love with pity, and so I "love" people I can pity and rescue.

Agree Disagree 8. It is hard for me to identify how I feel.

Agree Disagree 9. It is hard for me to feel or express feelings like joy, anger, or fear.

Agree Disagree 10. I am more a reactor than an initiator.

Agree Disagree 11. I judge myself and my actions harshly.

Agree Disagree 12. I often feel abandoned in the course of my relationships.

If you circled *Agree* more often than you circled *Disagree*, you've identified yourself with several codependent behaviors and feelings. If so, I hope you are aware of this concept:

> Codependency is not just a set of isolated feelings or behaviors.

Not a surface problem

Codependency is not a surface problem. Superficial solutions don't solve its problems. The deep hurt of an unmet need for love and acceptance either numbs you or drives you to accomplishments that please people and win their approval.

 Pretend you are writing to a friend with whom you once were close, but who you haven't seen in 15 years. Think about how you responded to the 12 statements above. Based on that impression, describe yourself to your friend.

_____

_____

_____

Codependent emotions and actions are designed to blunt personal pain and gain a desperately missed sense of worth. The problem is that codependent behavior yields only short-term solutions which ultimately cause more pain.

You don't have to struggle in codependency's grip the rest of your life!

Perhaps you've already tried some short-term solutions to understand the effects of tangled relationships in your life. The margin box contains several examples. Check all that you have tried.

Whatever you may have tried in the past, I know this with certainty. Your commitment to participate in your *Untangling Relationships* discovery group is not a superficial solution; it requires your time, your thought, your honesty, your personal insights, and your openness to the insights of your group.

While this course gives much attention to the problems and pain of codependency, its purpose is not to promote self-pity. The purpose is to promote objectivity, reality, and godly independence. Understanding the problem is only the first part of the process toward fixing it.

With understanding comes hope for change. And with understanding and hope, you can begin (or continue) a process toward spiritual, emotional, and relational health. These changes are not instant—but better than that—they are possible! You don't have to struggle in codependency's grip the rest of your life!

✎ **Pause now and identify how you feel at this moment about joining an *Untangling Relationships* discovery group.**

❏ I'm excited about being part of the group.
❏ I'm hopeful for answers to some tough questions.
❏ I'm afraid of feelings I may uncover that have been hidden.
❏ I'm distrustful of the group's commitment to confidentiality.
❏ I'm not sure the group will accept me.
❏ I can't identify any feelings about the group right now.
❏ other _____

✎ **What is one goal you have for yourself in this discovery group? Stop and pray about that goal. Seek God's direction and design of that goal. Write it on a separate piece of paper. If you are willing, plan to give it to your discovery-group leader at your upcoming session.**

Codependency blocks out hope like an eclipse blocks out the sun.

Codependency blocks out the sense of hope, the stability, the intimacy, and the vitality of life like an eclipse blocks the light of the sun. Remember what happens at the darkest moment of the eclipse? The sun begins once again to slowly emerge! In the same way, Christ's light can begin to shine in the darkness of codependency. You, or those codependents you love, can have a sense of hope, stability, worth, and intimacy—in relationships with others and in relationship with God.

✎ **Review this week's lessons. Find one statement in the text that helped you to understand better the codependent person(s) you love.**

Below rewrite that statement in your own words.

_____

_____

_____

Now, find one statement or insight you wrote that helped you to understand yourself better, whether or not you identify yourself as a codependent.

Below write it again, and describe how this new insight benefits you.

_____

_____

_____

Review the memory passage. Find it and check your memory. Then close your Bible and write the passage in this margin. What application have you made of this passage during your study of this unit? Below record your thoughts.

_____

_____

_____

Notes

[1]Melody Beattie, *Codependent No More* (New York: Hazelden Foundation, 1987), 31.
[2]Tim Sledge, *Making Peace With Your Past: Help for Adult Children of Dysfunctional Families* (Nashville: LifeWay Press, 1992), 16.
[3]Ibid., 10-14.
[4]Diana S. Richmond Garland, Kathryn Chapman, and Jerry Pounds, *Christian Self-Esteem: Parenting by Grace Parent's Guide* (Nashville: Family Ministry Department, The Sunday School Board of the Southern Baptist Convention, 1991), 75-76.
[5]Ibid., 84.
[6]Ibid.
[7]Adapted from a helpful analysis of adult children of alcoholics.

<table>
<tr><td>

UNIT

2

</td><td>

Lack of Objectivity

</td></tr>
</table>

Case in point

> ### CRITICAL OF EVERYTHING
>
> Helen had felt guilty and depressed since her family's last visit with her parents. She explained, "Our time with my parents was difficult. My mother was very critical of me and even of our children. I've felt really guilty since we left there."
>
> "Tell me about your parents," I probed. "My father is a wonderful man," she said. "He's loving and very supportive of me. My mother does a lot for me; she's very protective, but sometimes she is critical."
>
> Ken, Helen's husband, looked at her, "Sometimes?"
>
> "OK, more than sometimes."
>
> I asked, "When is your mother critical?" Helen thought and looked away as she answered, "When I was growing up, she criticized how I looked, the clothes I wore, my friends, my grades. Now she's critical of my husband, my children . . . just about everything." (Read more about Helen on page 30.)

What you'll learn

This week you will learn—

- two reasons why codependents lack objectivity;
- how codependents use five defense tactics to protect themselves from reality;
- eight sets of "blinders" codependents must remove if they are to regain objectivity;
- how to practice objectivity by reflecting on and evaluating childhood relationships with parents or parental figures.

What you'll study

Blinded to Reality	Results of a Lack of Objectivity	Blinders	Practicing Objectivity	Applying Objectivity
DAY 1	DAY 2	DAY 3	DAY 4	DAY 5

Memory verse

This week's passage of Scripture to memorize

I will lead the blind by a way they do not know, In paths they do not know I will guide them. I will make darkness into light before them And rugged places into plains.

–Isaiah 42:16

Blinded to Reality

Helen's story

"She criticized how I looked, the clothes I wore, my friends, my grades . . . just about everything."

Helen had felt guilty and depressed since her family's last visit with her parents. She explained, "Our time with my parents was difficult. My mother was very critical of me and even of our children. I've felt really guilty since we left there." I asked about her parents. She said, "My father is a wonderful man. He's loving and very supportive of me. My mother does a lot for me; she's very protective, but sometimes she is critical." Ken, Helen's husband, looked at her and said, "Sometimes?" She reluctantly admitted,"OK, more than sometimes."

I asked, "When is your mother critical?" Helen thought and looked away as she answered, "When I was growing up, she criticized how I looked, the clothes I wore, my friends, my grades. Now she's critical of my husband, my children . . . just about everything."

"I've failed her as her child."

"I just don't know how to get her to treat us well."

I asked how her father responds when her mother criticizes. She replied, "Oh, he goes into the living room and reads the paper. That's the way he copes when she nags him—which is just about all the time." She smiled weakly. "Daddy spends a lot of time reading the paper." But when I asked how Helen responds to her mother, she said: "Well, I've always tried to make her happy. I've always tried to please her, but I guess I just haven't been the daughter she wants me to be. I've really tried, though." Her voice trailed off. I said, "Helen, how do you feel when your mother criticizes you?" Helen replied, "Guilty, I guess . . . guilty I can't make her happy; guilty I've failed her as her child." Helen choked out the words, "Now she treats my children just like she treats me. Her criticism has never bothered me, but I don't want her to treat my children that way! I just don't know how to get her to treat us well." Her voice was trailing off again as she looked down.

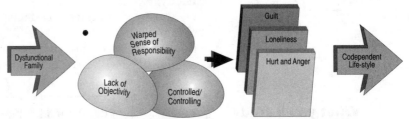

✎ **The course map above pictures the process of codependency. A lack of objectivity means the inability to see situations as they really are. Look back over Helen's story. Write at least three examples that indicate Helen was unable to see her situation objectively.**

1. _____

2. _____

3. _____

Helen showed her lack of objectivity in several ways. Your answers could have included: minimizing her mother's criticism with the word sometimes, her statement that she has failed her mother, her belief that she is responsible for her mother's happiness, or Helen's thought that she somehow could get her mother to treat her family well.

I asked Helen, "Do you think your mother has been loving toward you in all of this?" Helen looked stunned and said of course she had. I probed, "Do you show love that way, Helen?" She paused. "No, but I know my mother loves me no matter what I do." When I asked "How do you know she loves you?" Helen responded, "Well, I guess I . . . I've just assumed she loves me." I could tell my questions about her mother's love for her offended Helen.

"Maybe you're right . . . I hurt so bad, I feel so guilty . . . but I just know she loves me."

A few days later, we talked again. Helen began, "Maybe you're right . . . I hurt so bad, I feel so guilty all the time; but I just know she loves me." Helen began to cry. Ken put his arm around her. I asked if Helen had ever felt angry with her mother when she is critical. "No . . . no, I haven't." "Why not?" I asked. "Wouldn't anger be a normal response to someone who has condemned you and hurt you?" Helen said, "I guess so."

I asked how Helen wanted her mother to treat her. Her eyes brightened; she obviously had dreamed of this many times. "She would affirm me, love me even if I'm overweight, talk *to* me and not *at* me, listen to me. We'd be friends. We'd do fun things together." A pause, then, "She wouldn't slam the door of my room and leave me crying all alone." Helen raised her voice, "But she never did those kind and thoughtful things. Never! Even in high school she always made me wear the clothes she picked out for me." Then Helen broke into uncontrollable weeping. "She even made me take back a gown I'd bought for a big party and made me wear one she picked out. It was horrible! Everybody laughed at me!" Her voice calmed. "I haven't thought of that in years."

"It was horrible! Everybody laughed at me!"

Through several more conversations, Helen began to touch her deep hurt and repressed anger. It was the beginning of objectivity. It was the beginning of healing. Helen wore the glasses of codependency (remember day 5 in unit 1?). These glasses distorted reality and caused her to interpret life incorrectly. She thought she was responsible for making her mother happy. When her mother was unhappy, Helen felt guilty.

Practice the skill of being objective. Reread Helen's story. Use the margin box to describe this mother-daughter relationship in an objective—based on fact—manner. Write your description based on the details the story provides.

In either of the descriptions you have written put an * by any words that you believe Helen would not recognize (or admit) when she was denying reality about her relationship with her mother.

✏️ **At one moment in the story, Helen became offended. What offended**

her? _____

Helen took offense at the suggestion her mother did not love her. In the first unit, you studied our powerful needs to feel that we are loved and that we have worth. When Helen's need for love was not met, she lost any objectivity she might have had. The lack of love produced a lack of objectivity. Helen was an adult rearing her own family before she found the courage to admit that her mother did not treat her lovingly, and that she was angry and hurt about feeling unloved all her life.

Why can't codependents see reality clearly? Basically the reasons codependents lack objectivity are denial of reality and fear of reality.

Helen's attitudes and actions toward her mother were

_____

_____

_____

Her mother's attitudes and actions toward Helen were

_____

_____

_____

Denial of Reality

Codependents have an impaired ability to separate what's real and what's not. When families are filled with deception and denial, the members naturally will be deceived about and deny the reality of their families' pain. Learning to deny reality and practicing that denial starts in childhood. Children believe their parents are god-like. Therefore, they conclude that the way their parents treat them is how life is supposed to be. If parents are loving, children come to believe they are lovable. If parents are manipulative, condemning, or neglectful, children usually conclude that they and not their parents are somehow at fault. They see themselves as unlovable, unworthy of love and attention, but they still believe their parents always are good and right.

This twisted, distorted, and tragic perspective places enormous power in the hands of parents. Parents continue to exercise this power over their children even after the children are grown and gone. Helen's mother certainly had power to control Helen's feelings, attitudes, and responses. In the same way marrying or establishing any strong relationship with an addicted, troubled, or dysfunctional person slowly can erode a person's objectivity.

✎ **Read the Scripture in the margin and respond to the following questions:**

According to Deuteronomy 6:7-9, how important is good parenting?

_____

How much of the parents' time and attention do children need?

_____

How much time were your parents able to give you?

_____

> You shall teach [these words] diligently to your sons and shall talk of them when you sit in your house and when you walk by the way and when you lie down and when you rise up. and you shall bind them as a sign on your hand and they shall be as frontals on your forehead and you shall write them on the doorposts of your house an on your gates.
> –Deuteronomy 6:7-9

> Train up a child in the way he should go, Even when he is old he will not depart from it.
> –Proverbs 22:6

According to Proverbs 22:6 at left, how lasting are the results of good parenting?

❑ 1. Parents have little effect on their children's development.
❑ 2. The results of good parenting last for a lifetime.
❑ 3. The results last only while the child is in the home.

Both Scripture passages above show the importance of good parenting. Deuteronomy says children need to have the parents' time and attention in all the parts of daily life. Proverbs says that the results of good parenting last a lifetime (answer 2).

The harmful consequences of dysfunctional parenting also remain *to the third and fourth generations.* Denying the reality of childhood experiences will not make the harmful results go away. The opposite is true. Denying that anything was wrong is part of the problem. When codependents begin to look honestly at the effects denial produces in their lives, healing can begin.

The first reason codependents lack objectivity is that they deny reality in their lives and in the lives of people they love. Read the statements in the margin box. Circle the number of the statement which best describes this first reason.

Why they deny reality:

1. Codependents know what is real, and they ignore it.
2. Codependents would rather lie than tell the truth about their lives.
3. Codependents don't recognize reality because they've lived for a long time with people who don't admit what is true about life.
4. Codependents don't deny reality; they simply are too polite to point it out.

Of the four statements, the third best restates what denying reality means. Codependents live with people who constantly distort truth, who say:

- "It shouldn't hurt you," when it does.
- "He isn't drunk," when he is.
- "I'm doing this for your own good," when it makes you feel bad.
- "I am not angry," when she is.

The dysfunctional person lives a lie and expects others to live it too!

Remember: the dysfunctional person lives a lie and expects others to live it too! The codependent person lives a lifetime with those lies and learns to call them truth.

Fear of Reality

Codependents fear reality. Solving other people's crises drains so much of their energy that the prospect of any more pain or anger is frightening. Fleeting glimpses of reality are so painful, codependents are afraid of being overwhelmed by it in their own lives. Their perception is at least partially true. Often, objectivity does bring great pain and anger. Crawling inside an emotional turtle shell seems to provide temporary relief, but it ultimately brings more long-term pain and prevents the process of healing.

Crawling inside an emotional turtle shell seems to provide temporary relief, but it ultimately brings more long-term pain.

This fear of reality partly is the fear of losing one's identity. However broken and painful codependents' self-concepts may be, it is all they have! The fear of losing that morsel of identity is very threatening.

Fear of losing identity

Strangely, that fear leaves them clinging to a dysfunctional person who brings pain, abuse, and neglect, instead of facing reality, going through the healing process, and experiencing love, freedom, and strength. Lack of objectivity may sound fairly harmless, but it is powerful and destructive.

You have seen many things, but you do not observe them; Your ears are open, but none hears.
–Isaiah 42:20

Read the Scripture in the margin. Evidently, Isaiah learned from the Lord that many of Israel's troubles stemmed from the people's unwillingness to see and listen. Imagine that Isaiah, a trusted friend, had just said to you the words you just read. Use the margin box for your response.

➜ Find this unit's Scripture passage in your Bible. Mark it. Each day this week remember to spend a few minutes memorizing the unit Scripture passage.

How would you respond?

_____

_____

_____

_____

_____

SUMMARY STATEMENTS

- Codependency results in a lack of objectivity.
- Marrying or establishing any strong relationship with an addicted, troubled, or dysfunctional person slowly can erode a person's objectivity.
- Codependents fear reality. Solving other people's crises drains so much of their energy that the prospect of any more pain or anger is frightening.

Results of a Lack of Objectivity

Defense Tactic #1: One-way Perception

After reading the day 1 material about denial of reality, you may say, "I don't have this problem. My friends say I'm very perceptive." You may be correct about your ability to understand people. Many codependents are among the most perceptive people in the world! Usually they are perceptive about other people but not about themselves.

Usually codependents are perceptive about other people but not about themselves.

One friend of mine picks up other people's "vibes" incredibly well—almost reads their minds!—but has a very difficult time seeing the effects of his painful past on himself. People like my friend use perception as a defense mechanism. Such people have learned to recognize the desires of others very quickly and to become what others want them to be in an effort to please and gain approval. Although they "read" others very well, they don't see that they have become virtual puppets, dancing on the strings of those they want to please.

Codependents who are perceptive about others but not about themselves are like a man looking through the periscope of a submarine. He clearly sees the waves, the sky, and the ships around him, but he can't see himself or what's going on in the sub. He may be hit by depth charges from enemy destroyers, but he can't see the damage—he's still looking through the periscope. Don't forget: a submarine, like codependency, is designed to take you down!

Do you know persons who live "periscope up" and are very perceptive about others but not about themselves? In the margin box describe the negative qualities about themselves they do not see. Then describe the positive qualities about themselves they do not see.

You may be amazed by codependents' insight about others but confused by their blindness regarding themselves. They are just as amazed when their blindness is pointed out to them. Often, they simply do not believe it is true.

Negative traits:

_____

_____

_____

Positive traits:

_____

_____

_____

Defense Tactic #2: Emotional Walls

Other codependents have a different defense mechanism. Instead of developing a finely tuned perceptiveness about others, they go to the opposite extreme and build walls around themselves to block out their pain. They exist in a kind of emotional racquetball court—surrounded by walls. They appear unable to see how their words and actions affect others. Building these walls may block some of the painful emotions like hurt and rejection, but it also prevents people from experiencing many pleasant emotions like love, warmth, intimacy, and joy. Walls are not selective in the emotions they block—they block them all!

Walls prevent people from experiencing emotions like love, warmth, intimacy, and joy.

Defense Tactic #3: Extremes and Exaggerations

Codependents live life and understand life in its extreme or exaggerated forms. The two behaviors that best illustrate this defense tactic against reality are called black-and-white thinking and exaggerations.

No shades of gray

Therapists have come to call the codependent habit of seeing in the extremes "black-and-white" thinking. Codependents tend to see life in black or white, seldom in shades of gray. Life either is wonderful or awful. One friend described a co-worker: "He's doing a fantastic job! He is really mature and a hard worker. I'm so glad to be working with him!" But later, the co-worker fell from grace. My friend criticized him unmercifully: "I can't believe what a jerk he is! He's messed up everything he's touched!" I wondered, "Is this the same person he told me about a couple of months ago?"

I've realized I do the same thing. I was one of several presenters to a group of executives. In the discussion that followed, I thought, "I made the best presentation." My ideas were much better than those presented by the others. Theirs lacked insight and courage; they promised no success. My ideas, on the other hand, were brilliant! As the interaction continued, I saw these other people had shown keen understanding and were virtually certain of success. I started to feel angry and defended my proposal against their attack. Then I sat back and thought, "Wait a minute! Their ideas aren't that bad, and mine aren't all that good. In fact, these people may even be right!" A little objectivity does help us overcome our destructive black-and-white perspective.

✎ **People with this black-and-white view of life choose words, attitudes, and actions that prove their extreme perspective. Below, list some of the words, attitudes, and actions you have observed—in yourself or others—that signal a black-and-white perspective. I have given you an example:**

Words	Attitudes	Actions
you never	_resentment_	_withdrawal_

Perhaps you listed words like these: always, never, greatest, most awful, best, and worst. Attitudes you may have written could include: resentment, bitterness blind hatred, or undeserved loyalty. Some actions like those you listed might be: overcommitment of time and energy to the point of physical breakdown or extreme lethargy and depression.

Exaggeration

Making people or situations seem worse gives a feeling of importance.

Codependents often exaggerate. Making people or situations seem worse than they really are gives a feeling of importance. Exaggeration causes others to be more concerned than they might be if the objective truth were told. Similarly, describing people or situations better than they really are makes one look more impressive. The codependent's goals in relationships are to impress people or to get people to feel sorry for him or her.

Seeing good and bad

Objective persons see life as both good and bad at the same time. They realize good and evil exist in tension with each other. Codependents, however, give up one to embrace the other, leading to the extreme, black-and-white perspective. This exaggerated view of life causes wide emotional swings. The codependent's moods swing very quickly. Sometimes they do this when the situation hasn't changed at all!

Codependent perceptions

This chart shows how a codependent's perceptions differ from an objective person's view of the same situation:

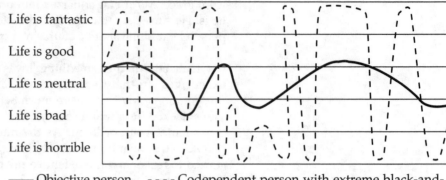

—— Objective person   - - - - Codependent person with extreme black-and-white perceptions

✎ **Which track on the chart most closely resembles your view of life? Would you prefer the other line to represent your life? ❑ Yes ❑ No**

Why or why not _____

_____

Defense Tactic #4: Believing the Unbelievable

Codependents believe others' distortions of reality.

Not only do codependents distort the truth, they also are likely to believe others' distortions of reality. How often has a codependent spouse or child heard the words, "I'll never drink again," and believed them, only to watch the alcoholic drink again, and promise again, and drink again . . . ? Codependents so badly want to believe the promises will be good, right, or true, that they completely deny obvious patterns of behavior in the dependent person's life. They grab hold of the grand pronouncements as facts. "Everything will be great now," they assume, only to be disappointed again.

Denying the obvious

When the dysfunctional person or anybody else fails, the promise of hope evaporates into bitterness. Codependents quickly go from one extreme to the other. Somehow, they have difficulty looking at the deeds instead of just hearing the words. They want so much to believe what they hear—the best—that they deny the reality going on right before their eyes.

✎ **Reread Helen's story at the start of day 1. What realities did she deny about her relationship with her mother?**

_____

✎ **What did she deny about her relationship with her father?**

_____

You noted that Helen denied that her mother had treated her less than lovingly, and she denied her anger toward her mother. When you first read the story, did you pick up Helen's denial concerning her father? She said he was "very supportive" of her, but then she said he abandoned her whenever her mother attacked Helen with criticism.

Defense Tactic #5: Daydreaming

Daydreaming is another sign of the codependent's extreme perspective. Codependents fantasize about making millions of dollars, being praised and respected, and having all the things they ever wanted, especially the love of the dysfunctional persons in their lives. Daydreams reflect either the negative, worst-case scenario, or the grand, glorious, best-possible scenario. These images can be quite detailed and emotional and can bring up all the dreams and/or self-pity hidden deep in codependents' hearts. In one moment, they may feel elated. In the next instant, an ambulance may roar by, and the codependent assumes a spouse, child, or parent is in it, critically injured and helpless. The codependent then likely assumes the reason for the accident was his or her neglect, compounding the fear with intense guilt.

Fear and intense guilt

Many daydreams include an escape from the abuse and neglect the compulsive person imposes on the codependent's life—like daydreams of escaping from the painful relationship to one with a tender, strong, wise, and comforting lover. The deeply anguished codependent even may daydream of killing the one who is hurting him or her. Reason has virtually nothing to do with these dreams and fears. The fantasies reflect the codependent's buried hurt, desire for affirmation, and fear of being hurt again.

The deeply anguished codependent may even daydream of killing the one who is hurting him or her.

✎ **Describe briefly several of your daydreams.** _____

_____

_____

What are some of their common themes? _____

_____

Your daydreams may focus on your hopes, fears, successes, or losses. They may be positive ones in which you are the hero or receive love or wealth. Or, they may be negative ones, centering on fears about yourself or your family.

For in many dreams and in many words there is emptiness.
—Ecclesiastes 5:7

✎ **Read the verse in the margin. Review this section on daydreams. Then jot down your responses to these questions:**

Why is emptiness an appropriate description of a life filled with daydreams (like the ones you've just studied)?

_____

What is the danger of such daydreams? _____

_____

_____

✎ **Review Helen's story in day 1. Helen used several defense tactics to shield her life from pain. But these prevented her from objectively seeing the truth about her life. Beside each defense tactic listed below, explain how Helen used it, or write her words that illustrate it.**

One-way perception: _____

Emotional walls: _____

Extremes and exaggerations: _____

Believing the unbelievable: _____

Daydreaming: _____

Helen demonstrated one-way perception by seeing what her mother wanted her to be and trying so desperately to become that vision. She used emotional walls to block out her anger so that she was out of touch with her own feelings. Helen's estimate of her father as "wonderful" and "supportive" of her showed extreme thinking. She believed the unbelievable in accepting her mother's estimate of her as a failure. Helen escaped into daydreaming by imagining her mother treating her with love.

SUMMARY STATEMENTS

- Codependents tend to be very perceptive about others while being blind to their own needs and motivations.
- Persons with a compulsion to please and control tend to live life and understand life in its extreme or exaggerated forms.
- Codependents want so badly to believe the promises they hear that they deny obvious patterns of behavior.

DAY 3

Blinders

You know what blinders are . . . those oddly shaped objects they place beside the eyes of racehorses. The owners put blinders on the horses for one reason only—to restrict the horse's view and remove any distractions. Blinders are a sign of the owner's control of the horse. Blinders ensure the horse has a one-track (no pun intended!) mind.

The blinders you'll read about in today's material do the same thing. Codependents wear these blinders, and you'll discover that they—

- restrict the codependent's view of life;
- remove "distractions"; in the codependent's case, they remove any new or helpful information which could challenge the blindness;
- represent control because codependents use these blinders to adapt their behavior and thinking to wishes of the dysfunctional persons in their lives. These blinders help keep codependents in bondage.

Like the defense tactics you studied in day 2 of this unit, these blinders restrict the codependent's view of life. They also restrict objectivity. In today's lesson we will consider the following types of blinders:

- Filtering information
- Defending the offender
- Redefining the pain
- Proclaiming perfect perception
- Keeping busy
- Exchanging emotions
- Pleasing people

Filtering Information

Removing painful truth

The codependent has a mental filter that removes a substantial amount of the truth. For example, when her bulimic sister says for the umpteenth time, "It's over; I'm never going to binge and purge again," the codependent wants to believe it so badly that she feels great relief and joy—even though her sister's record of keeping promises is abysmal. Or, codependents may hear and see only what they dread. If a codependent's performance review at work cites 20 things done well and one area needing improvement, he is heartbroken! That one area consumes his thoughts, not the good news about the great work he performs each day on the job.

 In the following chart three statements are about to pass through a codependent filter. Once they do, what do you think the codependent will hear? Write the filtered statement on the line on the right which corresponds to the examples on the left.

What codependents hear

"I'm impressed! Three hours work on that clunker, and now I only hear one small rattle!"

_____
_____
_____

On the annual check-up: "This person is physically fit. Eliminating salt from diet will enhance health."

_____
_____
_____

"Someday I hope to bake 36 cupcakes with only one lopsided one in the bunch! How'd you do that?!"

_____
_____

In the first case many codependents would hear: "What a poor job, it still rattles after all that work." The second might only hear: "You should stop using salt" or "you will die if you continue to use salt." The third may be embarrassed over the terrible lopsided cupcake.

Defending the Offender

The codependent usually defends the offender.

Instead of honestly feeling the hurt of betrayal and experiencing the anger of being abused or neglected, the codependent usually defends the offender. "It's not really her fault," he says. "She couldn't help it, and besides, it doesn't bother me when she curses me like that. I'm used to it by now." Another thinks, "Yes, it hurts when he treats me that way, but I feel so sorry for him. He wants to stop drinking, but he just can't."

People who defend the offender are also good at blaming the victim. Both blaming the victim and defending the offender excuse the one inflicting the hurt from any blame or guilt. The victim, or the codependent, not only bears the hurt but also bears the blame for the hurt.

The victim not only bears the hurt but also bears the blame for the hurt.

◆▸ We tragically see these blinders at work in the lives around us. Watch your local newspaper this week for stories, usually about domestic quarrels or crimes. If you find an article about a victim who "chooses not to press charges" or "refuses to testify," or some other action that excuses the offender, cut it out and clip it to this margin.

Redefining Pain

Being objective about deep hurt and seething anger produces both guilt and pain for codependents. But repressing the hurt and anger can make a person sick! Many who experience the stress of pain, anger, and guilt develop severe tension headaches. Instead of admitting their stress, they label these "migraine headaches."

Repressing the hurt and anger can make a person sick!

People use a host of other labels for their ailments. These labels shift the source of the problem from repressed emotions to purely physical causes. This of course does not mean repressed emotions cause every sickness a codependent experiences. But be careful. Buried emotions do lower our resistance to all kinds of disease.

 Look at this poor fellow in the drawing. Have you ever felt some of the symptoms he is feeling? If so, what did you call them? Write your responses beside the statements they match.

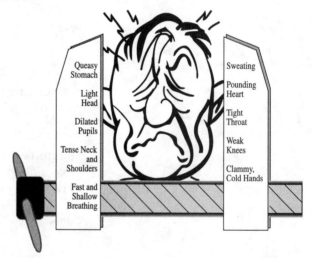

Queasy Stomach
Light Head
Dilated Pupils
Tense Neck and Shoulders
Fast and Shallow Breathing

Sweating
Pounding Heart
Tight Throat
Weak Knees
Clammy, Cold Hands

Did you write anything like: "I'm coming down with the flu," or "I'm having a heart attack"? Actually, all his symptoms are symptoms of stress. Admitting your body is showing the strain of constant stress is the first step to controlling its effects in your life. One man told me about his migraines. When I asked him to describe the pain, he did not mention one-sided, light-sensitive, throbbing pain—the typical symptoms of a migraine. He was having tension headaches but calling them migraine headaches. Redefining his pain freed him from dealing with his stressful life. After all, a migraine is a vascular problem; you can't blame a person for having that!

Fear of blame

Proclaiming Perfect Perception

Codependents often make statements intended to prove they understand life situations, even when they do not understand them at all. They may say, "Oh yes, I see it all now!" or proclaim, "I don't need her love and acceptance," or "It's never bothered me that he doesn't care about me." These kinds of statements show blindness to reality. They set up the codependent to continue the denial into the future. If we believe we are seeing accurately when facts prove we are not, then the perception prevents us from seeing reality and feeling pain. If one refuses to see the problem, no reason to change exists.

Time to come up for air! You've examined four of the seven blinders codependents use and that result in a restricted view of life. Review them by doing the activity in the margin box. On the blank following the examples, write the name we have given to each of the four blinders. You may review the descriptions you've just read.

These blinders provide a way to maintain the appearance of control. They don't stop the pain; instead they continue to freeze us into inaction. The answers were: 1. proclaiming perfect perception, 2. defending the offender, 3. filtering information, and 4. redefining pain.

Keeping Busy

Codependents use all sorts of activities to keep themselves too busy to reflect and feel. They may work 70 to 80 hours a week, participate in clubs and sports after work, watch television nonstop, even serve the church until all hours. The activity is not as important as is the fact that the codependent is busy and preoccupied with it. I've heard it said: "Activities are often the anesthetic to deaden the pain of an empty life." Most codependents are not aware that they are hurting. They may sense that something is wrong but have no idea what it is. They would reject out of hand the suggestion that they are living with repressed emotions. They are too busy to fiddle with such silliness!

Codependent believers need an application of grace. Grace is the free gift of God's love and acceptance. You can't stay busy enough to earn God's grace.

 Read Ephesians 2:8-10 (at left). What must come before "good works?"

_____

Our experience in salvation should teach us, as no other experience can, that busy-ness will lead to boasting. Not only is our salvation a gift we do not earn, but the faith we need to accept salvation is a gift! Only after this powerful, grace-filled experience does Christ free us to do "good works." Salvation must come before good works.

Exchanging Emotions

Because codependents haven't experienced true love and intimacy or genuine support and encouragement, they often substitute one emotion for another. For instance, one wife of an alcoholic equated worry with love. She always worried about her son, but she very seldom expressed affection for him. She

---

Identify the Blinder

1. Mike feels like he is faking his way through life because he cannot admit that he does not know how to do everything.

_____

2. Cheryl feels that the abuse she suffered at the hands of her father, and now her husband, is somehow her own fault.

_____

3. Bonnie only hears the bad things about herself and only the good things about her boyfriend.

_____

4. Bill finds himself missing more and more work due to illness as his relationship with his wife continues to deteriorate.

_____

For by grace you have been saved through faith; and that not of yourselves, it is the gift of God; not as a result of works, that no one should boast. For we are His workmanship, created in Christ Jesus for good works, which God prepared beforehand, that we should walk in them.
–Ephesians 2:8-10

What a great codependent word!
***Stoic**—it means not showing
your feelings.*

substituted the intensity of her worry for the love he actually needed. Some people use condemnation and praise to manipulate others rather than simply loving them. Some replace anger with a **stoic** calm that appears peaceful; but in reality, the calm denies the anger inside. Stoic is a great codependent word. It means not showing your feelings, especially feelings of pain or distress.

Perhaps the classic example of exchanged emotions is saying, "I'm frustrated" instead of "I'm angry." People seem to think frustration is OK, but real anger is not. Real anger is too threatening for codependents, so they alter it—call it *frustration*—to make their emotion less severe. The word *frustrated* is a perfectly good word describing a mildly negative emotional response, but it is much overused. In our office, we have agreed not to use this word; instead, we say we are *angry* when it is true. This was difficult at first, but after a few days, we found the honesty very refreshing!

Speaking the truth in love

✎ **The best way to remove the blinder of "exchanging emotions" is to learn to say what you mean. Recall specific conversations from the past day or two. Were you telling the truth? Record on the following chart three conversations. They could be with your spouse, a child, a coworker, an employer, or an acquaintance. Write *yes* beside the ones in which you said what you meant. Write *no* beside the ones in which you failed to speak the truth. Then rewrite the response to reflect better what you really felt.**

*"I wouldn't say mad; maybe miffed
is more like it."*

For example, imagine your spouse arrives late for dinner one night. He or she sits down and says, "You're not mad at me for being late, are you, Honey?" Suppose you reply, "I wouldn't say *mad*; maybe *miffed* is more like it." As you look at the statement, you decide you did not say what you meant. Then, write *no* beside the sentence, and rewrite it. In its more honest form, you might write, "I was mad when I realized the chicken and rice were drying out and wouldn't taste as good. If you'll call when you know you'll be late, I can start dinner at a different time."

Conversation:	What you really felt:

Pleasing People

Codependent adults compromise their own values as they develop a life-style of pleasing others.

Codependents' great need for others to accept them affects them at all stages of life. The intense peer pressure adolescents cope with is difficult even for the most stable youth. The added pressure a codependent youth feels is intense indeed. Dealing with both peer pressure and objective reality is a double whammy! Young adults have almost as much difficulty with the peer pressure of entering the "real world" after high school or college. Codependent adults compromise their own values as they develop a life-style of pleasing others.

Too often, objectivity doesn't occur until people are in their 30s, 40s, or 50s. By then they have wasted the wonderful years of youth in the oppressive combination of peer pressure, denial, rescuing, guilt, and pain.

✎ **You've now read about seven of the blinders codependents use and that result in a restricted view of life. Write your own description of the function of these blinders. Why do we continue to use them? What do they do for us? What is their long–term effect?**

_____

_____

The blinders do us short-term good but long-term damage. They help us to avoid the pain of reality, but they harm us because we never solve the underlying problems.

The Spirit of the Lord is upon Me, . . . He has sent Me to proclaim release to the captives, and recovery of sight to the blind . . .

–Luke 4:18

◆◆ **Read the Scripture in the margin. Pause and pray, thanking God that He is in the business of releasing captives and restoring sight. Ask Him to help you "recover your sight" by removing blinders that limit your ability to be objective.**

✎ **Begin removing the blinders in your life. On each scale below, circle the number which best indicates how often each blinder mentioned occurs in your life.**

Never 0 1 2 3 4 5 6 7 8 9 10 Always
Filtering Information

Never 0 1 2 3 4 5 6 7 8 9 10 Always
Defending the Offender

Never 0 1 2 3 4 5 6 7 8 9 10 Always
Redefining Pain

Never 0 1 2 3 4 5 6 7 8 9 10 Always
Proclaiming Perfect Perception

Never 0 1 2 3 4 5 6 7 8 9 10 Always
Keeping Busy

Never 0 1 2 3 4 5 6 7 8 9 10 Always
Exchanging Emotions

Never 0 1 2 3 4 5 6 7 8 9 10 Always
Pleasing People

A step to take—
_____
_____
_____
_____
_____

 Whether or not we are codependent, we all sometimes experience these blinders. Which blinder most frequently crops up in your life?

_____

Reread the section of material about the blinder you listed above. What is one step you can take this week, before your next discovery-group meeting, to begin removing that blinder from your life? What is one result you can expect from that step you will take? Write your answer in the margin box.

SUMMARY STATEMENTS

- Codependents use blinders to avoid pain, but in the process they avoid healing.
- Instead of honestly feeling the hurt of betrayal and experiencing the anger of being abused or neglected, the codependent usually defends the offender.
- Codependents use activities to keep themselves to busy to think and **feel**.

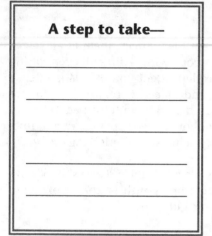

DAY 4

evaluate–v. to determine or fix the value of. (Webster's)

Evaluating is an important recovery skill—we determine what needs to be fixed or thrown away in our lives.

Practicing Objectivity

Your work these next two days will require you to reflect on your life. Be as objective in your thinking as possible. You will follow reflecting with **evaluating** (see definition at left). Again, be as objective as possible in your evaluating.

What you do today and on day 5 has two primary purposes:

1. To help you practice being objective, even about your family and your experiences in your family. That's difficult at times. You'll be filling in charts that may stir both warm memories and hurtful memories. Your objectivity is crucially important. You never may have been objective about some of your family experiences. Remember that now you are an adult. Now is the time to be objective and evaluate.

2. To provide you, through your own efforts, some powerful insights into who you were, who you are, and how God fits into the life you're living.

Your time will not be wasted as you proceed through each step. Answer every question. The fact that these questions are difficult shows the importance of an honest answer. May God bless you as you walk along memory lane.

Evaluating Your Relationship with Your Father

This exercise will help you evaluate your relationship with your father as it was while you were growing up. Perhaps your father was absent from your childhood home, but you may have had another significant, ongoing relationship with an adult man—perhaps a grandfather, uncle, or stepfather. If so, you also can fill in the chart below. As you respond to the exercise, seek to be as objective as possible. Choose words that describe your relationship as it was, not as you wish it had been.

Recall how this individual related to you when you were young; then check the appropriate square that best represents your answer. Take as much time as you need to fill it in honestly and objectively.

When I was a child, my father was—

Characteristics	Always	Very Often	Some-times	Hardly Ever	Never	Don't Know
Gentle						
Stern						
Loving						
Disapproving						
Distant						
Close, intimate						
Kind						
Angry						
Caring						
Demanding						
Harsh						
Trustworthy						
Joyful						
Forgiving						
Good						
Cherished me						
Impatient						
Unreasonable						
Strong						
Protective						
Passive						
Encouraging						
Sensitive						
Unpredictable						

1. **What does this inventory reveal to you about your father's . . .**

   . . . love for you? _____

   . . . opinion of your worth? _____

   . . . relationship to you? _____

2. **If you were an objective observer of the relationship . . .**

   what is one strength and one weakness of the man in the relationship?

   _____

how do his strengths and weaknesses impact this child? _____

_____

✐ 3. **If you were an adult present in the situation, what is one thing you would want to say . . .**

. . . to the father? _____

_____

. . . to the child? _____

_____

Evaluating Your Relationship with Your Mother

Repeat the exercise with your mother or relationship with another significant, adult woman—perhaps a grandmother, aunt, or stepmother. As you respond to the exercise, seek to be as objective as possible. Choose words that describe your relationship as it was, not as you wish it had been. Recall how this individual related to you when you were young; then check the appropriate square that best represents your answer:

When I was a child, my mother was—

Characteristics	Always	Very Often	Some-times	Hardly Ever	Never	Don't Know
Gentle						
Stern						
Loving						
Disapproving						
Distant						
Close, intimate						
Kind						
Angry						
Caring						
Demanding						
Harsh						
Trustworthy						
Joyful						
Forgiving						
Good						
Cherished me						
Impatient						
Unreasonable						
Strong						
Protective						
Passive						
Encouraging						
Sensitive						
Unpredictable						

✎ 1. What does this inventory reveal to you about your mother's . . .

. . . love for you? _____

. . . opinion of your worth? _____

. . . relationship to you? _____

✎ 2. **If you were an objective observer of the relationship you have just described,**

. . . what is one strength and one weakness the woman brings to the

relationship? _____

_____

. . . how does this strength and weakness impact this child? _____

_____

✎ 3. **If you were an adult present in the situation, what is one thing you would want to say . . .**

. . . to the mother? _____

. . . to the child? _____

⬥→ **Your work on today's content may have been emotionally draining for you. Take a five-minute break, breathe deeply, rub your neck muscles, walk outside for a moment—do whatever you consider relaxing and calming.**

Welcome back! You are almost finished for today. Try to identify how you feel since you completed those two inventories. In the margin box check all the feelings that apply.

Try to identify at least two reasons why you feel this way. If you are willing, call one of your discovery-group members or the group leader and talk with him or her about your feelings after doing these inventories.

✎ **Before the day is over, plan a time to pray about what you've learned and about how you feel. On the appropriate clock face below, indicate when that time will be:**

I feel—

❑ tired
❑ scared
❑ confused
❑ relieved
❑ guilty
❑ lonely
❑ peaceful
❑ thankful
❑ sad
❑ angry
❑ loved
❑ glad
❑ worthy
❑ hopeful
❑ other: _____

---

a.m.

p.m.

Applying Objectivity

You want me to be completely truthful, so teach me wisdom.
–Psalm 51:6, ICB

Let's use this inventory of personal characteristics once more—this time to help you evaluate your relationship with God. As before, your answers are not right or wrong; they are simply your answers. Answer openly and honestly. Let your answers reflect your personal experiences with God, not your theological knowledge about Him. You may feel God is displeased with a negative answer. Not so! Your honesty pleases Him, for only through honesty—through being transparent before Him—will you begin to grow. Pray the prayer of the psalmist from Psalm 51 (in the margin).

I feel that God is . . .

Characteristics	Always	Very Often	Some-times	Hardly Ever	Never	Don't Know
Gentle						
Stern						
Loving						
Disapproving						
Distant						
Close, intimate						
Kind						
Angry						
Caring						
Demanding						
Harsh						
Trustworthy						
Joyful						
Forgiving						
Good						
Cherished me						
Impatient						
Unreasonable						
Strong						
Protective						
Passive						
Encouraging						
Sensitive						
Unpredictable						

Knowing about God   ✐ What do your answers indicate you know about God? _____

_____

Feeling about God   What do your answers indicate you feel about God? _____

_____

Are "what you know" and "what you feel": ❑ alike?   ❑ different?

Explain your answer: _____

All people experience some gap between what they know or believe about God in their heads and what they feel about Him in their emotions. Most of the emotions people feel about God come from their parents or early caregivers. If one's parents were loving and dependable, then the person will feel that God is loving and dependable. If the parent or parents were critical and harsh, the person will feel that God is impossible to please and is cruel.

Many codependents have a spiritual life built on guilt.

Many recovering codependents say things like—"I always felt God was disappointed in me;" "No matter how hard I tried, I never seemed to be able to have a close relationship to God:" "I know God loves me, but I feel like He is ashamed of me." As a result, many codependents have a spiritual life built on guilt rather than on faith or love. They try so hard to please God and feel nothing but failure.

Your Father's Influence on Your Perception of God

Your relationship with your father (or the significant man you identified yesterday) was the basis for many of your ideas and feelings about God. The following exercise will help you explore this area of your life. On the following chart record the answers you wrote yesterday about your relationship with your father. Place your marks from the chart on page 45 in the shaded portion of the box beside each characteristic. When you finish transferring those marks, then transfer the marks you just made on the chart on page 48 evaluating your relationship with God. Place the marks about God in the white portion of the box beside each characteristic.

Your father and God

Characteristics	Always	Very Often	Some-times	Hardly Ever	Never	Don't Know
Gentle						
Stern						
Loving						
Disapproving						
Distant						
Close, intimate						
Kind						
Angry						
Caring						
Demanding						
Harsh						
Trustworthy						
Joyful						
Forgiving						
Good						
Cherished me						
Impatient						
Unreasonable						
Strong						
Protective						
Passive						
Encouraging						
Sensitive						
Unpredictable						

✎ List in the left column below the five characteristics you feel describe the way your father and your Heavenly Father are most alike. List in the right column the five characteristics with which you indicated your feelings for your father and your Heavenly Father are most different.

Alike   Different

_____   _____

_____   _____

_____   _____

_____   _____

_____   _____

Your Mother's Influence on Your Perception of God

Your relationship with your mother (or the significant woman you identified yesterday) also was the basis for many of your ideas and feelings about God. The following exercise will help you explore this area of your life. On the chart below, use the same procedure to compare your feelings about your mother with your feelings about God. Transfer the marks from the charts on pages 46 and 48.

Your mother and God

Characteristics	Always	Very Often	Some-times	Hardly Ever	Never	Don't Know
Gentle						
Stern						
Loving						
Disapproving						
Distant						
Close, intimate						
Kind						
Angry						
Caring						
Demanding						
Harsh						
Trustworthy						
Joyful						
Forgiving						
Good						
Cherished me						
Impatient						
Unreasonable						
Strong						
Protective						
Passive						
Encouraging						
Sensitive						
Unpredictable						

✎ List in the left column below the five characteristics you feel describe the way your mother and your Heavenly Father are most alike. List in the right column the five characteristics with which you indicated your feelings for your mother and your Heavenly Father are most different.

Alike	Different
_____	_____
_____	_____
_____	_____
_____	_____
_____	_____

On two separate sheets of paper, write a paragraph summarizing how your perception of God has been shaped by your relationship with your father and your mother. Write objectively; then add how you feel right now about what you have written. Place the sheets of paper in an unsealed envelope. Keep it nearby for the moment; you'll need it again.

✎ Review this week's lessons. Find one statement or insight you wrote that helped you to understand yourself better, whether or not you identify yourself as a codependent.

Below write the statement, and describe how this new insight benefits you.

_____

_____

_____

Review the memory passage. Look it up and check your memory. Then close your Bible and write the passage below. How have you made application of this passage during your study of this unit? Below record your thoughts.

_____

_____

_____

Notes

1These charts adapted from Jim Craddock, Scope Ministries International, which appear in *Your Parents and You* (Houston: Rapha Publishing, 1990).

A Warped Sense of Responsibility

Case in point

> **FROM ONE EXTREME TO THE OTHER**
>
> Susan's father ran his household like a boot camp. He made many demands, had a rigid set of expectations, and praised only the most outstanding behavior. Susan's mother lost all confidence in her own abilities and opinions. She lost her identity.
>
> Susan made straight A's through high school. Anything less would have been intolerable. She was, for the most part, a very compliant child. When Susan went to college, her father's artificial restrictions no longer were present to keep her in check. She began to do virtually all the things her father detested. She smoked, she drank, she experimented with drugs (and liked them!), and she hopped from bed to bed. She had imagined these things would bring her great freedom and pleasure, but they mostly brought confusion.
>
> Susan kept her father in the dark about most of her activities, but he knew she was spending more money than he had planned, and her grades were not what he had expected. He became furious. At Thanksgiving—their first face-to-face encounter since she had left for college—he exploded at her, but to his shock, Susan exploded right back! (Read more about Susan on page 53.)

What you'll learn

This week you'll learn to—

- recognize the unhealthy relationship to responsibility codependents and their families have;
- identify the behaviors and thoughts of the "fixer"—one who always wants to rescue others or fix their problems;
- explore the "savior complex" and the "Judas complex";
- understand the results of a warped sense of responsibility;
- evaluate these results in your own life.

What you'll study

Feeling Responsible	Codependents to the Rescue!	The Savior Complex/ The Judas Complex Part One	The Savior Complex/ The Judas Complex Part Two	Results of a Warped Sense of Responsibility
DAY 1	DAY 2	DAY 3	DAY 4	DAY 5

Memory verse

This week's passage of Scripture to memorize

For by grace you have been saved through faith; and that not of yourselves, it is the gift of God; not as a result of works, that no one should boast.

–Ephesians 2:8-9

Feeling Responsible

A psychiatrist once told me that in a dysfunctional family, one child may become quite irresponsible while another may have an overdeveloped sense of responsibility. This contrast is common.

One Family's Story

Susan's story

Susan's father was from a military background. He ran his household like a boot camp. He made many demands, had a rigid set of expectations, and praised only the most outstanding behavior. Susan's mother lost all confidence in her own abilities and opinions. She lost her identity. Susan made straight A's through high school. Anything less would have been intolerable. She was, for the most part, a very **compliant** child. When Susan went to college, her father's artificial restrictions no longer were present to keep her in check. She began to do virtually all the things her father detested. She smoked, she drank, she experimented with drugs (and liked them!), and she hopped from bed to bed. She had imagined these things would bring her great freedom and pleasure, but they mostly brought confusion.

compliant–adj. ready to conform or adapt one's actions to another's wishes. (Webster's) Codependent over-compliance is called "people–pleasing."

Susan kept her father in the dark about most of her activities, but he knew she was spending more money than he had planned, and her grades were not what he had expected. He became furious. At Thanksgiving—their first face-to-face encounter since she had left for college—he exploded at her, but to his shock, Susan exploded right back! For the next three-and-a-half years, their relationship was a blend of an armed truce—during the good times, and a guerrilla warfare most of the time. They played a game called subterfuge and sniping. The game involves hiding from—while shooting at—each other.

Like a war zone

After graduation, Susan had little to do with her family. She'd bring her new husband and her growing family for visits, but they were mechanical, required visits. Her basic attitude was, "Don't call me, I'll call you." When her parents needed help, they called on Rob, Susan's younger brother.

Rob grew up in the same environment, but his response in college and after graduation was entirely different. He always tried to please his parents. His mother appreciated what Rob did, but his father always expected more. So Rob tried to do more, to be more, to give more, to help more. His desire to please his demanding father shaped everything about his life. Even when he married, he focused more of his attention on his parents than on his wife. His excessive devotion to his parents' desires caused quite a strain in his marriage and in all of his relationships. No matter how hard he tried (and Rob tried very hard!), he couldn't do enough to please everyone, especially his father.

In the margin box write the names of the overly responsible child and the irresponsible child you read about in the above story.

 Read the story once again. While it's true that Susan and Rob are examples of out-of-balance responsibility, one example of balance exists in the story. Can you find it? List it here.

Identify—

The overly responsible child

was _____

The irresponsible child was

_____

Susan was the irresponsible one, and brother Rob the overly responsible one. Don't miss this—it's the "punchline" to this story. The family itself maintains its balance. Susan and Rob each chose different ways of coping with difficult, distant parents. When Susan rebelled and turned away from her parents, and the family was plunged into a storm, Rob helped calm the storm by turning toward his parents and working overly hard to please them. The family could accommodate Susan's irresponsibility because of Rob's overresponsiblity.

Both irresponsible and overly responsible behavior are characteristics of codependency. Both begin with the crushing burden of taking care of dysfunctional people and making them happy. One gives up. The other keeps trying. And somehow, the family itself adjusts, balances, and survives.

✎ Think of your immediate family. Which member or members behave in overly responsible or irresponsible ways? What do these persons do to make you think this about them?

Overly Responsible Person   Behaviors

_____   _____

_____   _____

_____   _____

Irresponsible Person   Behaviors

_____   _____

_____   _____

_____   _____

✎ In the margin beside each behavior, describe how you respond to that behavior when it occurs in your family.

✎ Think of your extended family. Who acts (or acted) in overly responsible or irresponsible ways? What do they (or did they) do to make you think this about them?

Overly Responsible Person   Behaviors

_____   _____

_____   _____

_____   _____

Irresponsible Person   Behaviors

_____   _____

_____   _____

_____   _____

You may have an alcoholic grandfather whose daughter (your mother) was a rescuer and caretaker for the family. You may have an abusive, selfish husband; a guilt-ridden, perfectionistic, driven child; or a child on drugs who is wasting his life. Most people can identify these traits fairly easily in their own families. The more dysfunctional the family system, the more warped and out of balance the sense of responsibility tends to be for each person.

✎ Review the exercises you've just completed, think about your family, and finish these sentences. Make the first sentence apply to you and the second to another family member. In the margin box I have given you an example.

"I am most like _____ when I _____

_____."

"_____ is most like me when he/she _____

_____."

➠ You have been doing some difficult work. Take a moment to pray. You may want to thank God for new insights or pray for courage. Be sure to thank Him for the hope and health He wants to bring families.

➠ In your Bible find the memory verse for this unit. Mark it and read it several times. Plan to begin and end every day of this unit by reading or repeating this verse. Use it as a prayer to God.

In my family—

"I am most like _my mother_

when I _Criticize my_

children ."

" _Art_ is most like me

when he _tries to_

please his parents.

SUMMARY STATEMENTS

- In a dysfunctional family, one child may become quite irresponsible while another may have an overdeveloped sense of responsibility.
- Both irresponsibility and overresponsibility are characteristics of codependency.
- Codependent behaviors are developed as members strive to maintain the balance of the family unit.

DAY 2

We felt responsible for solving the world's problems.

Codependents to the Rescue!

Ray, Diana, Joyce, and I were talking one day about our deep sense of responsibility for people. Diana said, "If only I hadn't had to take Christopher to the doctor last week, I could have kept those professors from being kidnapped in Lebanon." Ray chimed in, "Yeah, and it was all my fault that the hurricane hit Houston."

Someone else remarked, "We've *got* to do something about the budget deficit." And we all laughed. We were being facetious—sort of. Each of us felt responsible for solving the world's problems, fixing people's predicaments, and generally making everybody—literally everybody—happy. We were just stating our feelings in their logical extreme.

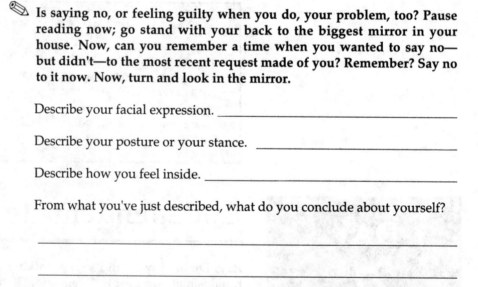

It was my fault that—

_____

_____

_____

_____

Suppose you had been in on this conversation. Write in the margin box a statement you would have made to show your feelings of responsibility for solving the world's problems.

Getting By Giving

As we have seen, codependents often feel unloved. They usually feel they don't have worth or value. How, then, can they gain the value, love, and respect they so desperately want? They seek worth _by helping others_. When they help somebody, it produces a temporary high. They conclude: "I am somebody. I am appreciated. I have value."

Other people, especially dysfunctional people, cooperate nicely and are glad for the codependent to solve their problems and rescue them. Life becomes a dance between a person with endless problems and a desperate problem solver, between a person in need and a person needing to rescue someone.

A consuming life-style

For overly responsible codependents taking care of others becomes a consuming life-style. In the role of caretaker, they again are like someone looking through the periscope of a submarine. They don't see the need to have their own identities, their own dreams, their own emotions, and their own schedules. They are driven to be and do and feel what other people want them to be and do and feel. They believe doing anything for themselves is selfish. Perhaps you've heard it said that codependents can't say no, but that isn't completely true. They can say no, but when they do, they feel guilty for being so selfish.

✎ **Is saying no, or feeling guilty when you do, your problem, too? Pause reading now; go stand with your back to the biggest mirror in your house. Now, can you remember a time when you wanted to say no— but didn't—to the most recent request made of you? Remember? Say no to it now. Now, turn and look in the mirror.**

Describe your facial expression. _____

Describe your posture or your stance. _____

Describe how you feel inside. _____

From what you've just described, what do you conclude about yourself?

_____

_____

In unit 2 you explored the effects of a lack of objectivity. Codependents who rescue lack objectivity. They cannot see what the dependent person really needs. Dependent people don't always—or even often—need to be rescued! They may need to be left alone. They may need to learn how to be responsible for themselves.

Dependent people often need to be left alone to learn to be responsible for themselves.

People need to learn to solve their own problems. They don't need to be rescued all the time. Rescuing only helps them continue in their problems instead of solving their problems. Rescuing is an attempt to meet the codependent's need for identity—the need to be needed. The codependent makes problems worse by looking for needs he or she can meet. If no needs exist, good codependents can create them. Codependents make little needs into big needs so they will feel more significant. They read every facial expression and tone of voice so they can say or do just the right thing to make someone else happy. Then, when they have rescued the victim of their attention, they feel great for a while. If they fail, they feel miserable because the very basis of their self-worth has been shaken.

Assumptions

Emotionally dependent

The emotions of a codependent depend on the responses of other people. For instance, codependent thinking goes something like this:

> - If he is angry, it must be my fault. I feel guilty.
> - If she is sad, I must have done something to hurt her feelings.
> - If she is afraid, I need to comfort and protect her.
> - If he is happy, I must have helped him!

Or, even more personal for the codependent, are these thoughts:

> - If I am angry, he needs to change how he treats me.
> - If I am sad, it's her fault.
> - If I am afraid, he needs to protect me.
> - If I am happy, it is because she appreciates me.

Codependents expect others to make them happy.

Besides assuming the responsibility of making others happy, codependents expect others to make *them* happy. Personal responsibility—each person being responsible for himself or herself—is out!

We Christians may be uncomfortable with this discussion about responsibility. After all, Scripture teaches us to love and care for others and to regard others' needs before our own needs. Scripture also teaches us to love others as we love ourselves, to provide for ourselves so others do not have to, and to be careful we don't cause others to stumble because of our actions or choices. So how do we, especially when we are codependent, model personal responsibility without it appearing selfish or conceited? Perhaps Margaret Rinck's observations of codependency can help here—

Is it really love to act out of fear of abandonment or fear of rejection?

> *Is not the codependent person who is acting needy; who manipulates through kindness and guilt; who controls others with smiles and by making others dependent on him—is not this person equally selfish? Is it really acting out of genuine love to do things for someone solely out of fear of abandonment or rejection? Is it less selfish to control others by doing things for them that they should do for themselves? . . . Codependent people who go into recovery are always stunned at how controlling and manipulative (selfish) they have been. They also want someone else to be as obsessed with them as they are with the other person. Obsession is love to them, and so if they "love" someone, they are obsessed with them, and feel "hurt" or "rejected" if the obsessive attention is not returned.[1]*

✎ **Reread the quote from Margaret Rinck. How is "obsessive love" for another person described in it? Write your thoughts here.**

_____

_____

Obsessive love is destructive because it is selfish; because we so desperately need to be needed, we end up destroying the other person.

Obsessive love is not genuine love. How would you describe "genuine love" for another person? In the margin box write your thoughts about this.

➤➤ **Pause now and telephone one person in your discovery group. Discuss with that person the two descriptions you have just written; ask for his or her ideas about obsessive and genuine love.**

(While you've got that group member on the phone, each of you practice saying your memory verse to each other!)

Being personally responsible means I have accepted the fact that I am ultimately accountable only for myself—my actions, my choices, my relationships, my behavior. I am not accountable for others' actions, choices, relationships, or behavior.

✎ **Practice personal responsibility by rewriting some of the assumptions codependents often make (from the boxes on page 57). Change the assumptions to statements reflecting genuine love for other people and personal responsibility for yourself.**

For example: If he is angry, it must be my fault. I feel guilty. I've rewritten this as: He seems angry. I probably would feel angry too in the same situation. Perhaps I can be a listening ear or an encourager to him.

Now, you rewrite the rest:

If she is sad, I must have done something to hurt her feelings.

_____

If she is afraid, I need to comfort and protect her.

_____

If he is happy, I must have helped him!

_____

If I am angry, he needs to change how he treats me.

_____

If I am sad, it's her fault.

_____

Genuine love is—

_____

_____

_____

_____

_____

Children to the Rescue—Parenting Their Parents

Sometimes children become parents to their parents.

When children in a dysfunctional family take responsibility for their parents' happiness, they in effect become parents to their parents. Instead of the parent nurturing, protecting, and providing for the child, the child becomes responsible to nurture, protect, and provide for the parents. Roles are reversed: the parents are needy, and the child is forced to assume adult responsibilities. The child isn't allowed to go through a normal, healthy process of developing self-concept and identity. The child learns to deny and control his or her "childish" emotions; sadly, this stops the healthy process of emotional development. The child's chance for a maturing relationship with the parents is lost. The resulting damage is deep and prolonged. When children who have "parented" their parents become parents themselves, they often expect their children to "parent" them, and the cycle continues.

Cycle of damage

Codependents to the Rescue—Fixing Their World

Codependents' desire to make people happy extends far beyond their own family. They feel responsible for making everybody happy. I understand this! I used to be what salesmen call "an easy mark." I'm quite sure all the door-to-door salesmen held a convention and marked our house with a big red pin. They would tell each other: "This guy will buy anything—car-wash solution, magazines, Girl Scout cookies, oranges, anything!" I remember one man who came to our door a few years ago selling a "wonder cleaning fluid." "It only costs $35 a gallon, and you would really be helping me out (the magic words!) if you would buy some." He did have a slightly pitiful expression. Now, who would buy something like this? Who would buy something (when it is obviously overpriced) he doesn't need from somebody he doesn't know, just to make somebody feel better? That would be ridiculous, wouldn't it? (I've still got about half a bottle left, if you want to try it!)

When we codependents help someone, we feel great; but when we fail, we feel like we have betrayed the other person. These two extremes form a consistent pattern in our lives. From your study of day 1 and day 2 in this unit, use the margin box to describe how a codependent "rescues" another person.

> **How a codependent rescues—**
>
> _____
>
> _____
>
> _____
>
> _____

✎ **Even if we are not actually codependent, all of us have rescued at some time. Try to list three examples of words you've said and actions you've used to try to rescue others.**

Words	Actions
_____	_____
_____	_____
_____	_____

In the margin you may have written something like, "to rescue means to take care of others—no matter who they are—and their problems—no matter what they are! Codependents feel compelled to solve others' problems without even being asked to do so."

Maybe you listed examples like these: giving others money when they have irresponsibly spent all they had; telling someone what to think and feel, or how to act; controlling others' decisions "for their own good"; making excuses for others' bad behavior.

✎ From the examples you just gave, choose the one that is most recent. Use it to fill in the front-page story below about you and your "amazing rescue!"

Super Nice Person Completes Successful Rescue!

Who was rescued?
_____
_____

When did it happen?
_____
_____

Where did it occur?
_____

What actually happened?
_____
_____
_____

Why was the rescue necessary?
_____
_____
_____
_____

How did you recognize the need?
_____
_____
_____

SUMMARY STATEMENTS

- When codependents say no, they feel guilty for being so selfish.
- People need to learn to solve their own problems. Rescuing only helps them continue in their problems instead of solving them.
- Besides assuming the responsibility for making others happy, codependents expect others to make *them* happy.
- When children have "parented" their parents, they often expect their children to "parent" them, and the cycle continues.

DAY 3

The Savior Complex/ The Judas Complex (Part One)

Linda explained to me that she feels responsible for her parents, her husband, her friends, her job, and everything else she touches. She said, "I feel like I need to solve everybody's problems. Nobody else will do it if I don't." A striking parallel hit me. "You feel like a savior, don't you?" I asked. Her eyes lit up; then she smiled. "Yes, I do. I guess I'm taking somebody else's role." She laughed at her insight.

A codependent feels either like a savior or a Judas—one who rescues or one who betrays, one who helps or one who fails to help. Often, these black-and-white perceptions of self change in a heartbeat, depending on whether other people are happy or angry with the codependent.

The Savior Mode

Codependents in the savior mode believe they can do no wrong and can rescue everyone who is in need. The codependent's creed is:

- "If someone has a need, I'll meet it!"
- "If a need doesn't exist, I'll find one, and then I'll meet it!"
- "If there's a small need, I'll make it a large one. Then I'll feel even better when I meet it!"
- "Even if nobody wants help, I'll help anyway!"
- "When I've helped, I'll finally feel good about myself!"

The codependent's family complicates the problem. Family members say, "We knew we could count on you!"

Persons with a savior complex think they are indispensable.

Persons with a savior complex think they are indispensable. They believe whatever they are doing is absolutely the most important thing in the world! Nobody else's work or effort even comes close.

 Perhaps you know some folks with such "savior-like" thoughts. By the statements above write their names or initials.

The Judas Mode

In the Judas mode, the codependent's outlook is quite different. The mood is one of failure and despair. One man explained, "I feel like I have to rescue people, but I'm so afraid of failing that I'm paralyzed." He lives with tremendous tension and heartache. Paralyzing fear and withdrawal prevent persons with a Judas complex from actively rescuing. Therefore, they may not see themselves as codependent. Their analysis is mistaken, however. They desperately want to rescue others just like codependents in the savior mode do, but they can't. Their creed becomes:

"I'm so afraid of failing that I'm paralyzed."

- "People need me, but I can't help them."
- "Their needs are enormous, and I feel awful that I can't help."
- "Every time I try to help, I mess up."
- "No matter what I do, it's wrong."
- "If I try, I fail. If I don't try, I fail. I am a miserable failure."

This time the family's message to the codependent is, "We thought we could count on you, but I guess we can't."

 You probably also know some folks with these "Judas-like" thoughts. By the statements above write their initials.

And how do persons with a savior complex nose dive into a Judas complex? Three basic ways exist. Codependents may—

The nose dive

> • try to help, but fail;
> • try to help, but not be appreciated;
> • not even try because they are sure they will fail.

In any of these situations, the result is usually withdrawal, guilt, loneliness, anger, self-condemnation, and hopelessness.

 When do you feel like a savior? How do you act?

_____

_____

Most of us feel like a savior when someone needs us or when we solve another's problems. We may act with supreme confidence to "assume command" of the person or situation, but inside we are afraid we may fail or we may not be appreciated for our efforts.

 When do you feel like a Judas? How do you act?

_____

_____

You may feel like a Judas when you feel needed, but you also may feel inadequate to meet the need. At such times you may withdraw quietly into self-contempt, or perhaps you may blame others because you are unable to meet their needs.

How do you feel when you say no to others? Read the responses in the margin box and check all that apply.

When I say no, I feel—

❑ selfish
❑ guilty
❑ insensitive
❑ mean–spirited
❑ uncaring
❑ ashamed

What do you want *no* to mean when you say it to others? Circle the one statement that best expresses your feelings.

"I understand my physical limits."
"To do a good job with my other commitments, I must say no to this one."
"Thank you for considering me competent and capable for this opportunity. I'd like to help out another time."
"Your emergency is not my emergency!"
"I love you too much to make your decisions and straighten out your life."
Other _____

Take time to make a bookmark for a Bible. Use your creativity to make it attractive. Somewhere on it, or attached to it, write this unit's memory verse. Present it to your favorite codependent person (other than yourself, if you happen be your favorite codependent person!)

SUMMARY STATEMENTS

- Codependents tend to feel like either a savior or a Judas.
- Codependents in savior mode feel like they are indispensable and that they can do no wrong.
- Codependents in Judas mode feel failure and despair.
- The savior-Judas pattern is an expression of black-and-white thinking.

DAY 4

The Savior Complex/ The Judas Complex (Part 2)

Talk about extremes! Could there be anything more different than feeling like either Jesus or Judas? I don't think so. Since completing your day 3 study, you likely are beginning to see how difficult it is on the codependent who either feels like a savior, feels like a Judas, or feels the extremes of sometimes being a savior and other times being a Judas. The following charts show the extremes codependents experience in their self-concepts.

Persons who are very skilled at pleasing people may be in a chronic savior pattern.

Persons who are very skilled at pleasing people (or who are very young and haven't experienced enough crushing blows of failure) may be in a chronic savior pattern and recall only a few times of feeling like a Judas. Often, persons in this condition see themselves as very healthy and successful, not as the persons they really are. Their charts look like this:

Chronic Savior Pattern

Savior
(I can help you.)

Judas
(I'll let you down.)

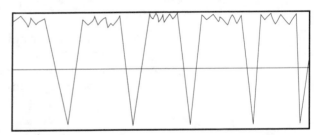

Persons gradually lose confidence in themselves.

Persons who have experienced more criticism gradually lose confidence in themselves. They begin to feel less like a savior and more like a Judas. Their charts may look like this—

Mixed Savior/Judas Pattern

Savior
(I can help you.)

Judas
(I'll let you down.)

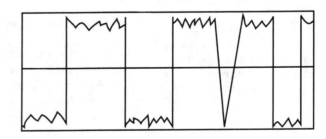

A person's self-concept may erode to a point where it is characterized almost completely by guilt.

Through any number of painful circumstances and with the help of manipulative, condemning people, a person's self-concept may erode to a point where it is characterized almost completely by guilt, despair, anger, loneliness, and hopelessness. This may happen during childhood, or it may happen much later. The codependent person's life then will be marked by a chronic Judas pattern:

Chronic Judas Pattern

Savior
(I can help you.)

Judas
(I'll let you down.)

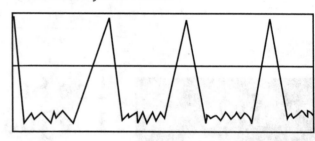

Sides of same coin

The savior and Judas complexes are flip sides of the same coin—the need for a sense of worth—the need to be loved and accepted. The savior feels he or she is accomplishing this goal. The Judas fears he or she can't.

 Which of the three patterns above best describes your life and experience?

_____

Which of the three patterns above best describes the life and experience of the codependents you love?

_____

Do they recognize this pattern being lived out in their lives?
❑ Yes   ❑ No

Many of us can identify the patterns of our compulsion to rescue and our sense of failure when we can't fix people's problems. This observation can help us understand our mood swings, our desire to be around people who appreciate our rescuing and our withdrawal from those who don't.

Who Is the Savior?

Jesus asked his disciples, "Who do you say I am?" Simon Peter answered, "You are the Christ, the Son of the living God."
–Matthew 16:13-16, NIV

The first two Scriptures in the margin make it very clear. He is God! He does for us what we cannot do for ourselves. He is utterly unique; no other person is like Him. You and I cannot duplicate who He is or what He does.

Here is a trustworthy saying that deserves full acceptance: Christ Jesus came into the world to save sinners.
–1 Timothy 1:15, NIV

Who Was Judas?

Judas was the selfish disciple. He limited himself to what he wanted to see. When reality didn't match his personal vision, he decided he'd signed up for a losing cause. That's when he tried to "fix" reality. Betraying the Savior was the result. Judas accepted 30 pieces of silver to betray Jesus. In those days that was the cost of an ordinary slave.

Judas Iscariot went to the chief priests and asked, "What are you willing to give me if I hand him over to you?" So they counted out for him thirty silver coins. From then on Judas watched for an opportunity to hand him over.

–Matthew 26:14-16

When Judas saw that Jesus was condemned, he was seized with remorse and returned the thirty silver coins to the chief priests and the elders. "I have sinned," he said, "for I have betrayed innocent blood"

–Matthew 27:3-5, NIV

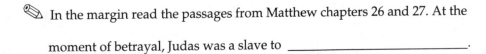 In the margin read the passages from Matthew chapters 26 and 27. At the moment of betrayal, Judas was a slave to _____.

You may have concluded that Judas was a slave to his greed or his selfishness. He seems to have wanted to be in control. When Jesus didn't do what he wanted done, he betrayed the Savior. Stated like that, Judas sounds like a very selfish man. He was, and when we act like Judas, we are, too. If we remain in the Judas mode, we betray ourselves—because we are not responsible for ourselves, and we betray others—because we are seeking to control them and run their lives.

➡ **Pause now and pray. Thank God for providing Jesus—the only Savior the world needs. Then, ask Him to forgive you when you betray yourself or others.**

SUMMARY STATEMENTS

- When we are in savior mode we feel we are important, powerful people that others cannot do without.
- When we are in Judas mode we feel that we are worthless and hopeless.
- Both the savior and Judas pattern come from the need at the core of codependency—the need to prove our worth.

DAY 5

Results of a Warped Sense of Responsibility

Trying to rescue people, or failing to rescue them, results in the following personal and relational problems:

1. Codependents prevent others from developing responsibility.
2. Codependents neglect themselves.
3. Codependents resent being saviors.
4. Codependents threaten but continue rescuing.
5. Codependents lack objectivity about serving and helping others.
6. Codependents take themselves too seriously.

Let's look one at a time at these results of codependency.

1. Codependents prevent others from developing their own sense of responsibility.

We keep addicted, needy people addicted and needy—dependent

By constantly solving, fixing, helping, and rescuing, codependents keep others from developing their own sense of responsibility. That keeps addicted, needy people addicted and needy—dependent on the codependent, and the cycle continues. Codependents need to let others do things for themselves!

2. Codependents neglect themselves.

Neglected needs

By focusing on others' needs, codependents fail to see their own needs. They try to get their self-worth from the opinions of others. They use all of their resources to please others. But their greatest needs are to develop their own identity, to recognize their own opinions, to manage their own time, to have their own friends, and to feel their own feelings. Codependents need to do things for themselves!

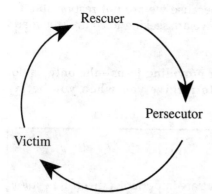

Rescuer

Persecutor

Victim

"That's the limit! That's as far as I go!"

3. Codependents resent being saviors.

Codependents rescue others to feel good about themselves, but this feeling often goes away rather quickly. They rescue; then they get angry that someone has taken advantage of them; then they feel sorry for themselves.[2]

4. Codependents threaten but continue rescuing.

When codependents feel anger and self-pity, they will threaten to stop helping someone, especially another codependent or a person with a compulsive disorder. They say, "That's the limit! That's as far as I go! You have to change your behavior!" But when more fixing, solving, and rescuing follow these threats, the words become meaningless. The ones being threatened learn they can continue to do as they please. They know someone eventually will rescue them!

5. Codependents lack objectivity about serving and helping others.

Because they spend so much of their lives in helping others, codependents often see themselves as humble (or abused) servants. But a great difference exists between helping people because you want to and feeling you have to help others to prevent a loss of value and worth. One is loving service; the other is codependency.

6. Codependents take themselves too seriously.

Lighten up!

Earlier I shared the comments of a co-worker who told me, "Pat, you take yourself too seriously. Lighten up!" "Fine," I remember thinking, "I'll just give up trying to have a sense of self-worth by accomplishing enough to win the respect and approval of other people. That will help!" He was right, of course. I was much too serious (and probably still am), but telling me not to take myself seriously didn't solve my problem. The condition of a person's self-worth is serious, but codependent behavior is not the solution. It is part of the problem!

✎ **Review the six consequences for codependents of a warped sense of responsibility. As you do, write here the verbs in each statement.**

_____

_____

Your list probably includes these words: prevent, neglect, resent, threaten, lack, and take. Just by reading these verbs and thinking about their impact, describe a person who is codependent.

_____

_____

After studying this unit, do you think you have a warped sense of responsibility?   ❏ Yes ❏ No

If you answered yes, which of the six statements on page 65 best explains the results of this in your life? Number ____. Now, in the blank below, rewrite in your own words that statement.

_____

How does this affect your self-concept? _____

_____

How does this affect your time? _____

_____

How does this affect your values? _____

_____

How does this affect others and their lives? _____

_____

Take plenty of time to reflect on these issues. This reflection may be painful, but it will help you gain objectivity about yourself and see your choices more clearly. Now, determine two positive thoughts or actions you could begin this week to prevent this consequence from occurring in your life. Below describe these thoughts or actions.

1. _____

2. _____

Consider sharing with your discovery group these plans. You also may want to talk to your discovery group or a trusted friend to get additional perspective on your sense of responsibility.

Do you believe your life would be different if you weren't compelled to help, fix, and rescue others? It's true! Most of us would experience many changes in both our outward behavior and in our inner lives. Our choices would be based on wisdom, not on compulsion. We would experience more peace, genuine love, and true joy. At the same time, our emotions would reawaken; we'd find we could grieve over our losses, and we could forgive rather than become bitter.

✎ **Review this week's lessons. Find one statement in the text that helped you to understand better the codependent person(s) you love.**

Below rewrite that statement below in your own words.

_____

_____

_____

Now, find one statement or insight you wrote that helped you to understand yourself better, whether or not you identify yourself as a codependent.

Below write it again, and describe how this new insight benefits you.

_____

_____

_____

Review the memory passage. Look it up and check your memory. Then close your Bible and write the passage below. How have you made application of this passage during your study of this unit? Below record your thoughts.

_____

_____

_____

_____

Notes

[1]Taken from the book, CAN CHRISTIANS LOVE TOO MUCH? by Margaret Josephson Rinck. Copyright © 1989 by Margaret Josephson Rinck. Used by permission of Zondervan Publishing House.
[2]Claude M. Steiner, *Scripts People Live* (New York: Grove Press, 1974), quoted in Melody Beattie, *Codependent No More*, 77. This cycle of rescue-anger-self-pity, or rescuer-persecutor-victim, is the insight of Stephen B. Karpman and is called the Karpman Drama Triangle.

Controlled/Controlling

Case in point

> ## ADDICTED TO AN ABUSER
>
> Charlotte's husband, John, was both a charmer and a beast. Like a drug addict, Charlotte tolerated the deterioration of almost everything else in her life for the rush she felt when John treated her well.
>
> He was good to her at times, but he also was physically and psychologically brutal. Right-handed blows to her face didn't hurt as badly as did his moodiness and silences triggered by her smallest breaking of the rules. Instead of blaming her husband for his selfish and immature behavior, Charlotte blamed herself, and her self-condemnation turned to self-hatred.
>
> Sometimes John could be charming. He would tell her how beautiful she was, and he would make wonderful promises. Charlotte believed each time that this was it! Now they would be happy! But the dream always died. She lamented, "It's hard to explain how depressed you feel when you realize that things haven't really changed when you thought they were going well."[1] (Read more about Charlotte on page 73).

What you'll learn

This week you will—

- explore how easily guilt and comparison control codependents;
- face the possibility that controlling behavior can become abusive behavior;
- understand how codependents suffer consequences when they control each aspect of their lives;
- describe how codependents also may become very controlling of other people;
- identify several key patterns that emerge from the controlled and controlling lives of codependents.

What you'll study

Controlled by Others	Tolerating Abusive Control	Controlling Yourself	Controlling Others	Patterns of Control
DAY 1	DAY 2	DAY 3	DAY 4	DAY 5

Memory verse

This week's passage of Scripture to memorize

For the love of Christ controls us, having concluded this, that one died for all, therefore all died; Therefore if any man is in Christ, he is a new creature; the old things passed away; behold, new things have come.

–2 Corinthians 5:14,17

DAY 1

Codependents want to be in absolute control of their lives so that they won't fail.

Winning others' approval

Controlled by Others

Without the secure anchors of love, acceptance, and significance, the codependent feels responsible for everyone but feels confident in no one. The codependent feels responsible for everything but feels confident in nothing. Codependents try to find security by pleasing people, by being right, and by doing right things in the right way. Their actions become like those of a puppet, dancing on the strings of praise and condemnation and easily controlled by the desires of others. Codependents need to be in control. They want to be in absolute control of their own lives so that they won't fail, while they want to control the behavior of others so that the others will add to and not subtract from their ability to perform well and please people.

Codependents Are Easily Controlled

Like everyone else, codependents need love and respect. Because they've been deprived of those desperately needed items, they are determined to do whatever it takes to win the approval and value they crave. Their means to that end is to make people happy. Their chief fear is that people will be unhappy with them.

 In the paragraph above, underline the codependent's strategy for winning the approval of others. Circle the codependent's greatest fear in implementing that strategy.

Codependents feel pressured to do more and to be more for others. You probably underlined the statement expressing the idea that making people happy becomes codependents' strategy for winning approval. Did you circle "they fear that others will be unhappy with them?"

Those around them quickly learn where the codependent's buttons are and how to push them. Skillful use of praise and condemnation manipulates the codependent as artfully as a puppeteer manipulates a puppet. Those around codependents may make statements to them like this:

- An "A" on an exam isn't good enough.
- I wish you'd get that promotion. I'll be so proud of you!
- I'm proud of you for doing so well. I can't wait to tell my friends!
- You are so wonderful to help me. I wish your sister was as kind as you are.
- You wouldn't be stupid enough to vote for somebody like that, would you?
- I wish you had come to visit me; I really needed you.
- My goodness, what an unusual hair style; I'm sure it will look better when it grows out.

Choose the statement above that really "pulled your strings," the one that affected you most when you read it. Use the margin box to explain how the statement is an attempt to control you. Individuals attempting to control the codependent probably believe they are doing a great favor. They justify their control with statements such as these:

- I'm only saying this for your own good . . . because I love you.
- I'm your mother. If I can't say this to you, who can?

The statement that "pulls my strings"—

_____

_____

_____

_____

- I know you better than you know yourself.
- If it weren't for me, who knows what kind of mess you'd make of your life!

In the margin box, name the feelings you have when someone makes to you statements like the four you just read.

 Have you ever made such statements to another person? ❑ Yes ❑ No

If yes, to whom were you speaking? _____

What was the situation? _____

How were your words meant to control either the situation or the person to whom you said them?

_____

These and many other statements range from tender to total manipulation. Each one, taken alone, may sound like a harmless question or statement. But in the context of codependency, in which one feels worthless and desperate for love and affirmation, the statements represent an attack. The attack is designed to change another's behavior through praise or condemnation. And the attack works! People use two types of control to manipulate codependents. Codependents are susceptible to control by guilt and by comparison.

1. Motivation By Guilt

Guilt is a primary motivator which produces a "have to" mentality. Often codependents feel no freedom to fail because they see the risks of losing love and/or respect as too great. Consequently, codependents are driven. In extreme cases this drive for perfection even can lead to **obsessive-compulsive** behavior. Codependents have to do the right thing, make the clever remark, wear the right clothes, look the right way, and, in short, be perfect. (That's not asking too much, is it?) Besides being driven, they want to please so much that they are compliant or submissive. They set aside their own wishes, ideas, and judgments rather than offend. At least for a while codependents will do anything for anybody at any time with a smile.

obsessive-compulsive–An idea or an emotion that persists in an individual's mind and cannot be dislodged by any conscious process is an obsession; one form of an obsession is the driving need a person feels to perform a particular act over and over again. Codependents frequently exhibit obsessive-compulsive behaviors and thoughts as a way to cope with life. Being obsessive-compulsive seems to provide control in a life that is frequently out of control.[2]

Guilt-driven persons can learn the lesson of 2 Corinthians 5:14-15. The apostle Paul says, "Christ's love compels us, because we are convinced that one died for all, and therefore all died. And he died for all, that those who live should no longer live for themselves but for him who died for them and was raised again" (NIV).

 Reread 2 Corinthians 5:14-15. What is the difference between being motivated by love and being driven by guilt?

_____

You may have written one of many differences between guilt and grace motivation. Did you notice the one identified in the Scripture passage? The words "for themselves" show the self-focus and self-protection of guilt motivation.

Reread the definition of *false guilt* **in unit 1 on page 12. Then ask yourself: "Do I usually feel the guilt of not pleasing God which is sin, or do I usually feel the guilt (or shame) of not pleasing others?" Pause now and pray for God's ability to understand clearly the guilt the Holy Spirit produces to convict you of your sin and the false guilt you impose on yourself when your life is not perfect and controlled.**

2. Motivation by Comparison

Comparison motivates codependents. People compare them to other members of the family, to co-workers, to relatives, and to anybody else that might inspire them or shame them into doing more. A friend told me what her mother tells her every month or so: "My friends' children always are doing nice things for them. They buy them clothes, jewelry, and nice furniture. They take them on vacations. Their children are there whenever they are needed. I guess I'll just have to take care of myself." Is that a neutral statement of fact, a statement of independence? No way! This mother is using comparison to manipulate her daughter!

The goal is to inspire them or shame them into doing more.

Pause now and read the verses from Psalm 139 in the margin. Allow King David's words of praise to be your words of praise, too. David celebrated the joy of being known by God, of being created by God, and of being utterly unique. In the psalm underline any words or phrases which particularly touch you today and give you hope.

The next time someone uses the weapon of comparison against you, like the mother did in the story above, pray the prayer David prayed as he concluded this psalm. You have those words printed in the margin. Ask God, not your accuser, to reveal any "offensive way" you are following and to lead you.

Describe a situation in which you felt manipulated by guilt and a situation in which you felt manipulated by comparison. To do this answer the questions in the following chart about the two situations.

O Lord, you have searched me and you know me. You know when I sit and when I rise; you perceive my thoughts from afar. For you created my inmost being; you knit me together in my mother's womb. I praise you because I am fearfully and wonderfully made; your works are wonderful , I know that full well . . . your eyes saw my unformed body. All the days ordained for me were written in your book before one of them came to be.
    –Psalm 139:1-2,13-14,16, NIV

Search me, O God, and know my heart; test me and know my anxious thoughts. See if there is any offensive way in me, and lead me in the way everlasting.
    –Psalm 139:23-24, NIV

	Guilt Situation	Comparison Situation
Who manipulated you?		
How did he or she manipulate you?		
What did you gain or lose by permitting yourself to be manipulated?		
How did you respond?		
How did your response make you feel?		

If manipulation by guilt or comparison motivates you—or codependents you know—keep this in mind:

> Manipulation is not harmless.
> Manipulation is evil, seductive, and destructive.

❖ **Begin today to memorize the unit memory verse.**

SUMMARY STATEMENTS

- Codependents need to be in control. They want to be in absolute control of their own and others' lives so that they won't fail.
- Codependents are easily controlled because they feel the need to please other people.
- Guilt and comparison are two methods frequently used to control and manipulate codependents.

Charlotte's story

Tolerating Abusive Control

Shattered Dreams

To an objective bystander, the control abusive persons exercise in their families is almost unbelievable. But the family is not objective. No matter how much abuse and neglect the family members endure, their overwhelming thirst for the abuser's acceptance keeps them coming back for more.

In her book, *Shattered Dreams*, Charlotte Fedders described the details of her relationship with her abusive husband. Charlotte's husband, John, was both a charmer and a beast. Like a drug addict, Charlotte tolerated the deterioration of almost everything else in her life for the rush she felt when John treated her well. He was good to her at times, but he also was physically and psychologically brutal. Right-handed blows to her face didn't hurt as badly as did his moodiness and silences triggered by her smallest breaking of the rules. Instead of blaming her husband for his selfish and immature behavior, Charlotte blamed herself, and her self-condemnation turned to self-hatred.

Sometimes John could be charming. He would tell her how beautiful she was, and he would make wonderful promises. Charlotte believed each time that this was it! Now they would be happy! But the dream always died.

Charlotte believed each time that this was it! They would be happy!

She lamented, "It's hard to explain how depressed you feel when you realize that things haven't really changed when you thought they were going well. I was so sure that we were making progress, and then John would be moody or silent and we were back to square one. It would make me crazy and so desperate." Charlotte wasn't able to be objective until later—then her desperation only made her more easily controlled by John.[3]

1. One-way Perception
2. Emotional Walls
3. Extremes and Exaggerations
4. Believing the Unbelievable
5. Daydreaming

 In the margin you will find the five defense tactics codependents often use. You first learned these in unit 2, day 2. Review them if necessary; then below write which one(s) you see in Charlotte's story.

_____

_____

 In a codependent's life what result occurs from using these defense tactics?

_____

The answer to the first exercise could have included: one-way perception (because Charlotte blamed herself), and extremes and exaggerations and believing the unbelievable (demonstrated by Charlotte's believing John's promises). The answer to the second exercise was the title of unit 2. The codependent suffers a growing lack of objectivity.

Always Reacting

Many of us have so little self-confidence that we seldom have or express our own ideas and desires. We only respond—or react—to the ideas and desires of others. We are like a ball in a pinball machine—being forced in one direction, then another; always doing what the outside force demands; never able to determine its own course. We learn to react to the slightest hint of praise or condemnation. In fact, we don't even wait for a hint. We anticipate what others might want from us, and we act accordingly.

Repeatedly giving in

Although codependents eventually tire of this game, they lack the objectivity to stop playing. They become angry as they realize they are being pressured to perform, and they repeatedly give in to that pressure.

As a result, they hate themselves for their foolishness, and they hate the dependent person for manipulating them. But because this is the only game they know, they keep playing. Their desperate need for approval keeps codependents on a seemingly endless treadmill of need–manipulation–anger. They may even become openly hostile.

passive-aggressive–A controlling form of noninvolvement because it forces others to "take charge." A person mentally or emotionally refuses to make a decision, perform an action, or do a certain behavior, forcing someone else to fill the gap where those things are needed. So, the first person seems "passive" since he or she has done nothing, but actually this person is "aggressive" because the inactivity pushes on another person.

More likely, they will become **passive-aggressive**—refusing to be honest and also refusing to respond. Although they may appear passive, the real goal is to hurt the one who has been controlling them.

Continued Dependence and Submission

Occasionally, the dependent person will tolerate to a certain extent or even encourage the independence the codependent demonstrates. But beyond that point, it is strictly taboo. Past that point, the dependent person may explode in anger and say, "How could you be so selfish?" Or the dependent person may take the much more subtle approach, "We need to talk," meaning, "We need to talk so I can convince you to go back to being dependent on me, submissive to me, and easily manipulated by me. No limits should exist to what you will do for me. After all, pleasing me is your way of gaining self-worth."

One woman, describing her relationship with her alcoholic husband, stated emphatically, "I'm independent now. I don't tell him anything!" But her description of their relationship was not one of her growing sense of self-worth. She was so hurt that she simply withdrew from him. Her identity and sense of self-confidence weren't any better. She was still "dancing on his strings,"—doing what he wanted her to do. She didn't talk to him as much as she used to, but that really did not represent progress for her self-worth or their relationship.

How do you feel when you give in to someone's manipulation? In the margin box describe your feelings. Then describe how you feel when you refuse to give in to the pressure when someone tries to manipulate you. When you give in you may feel immediate relief that the pressure is over, but soon, you may feel self-pity and self-contempt for your failure to be strong. You also may feel resentment toward the one who pressured you. On those occasions when you stand up for yourself you may feel strong, but at the same time you may feel guilt, as if you had betrayed the other person. You also may feel bitter toward the one who tried to control you.

Only one person has controlling rights in your life—and He is Jesus Christ. He earned those rights through self-sacrifice, but He will not exercise them without your permission. His respect for you and love for you are total and complete.

 On five separate index cards write the unit memory passage five times. **Tape each card on some item that represents an area you carefully control in your life. You may find yourself taping cards to your calendar, your steering wheel, your checkbook, your workshop door, or your computer screen. Leave the cards in those places during the remainder of this unit. Each time you see a card, take time to read and memorize the verse. Then pray a prayer asking God to take control of that area of your life.**

Read again Charlotte's story at the beginning of this day's content. Does her story have any similarity to your life today? In the box below read some important words of warning.

When I give in I feel—

_____

_____

_____

When I don't give in I feel—

_____

_____

_____

> If the control issue in your life has gone so far that you are being abused, it needs to stop now. The abuse you tolerate may be emotional, verbal, sexual, or physical. Be aware that when we start saying no to other people's abusive behavior, they often become more abusive rather than less. Their desire is to force us to become compliant again. We can be prepared for this result.
>
> I strongly encourage you to take a step today to prevent any more abusive behavior directed against you. You possibly may need legal help or physical protection. Call your discovery-group leader or minister and ask these individuals to refer you to a competent counselor.
>
> Ask for their prayer support. No one—including you—ever deserves or needs to be abused or to tolerate abuse.

If you are not sure whether you are being abused, then turn down the corner of page 75. Write on that corner, "Reread at the end of unit 5." Unit 5 will deal in more depth with the hurt and anger an abusive relationship produces.

After studying that unit, read this material again. If you recognize that you are being abused, I urge you again to take the steps outlined previously to see that the abuse never occurs again. May God bless you with insight and courage.

> **SUMMARY STATEMENTS**
>
> - Compulsive rescuers tolerate abuse because their lack of objectivity blinds them to the abuse.
> - Many of us have so little self-confidence that we seldom have or express our own ideas and desires.
> - The compulsion to control leads to a cycle of need-manipulation-anger.

DAY 3

Controlling Yourself

The Compulsion to "Be Right"

Codependents define themselves by what they do, how they look, and how well they accomplish tasks in life. They don't perceive failure as an option. They have to be right. They have to be in control of their lives. Why? Because the rest of their lives are so chaotic, with a dependent parent or spouse, that they have a strong need for an area of their lives that they can control.

As is usually the case with codependents, two extremes of behavior appear. Some codependents become obsessive-compulsive to gain control of life; others give up and withdraw from life.

Some codependents must have order in their lives. Things are in boxes—neatly labeled, of course—the home is tidy, clothes are immaculate, makeup is worn perfectly, every hair is in place, the car is clean and its tank filled, work is done on time and with excellence. Schedules are meticulously drawn up to aid maximum efficiency and minimize distractions. At best, their sense of satisfaction for doing a job well is very short-lived. It has to be done again tomorrow, and next week, and next month, and . . .

A pastor's story

A pastor tells how this effort to control became obsessive-compulsive and took over his life.

"When I was about 8 years old, I received a Bible for Christmas. This Bible had a schedule in the back for reading the Bible through in one year. I made a New Year's resolution to read the whole Bible by following this plan. In the mornings I read from the Old Testament, and in the evenings I read from the New Testament.

"As I read, something unusual started to happen, which I now believe was a symptom of the emotional pain I felt in my family.

Not perfect

"As I read my Bible, I would read a section once and then say to myself, 'That wasn't good enough.' So I would read a phrase aloud. It didn't sound right to me. Maybe I didn't pronounce a word just right. I would read it again. Soon I was reading a phrase aloud over and over again, sometimes stuttering. Finally, I would move on to the next section of Scripture. It took a long time to complete the daily readings.

"When I had finished reading, I would go to my desk. I kept my Bible and my Sunday School book on the lower right corner of my desk. I would make sure that the side of the Sunday School book was half an inch from the side of the desk and that the bottom was half an inch from the front of the desk. I would place the Bible on top of the Sunday School book, with every corner matching in perfect alignment. Then I would recheck the Bible and the Sunday School book for alignment as many as 50 times.

Crying out to God

"My father was getting drunk. I didn't understand, and I was crying out to God: 'God, I don't understand what is going on in my family. I know that my parents love me, but something is wrong. I don't understand it. Help me, God. Look at me, God. Look how hard I'm trying.'"[4]

✎ **What evidence did you find in this story of the powerful need to "be right"?**

_____

_____

Do you also find evidence of withdrawing from life? What is it?

_____

The boy's need to be right was so strong that he spent great amounts of time seeking to pronounce words perfectly and stack books precisely. His time spent performing rituals was a form of withdrawal. By reading his Bible he temporarily could escape the chaos of his home.

Relating to Children

Obsessive-compulsive persons want the people in their lives to be in control, too. They need their spouses, children, coworkers—everybody—to contribute to their compelling need for a well-ordered life. Precisely because they are so uncontrollable, young children often cause obsessive-compulsives a lot of problems.

When a child cries, an obsessive-compulsive interprets the crying to mean, "There's something wrong. Things are out of control and it's your fault, Mother (or Father)!" Their crying or spilling something—disruptive behavior—can be a threat to obsessive-compulsives' stability and significance because noises or actions like this communicate to them that things are out of control.

Take a study break! Go to a nearby park, playground, or schoolyard where you can observe young children at play. Use the margin box to record what you see and hear as you observe their childlike play.

I see

_____

_____

_____

I hear

_____

_____

_____

At that time the disciples came to Jesus and asked, "Who is the greatest in the kingdom of heaven?" He called a little child and had him stand among them. And he said: "I tell you the truth, unless you change and become like little children, you will never enter the kingdom of heaven. Therefore, whoever humbles himself like this child is the greatest in the kingdom of heaven."

–Matthew 18:1-3, NIV

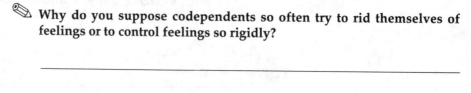 Look at what you've just written; read the verse in the margin. What positive things about young children—and about being childlike—have you discovered?

_____

_____

As you watched children at play, did you observe a child's lack of self-consciousness? Were the children concerned about how they looked or what someone else thought of them, or were they more concerned with having a good time? Is it possible that the childlike quality of which Jesus spoke included absence of worry about performance and others' opinions?

Relating to Feelings

The obsessive-compulsive also controls his or her emotions—not too much crying (maybe none at all) and not too much laughter either. Anger is expressly forbidden. Being angry means you really are out of control.

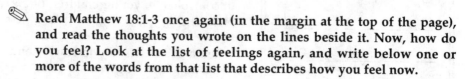 Why do you suppose codependents so often try to rid themselves of feelings or to control feelings so rigidly?

_____

_____

You may have written something similar to the following—
- Codependents learned to live through others' feelings rather than to feel their own.
- Their families, then and now, may have discouraged expressions of feelings or may have punished them when certain feelings were expressed.
- The rules in their families—usually unstated rules—said some feelings were acceptable and others were not.
- As a result of any or all of these, their emotional systems simply may have shut down, even though they have had intense feelings in the past.[5]

Reading this section may have caused you to have some strong feelings or some different ones than you've experienced in the past. What are you feeling right now as you've read this section? In the margin box, check all the feelings that apply. Then try to describe why you are feeling those emotions.

Read Matthew 18:1-3 once again (in the margin at the top of the page), and read the thoughts you wrote on the lines beside it. Now, how do you feel? Look at the list of feelings again, and write below one or more of the words from that list that describes how you feel now.

_____

Pause now to thank God that you can feel—even if you are feeling sad or angry or confused. Feelings are His gift to help us understand ourselves and our lives. Learning to name them and to admit to having them is the first step in learning to express these feelings and to deal with them appropriately.

Right now I am feeling—

❑ Sad
❑ Angry
❑ Lonely
❑ Ashamed
❑ Guilty
❑ Confused
❑ Afraid
❑ No feelings
❑ Other _____

I'm feeling this because—

_____

_____

Relating to God

A codependent's relationship with God also is likely to be obsessive-compulsive and highly controlled. The relationship is often—

Rigid and ritualistic

- rigid and ritualistic;
- filled with good activities;
- but has little spontaneity and warmth.

✎ **Read the pastor's story on pages 76-77 again. Find in it evidence of the three characteristics just mentioned, and write those characteristics in the story's margins.**

Why do you suppose religious activity appeals to many codependents? Write your thoughts here and consider sharing them with your discovery group.

_____

_____

Codependents trying to manage the twin burdens of always being right and always being in control have one of two looks. They may appear selectively perfect, or they may seem broken and hopeless.

1. Selectively Perfect

Of course, people cannot be in complete control of their schedule, work, relationships, and emotions all the time, so obsessive-compulsives are forced to choose which areas they will concentrate on (and get their self-worth from) and which areas to let slide (and say they don't care about).

Using the margin box give an example of ways you try to control your schedule, relationship, emotions, or other parts of your life.

✎ **Do these controlling behaviors show your own search for perfection in your life?   Yes   No   (Circle one) On the lines below explain your answer.**

_____

_____

Many of us try desperately to control ourselves because the rest of our relationships are so out of control. We may become rigid and legalistic in some areas, but we may neglect other areas completely. The results often are a mixture of pride about our ability to control part of our lives and denial or shame about the part that we neglect.

✎ **In what ways do you try to be selectively perfect?**

_____

Do you feel there's something you'd like to change about that behavior?

_____

Ways I control—
my schedule _____
_____
my relationships _____
_____
my emotions _____
_____
other _____
_____

2. Being Broken and Hopeless

For some codependents, the crushing weight of being right and neat and in complete control at all times is simply too much. They become immobilized because the job of rigidly controlling life is such a massive task. They appear to be very irresponsible when, in fact, they have broken under the strain of striving for perfection. They've given up, but they still have no feeling of freedom or relief.

> Praise the Lord. How good it is to sing praises to our God, how pleasant and fitting to praise him! He heals the brokenhearted and binds up their wounds. His pleasure is not in the strength of the horse, nor his delight in the legs of a man; the Lord delights in those who fear him, who put their hope in his unfailing love.
> –Psalm 147:1,3,10-11, NIV

✎ **Read the passage in the margin. Name someone you know who is**

brokenhearted. _____

Name someone you know who is hopeless. _____

➤ **Pause now and pray for these two persons. In your prayer use the psalmist's words.**

Some obsessive-compulsives feel guilty and hopeless. They believe they are terrible failures. Others feel powerful and in control when they have achieved their rigid goals. Either way the cycle is perpetuated. Some of them look very successful. Others appear lazy and passive. In reality, both kinds have defined life and its purposes by their beliefs about control. Although they illustrate the extremes of control's effects in people's lives, both kinds of persons are hurting.

SUMMARY STATEMENTS

- Codependents define themselves by what they do, how they look, and how well they accomplish tasks in life.
- Codependent believers tend to have a relationship with God that is highly controlled.
- Some persons appear to be very irresponsible when, in fact, they have broken under the strain of striving for perfection.
- Some driven people feel guilty and hopeless. They believe they are terrible failures; others feel powerful and in control.

DAY 4

Controlling Others

How codependents relate to others usually is a mirror of their relationship with the addicted or needy persons in their lives. They may hate the way others treat them, but modeling and experience are powerful teachers. They shape our patterns of behavior, including how we treat others.

Two Extremes

The codependent's attempt to control people usually produces one of two extremes of behavior. At one extreme, codependents may try to act like a smothering parent and shape their opinions and habits by constant attention with both praise and criticism. Or, codependents may become like dictators—barking orders and exercising any real or perceived authority in their lives.

The other extreme is withdrawal. Persons may become so tired of trying to control others, or may feel so inadequate and worthless from the effort, that they believe no one will do what they want them to do. Their poor self-concept overcomes the desire to manipulate, and they give up.

Inadequate and worthless

✎ **Identify the three most important people in your life. Then, on the continuum below, write their names across the line at the point that best describes the amount of control you attempt to exercise in their lives.**

Constant   Withdrawal
Attention _____

Doing Unto Others . . .

Codependents manipulate others by using the same techniques of praise and condemnation that have been used on them. For example, they'll use their wit and humor to impress people. Remember, codependents usually have excellent minds and develop strong communication skills to win acceptance. Or, they'll use sarcasm, sometimes to cut people to ribbons. And of course, they'll use praise, anger, and withdrawal to get people to do what they want them to do. These techniques worked on the codependent; they'll work on others most of the time, too.

So in everything, do to others what you would have them do to you.
　　　　　–Matthew 7:12, NIV

✎ **Read the Scriptures in the margin. What do the passages say about controlling other people?**

_____

_____

The entire law is summed up in a single command: "Love your neighbor as yourself."
　　　　　–Galatians 5:14, NIV

These and other Scriptures say that we are to love others and treat them as we would want to be treated. We are told to do no harm, but controlling is harmful to others. Controlling others' behavior is the opposite of simply loving them.

Love does no harm to its neighbor. Therefore love is the fulfillment of the law.
　　　　　–Romans 13:10, NIV

The Paradox

The paradox for codependents is this: while they are trying to control others, they are being controlled by the persons they try to control. They want others to perform and appreciate them, but they still get their self-worth from the other person's approval.

One man tried to get his wife, who was addicted to prescription drugs, to pull her act together. Her behavior might cost him a promotion. But she still had him on a string. She could be happy when she wanted or angry or sad when she chose. In those ways, she could get him to do almost anything for her. The tables were turned: the rabbit was chasing the dog.

Taking Off the Controls

We need to stop attempting to control other people. We need to let them make their own decisions and live with the consequences. We need to get our self-worth from something other than their approval. We need to cut the strings. Letting people make their own choices can be hard.

Taylor's story

Every week I give my children, Catherine and Taylor, a small allowance. They put it into boxes labeled save, spend, and give. My wife Joyce and I tell them they can use the spending money any way they choose. Catherine usually uses her money to buy toys like shoe skates that are more lasting. But Taylor has a habit of spending his money (that's a key term in this story: *his* money) on things he plays with for a day or two and never takes out of the closet again. A few months ago, we went to the store to buy batteries (the 742,932nd we'd bought in the last eight years!), and Taylor spied a toy he wanted. It was a transformable little man in a shark-shaped container. He loves sharks, and he really wanted this toy. I said, "Son, it's your choice how you spend your money, but I don't think it's a good idea to spend $9 on this. Now, what do you want to do?" "I like it, Daddy. I'm going to get it." Round one was lost.

Round two started. "Son, you can do whatever you want. It's your money, but you've bought other toys like this before. Where are those toys now?" "I want this one, Daddy." Not a hint of frustration in his voice.

Round three: "Taylor, it's $9! You can find something else you'd enjoy a lot more for that much money. I don't think it's a good idea to get this." To his credit, he stood his ground. He picked it up and said, "This is the one I want." He took out the wad of dollar bills in his pocket and paid for the toy. He beamed with joy as he walked out of the store.

I quickly realized the error of my ways and apologized. Stating my opinion once and giving him some helpful advice was fine, but I had gone well beyond that point. I was demanding and was trying to manipulate Taylor, but he was his own man. He made his own choice. Next time, I hope I give him the freedom to do that without interfering.

Write in the margin box examples of ways you try to control others' schedules, relationships, emotions, or other parts of their lives.

🖉 **Do these controlling behaviors signal your own search for perfection in your life?** ❏ Yes ❏ No **On the lines below explain your answer.**

_____

_____

You may use the same techniques used on you, or you may do the opposite. For instance, if you have been smothered and controlled too much, you may be too permissive with your children. You may hope to help them avoid the same pain you experienced as well as avoid the guilt you would feel if you smothered them.

What are the results of your controlling behavior? _____

_____

_____

Ways I attempt to control others'—

schedules _____

_____

relationships _____

_____

emotions _____

_____

other _____

_____

How would you change your own controlling behavior?

_____

_____

Your inner guilt, fear, or shame may have prompted the abuse.

Perhaps you have now acknowledged to yourself—whether for the first or for the 50th time—that you are using abusive behavior to control other people. You may have used emotional, verbal, sexual, or physical abuse against other persons in your family or your community. Your inner guilt, fear, or shame may have prompted the abuse. Reasons from your own dysfunctional past may have contributed to your behavior, but those reasons do not excuse your behavior. You are responsible.

I strongly encourage you to take a step today to prevent yourself from ever abusing another person. Call your discovery-group leader or minister and ask these individuals to refer you to a competent counselor or treatment facility. Ask for their prayer support. No one ever deserves to be abused—no one.

SUMMARY STATEMENTS

- Codependents manipulate others by using the same techniques of praise and condemnation that others have used on them.
- The paradox for codependents is this: while they are trying to control others, they are being controlled by the persons they try to control.
- We need to let other people make their own decisions and live with the consequences.

DAY 5

Patterns of Control

Whether being controlled or controlling others, certain patterns develop in a person's life. Some people are so afraid to be wrong in any given decision that they become passive and indecisive. They are paralyzed by fear of making a mistake. Others feel such a strong need to be right that they state their opinions dogmatically, demanding others choose to be for them or against them. Between these extremes is mature moderation, the ability to form and state opinions without demanding that others agree.

"I'm Afraid To Be Wrong"

I have a friend that I go to lunch with sometimes. When we get together, I ask him where he wants to go to eat. He invariably says, "I dunno. Where do you want to go?" I say, "I don't care. I decided last time. Why don't you decide this time." After we go back and forth a few times, one of us finally makes a concrete suggestion. Behind this indecision is the fear of making the wrong choice and the fear of someone else's knowing my choice was wrong.

"I Have To Be Right"

To illustrate the other end of the spectrum, I know a man who never has been wrong (according to his own testimony) in his life! He always seems to be one step ahead of the rest of us and always seems to have thought things through a little more than we do. He is bright, articulate, and persuasive, and when he speaks, he states his opinions as if any sane person would agree with him and only an imbecile would disagree! The people who follow him think he is wonderful. Others avoid him, especially if they have been branded as enemies in one of his black-and-white statements.

He forces people to take a stand for him or against him, almost like Colonel Travis drawing a line in the dirt at the Alamo and saying, "If you are with me, cross over this line." Travis, however, allowed people to decide if they wanted to try to escape and save their lives. He gave them an option. He wasn't demanding a response. My codependent friend demands the right response.

Travis allowed people to decide if they wanted to try to escape and save their lives.

Why does he act this way? Probably because he is insecure. Though he appears to be one of the most secure people in the universe, he probably feels that he needs strongly defined convictions to designate who he is. And he needs for others to affirm him, so he takes the risk of offending some to win others' approval.

 When you encounter such a person as this man, what path do you typically take? Draw yourself (or a reasonable facsimile!) on the path that best represents your typical response.

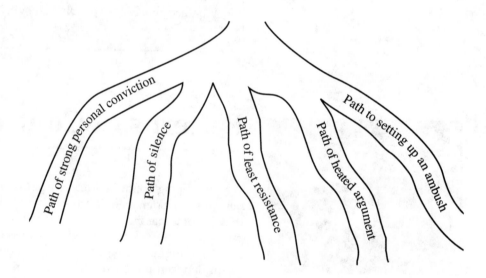

Strong Motivations

Codependents desperately need to be loved. They desperately need to feel that they are loved and have a sense of worth. When these needs are unmet, some will try to avoid the pain by being indecisive and passive, while others will try to win approval by being right. Most of us are a blend of the two. Certain people or certain situations exist which will cause us to withdraw into passivity, but at other times we will take a stand, state our opinions forcefully, and hope people like what we've said. Both avenues are designed to get us to the same goal: avoiding pain and winning approval.

✎ **You may or may not be a codependent, but all of us exhibit codependent behaviors at times because we're human and unsure of ourselves. Answer the following questions and try to gain new insight about yourself.**

How did (does) your family try to control you? _____

_____

Do you ever use such behavior to try to control others?   Yes   No   (circle one)

Give an example.   _____

Your family may have used praise, rewards, condemnation, withdrawal, or many other techniques to make you fear their disapproval. You may use the same or very different methods.

Describe two situations in which you become passive and indecisive because you are afraid to fail.

<table>
<tr><td>Situation #1</td><td>Situation #2</td></tr>
<tr><td>_____</td><td>_____</td></tr>
<tr><td>_____</td><td>_____</td></tr>
<tr><td>_____</td><td>_____</td></tr>
<tr><td>_____</td><td>_____</td></tr>
</table>

Many of us become passive and indecisive around powerful people, people who threaten us, or those around whom we are afraid to fail.

✎ **Describe two situations, one where you feel you have to be right and one where you feel people have to agree with you.**

<table>
<tr><td>Situation #1</td><td>Situation #2</td></tr>
<tr><td>_____</td><td>_____</td></tr>
<tr><td>_____</td><td>_____</td></tr>
<tr><td>_____</td><td>_____</td></tr>
<tr><td>_____</td><td>_____</td></tr>
</table>

We may cover our fears and insecurity by being dogmatic about our opinions. We demand that people agree with us because we feel their disagreement is a threat to our security.

✎ **Review this week's lessons. Find one statement in the text that helped you to understand better the codependent person(s) you love.**

Below rewrite that statement in your own words.

_____

_____

_____

Now, find one statement or insight you wrote that helped you to understand yourself better, whether or not you identify yourself as codependent.

Below write it again, and describe how this new insight benefits you.

_____

_____

_____

Review the memory passage. Look it up and check your memory. Then close your Bible and write the passage in this margin. How have you made application of this passage during your study of this unit? Below record your thoughts.

_____

_____

_____

Notes

[1] Charlotte Fedders and Laura Elliot, *Shattered Dreams* (New York: Dell Publishing, 1987), 87.
[2] Samuel L. Andelman, *The New Home Medical Encyclopedia*, Illustrated ((New York: Quadrangle Books, Inc., 1973), 865.
[3] Charlotte Fedders and Laura Elliot, *Shattered Dreams* (New York: Dell Publishing, 1987), 87.
[4] Tim Sledge, *Making Peace With Your Past: Help for Adult Children of Dysfunctional Families* (Nashville: LifeWay Press, 1992), 35.
[5] Ibid., 24.

Hurt and Anger

AN EMOTIONAL ORPHAN

Although most people would describe Connie as healthy and mature, she thought she was losing her mind. Though she had many friends and although many people considered her successful, she was dying inside.

She described the home of her childhood. On the surface it seemed normal enough: no alcoholism, no divorce, no addictions. Yet, she remembered her parents' relationship as being cool and aloof, like an armed truce. Their relationship with each other was duplicated in their relationship with her. Though no outward signs of a dysfunctional family existed, the family was quite dysfunctional. She had been left an emotional orphan—fending for herself and lacking the love, protection, and support every child needs.

She wept, "My father never held me. He never told me I was his special little girl or anything. I wanted to be loved so much, but no matter what I did to please him, I never felt he loved me." (Read more about Connie on page 92.)

What you'll learn

This week you will—

- learn how abuse deeply wounds its victims;
- analyze numbness and pain without gain—two ineffective ways people attempt to manage hurt and anger;
- explore ways people use excusing the offender/blaming themselves and displaced anger to manage hurt and anger;
- understand how people use outbursts of anger and self-pity with anger to manipulate others and manage hurt and anger;
- recall memories of parents and childhood to discover potential sources of hurt and anger.

What you'll study

Deep Wounds	Responding to Hurt and Anger Part 1	Responding to Hurt and Anger Part 2	Responding to Hurt and Anger Part 3	Memories
DAY 1	DAY 2	DAY 3	DAY 4	DAY 5

Memory verse

This week's passage of Scripture to memorize

For we do not have a high priest who cannot sympathize with our weaknesses, but one who has been tempted in all things as we are, yet without sin. Let us therefore draw near with confidence to the throne of grace, that we may receive mercy and may find grace to help in time of need.

–Hebrews 4:15-16

Deep Wounds

Abuse comes in many forms. Physical and sexual abuse are not the only ways abuse exists. Author Dr. Susan Forward defined and described how some men abuse their wives or lovers. Her definition applies to all other relationships as well. In her book, *Men Who Hate Women and the Women Who Love Them*, she wrote:

> Abuse is defined as any behavior that is designed to control and subjugate another human being through the use of fear, humiliation, and verbal or physical assaults. . . . (It is) the systematic persecution of one partner by another. . . . they wear down their partners through unrelenting criticism and fault-finding. This type of psychological abuse is particularly insidious because it is often disguised as a way of teaching the woman how to be a better person.[1]

Results of Abuse

The predictable results of such abuse are—

- self-condemnation;
- lack of confidence;
- passivity;
- tendency to be easily manipulated;
- morbid introspection;
- lack of security;
- rigidity;
- other emotional and relational problems.

Passive abuse

Active physical and/or verbal abuse in a dysfunctional family leaves codependents feeling deeply hurt and angry toward the ones who have hurt them. But the passive abuse of neglect and withdrawal are equally devastating. The family ideally provides warmth and worth, but the abusive family provides pain. Codependents then try to please and rescue the one(s) who are hurting them in an attempt to win the love and approval codependents so desperately need.

Codependents temporarily may be rewarded for their attempts to rescue, but this reward will not meet their needs for unconditional love. Their hurt and anger will continue to grow. A system traps them, and this system fuels their compulsion to rescue by withholding love and affection.

✎ **Look over the following list of abusive behaviors. Place an *A* by the ones you consider Active and a *P* by the ones you consider Passive.**

___ 1. Name calling
___ 2. The "silent treatment"
___ 3. Disapproving looks
___ 4. Rage

___ 5. Belittling comments
___ 6. Verbal threats
___ 7. Throwing objects
___ 8. Slapping

✎ **Have you ever experienced any of these or other abusive behaviors directed against you? If so, write the behavior in the margin.**

Numbers 1, 4, 5, 6, 7, and 8 are active forms of abusive behavior. Numbers 2 and 3 are passive.

 Now, look on the previous page at the list of results of abuse. Did you also experience any of these results at the time you experienced the abuse? If so, write the result next to the behavior(s) you've written in the margin on the previous page.

Has the exercise above given you any new insight about any hurt or anger in your life? Use the margin box to record your thoughts.

The offenses a non-codependent person experiences are like a fist hitting an arm. The blow causes pain for a while, but the pain soon disappears. The same blow to a codependent is more severe. The codependent's emotional arm already is broken, so the pain of being hit is much more terrible. It inflicts greater injury, and the injury takes much longer to heal.

Hurt and Anger

Hurt and anger go together. Hurt results from not feeling loved and not being valued. It comes from feeling abandoned, used, and condemned. Anger is the reaction toward the source of the hurt. These painful emotions not only are the products of the codependent's past, they are a part of everyday reality. The need for a sense of worth leads codependents to try to rescue the very ones who have hurt them. As a result, the codependents are hurt again and again. Sooner or later, they feel angry.

Marianne's story

Marianne's husband, Kyle, is an alcoholic. Under the pressure of her pleas and coaxing, he stopped drinking at times, only to slide back into the dark pit again. Marianne made excuses for him. She worked to support the family because he couldn't keep a job. She repeatedly explained to their children, "Daddy is sick today. We have to be quiet and get him whatever he needs."

Occasionally, Marianne reached her limit. She'd had enough! She'd tell him she wasn't calling in to say he was sick today. He'd have to call this time. But his response usually was something like, "How can you be so selfish? I'm only asking you to do one little thing for me, and you won't do it. If you loved me, you'd do it for me."

Calling a codependent selfish is the worst possible insult.

Codependents live by rescuing. Calling a codependent selfish is the worst possible insult. Marianne gave in and made the call—of course! Then she realized he had done it again. He had gotten his way. He had manipulated her into doing what he wanted her to do! She was furious! But she was not furious enough to refuse to rescue him the next time, and the next, and the next.

Marianne's codependent relationship with Kyle robbed her of the ability to objectively understand their tangled relationship.

 Is Kyle's abusive behavior ❑ active or ❑ passive? Check the answer which applies; then explain your answer.

_____

_____

What results of Kyle's behavior occur in Marianne's life? (Refer to the list on page 88 of predictable results of abuse.)

_____

_____

Passive abuse

Kyle's abuse is primarily passive. He controls Marianne with his helplessness. He plays on her guilt and demands that she take care of him. This behavior prompts Marianne to take Kyle's responsibilities for him. You certainly could have included among your answers self-condemnation, lack of confidence, and the ability to be easily manipulated.

 Fill in the sketch below with words Marianne could say next time Kyle wants her to make excuses for his drinking. Choose words that will break Marianne and Kyle's typical codependent pattern.

Layers of Protection

A great well of anger exists in a codependent's soul. The codependent builds elaborate defense mechanisms to block pain and to control anger. These defenses include—

Overwhelming anger

- denying reality;
- pleasing people;
- being in control;
- keeping people at a distance;

- being numb to feelings;
- displacing anger;
- excusing the offender(s);
- and many other variations.

Some of us use different defenses for different circumstances, but most of us have developed several layers to ensure our protection. In days 2, 3, and 4 of this unit you will explore these ways of managing hurt and anger.

These defense mechanisms bring some short-term gains because they help us block out pain and control anger to some degree. But over the long term, we lose. These same strategies that seem to protect us from the deep wounds of tangled relationships also protect us from the healing process such wounds require. Just like the thin layers of an onion, these defense mechanisms surround us with insulating layers and separate us from our wounds. What happens if we peel away these layers? Our hurt and anger will be exposed. This will be painful. But the fresh air and light on our pain and anger will begin the healing we need. Many codependents grow up in and continue to live in relationships characterized by manipulation, abuse, abandonment, poor resolution of conflict, and other behaviors which wound them deeply.

The fresh air and light on our pain and anger will begin the healing we need.

 Look at the drawing of the onion in the margin. Draw an arrow to the heart of the onion and label it *deep wounds*. What benefits do codependents get from keeping their deep wounds hidden under the protective layers of the defense mechanisms this study mentions?

_____

_____

The reality of pain and anger is too threatening to codependents and to their important relationships. No one has taught or allowed them to process their pain. No one has taught them the joys of love and forgiveness. Almost by default, their only solution for dealing with the pain of deep wounds is *not* to deal with them but to repress them. Codependents use these to block pain and to continue to be irresponsible. That is the false benefit of the mechanisms.

 Find in your Bible this unit's Scripture passage to memorize. Mark it. Read it five times. Pray for persistence this week to memorize it.

SUMMARY STATEMENTS

- Any behavior designed to control and conquer another human being is abusive.
- The passive abuse of neglect and withdrawal can be as devastating as can active abuse.
- Elaborate defense mechanisms help the codependent control anger and avoid dealing with emotional pain.

DAY 2

Responding to Hurt and Anger

Remember the first characteristic of codependency unit 1 identified? "Lack of objectivity," you say? You are exactly right! Regaining some objectivity about life and your responses to it is an important first step toward untangling relationships and healing deep wounds in your life. As you read below about six common responses, or defense mechanisms, codependents use to manage their hurt and anger, you have important work to do. You need to—

- read for *understanding* about each response;
- read for *application*. About each response objectively seek to answer the question, "Do I typically respond to hurt and anger in my life in this way?"

1. Numbness

Superficial relationships

"I don't want to feel this way, so I won't," is a personal philosophy for some of us. When our pain is too great, we block it out. When our anger is too frightening, we act like it's not there. Daily we force life to the surface emotionally because what we feel deep down simply is too much to bear. We have superficial emotions and superficial relationships.

Anna's story

Anna's parents divorced when she was 7 years old. Her father remarried and moved away. For a couple of years after he left her father sent Anna gifts, but gradually he faded from her life. Her mother went to work to support Anna and her brother. As an abandoned, working, single parent, her mother was frazzled and frantic. I asked Anna how her parents' divorce affected her. "Not much at all" Anna replied. I asked if she missed her father. She replied, "No, not really."

I asked whether Anna felt especially close to her mother since her mother had taken care of Anna so well. "Yeah, I guess so, but we're not that close," she replied. Anna seemed a bit detached from her situation, so I asked a different question. "What makes you really happy? What do you really enjoy?" She thought for a minute. "I can't think of anything." She said nothing much made her angry or upset. "I don't feel much of anything." Over the next several months we talked more about her past, and she began to feel more. Some of the feelings were painful; some were pleasant, but through finding them she was able to get in touch with more of her life.

She said nothing much made her angry or upset. "I don't feel much of anything."

Numbness keeps us emotionally distant from what's happening in our lives. This distance doesn't put things in perspective by providing the wide-angle view; it's the kind of distance that blurs and confuses things, leaving us emotionally blinded. Sometimes people conclude that since feelings are painful, they must be wrong. They try to make others happy and suppress their own feelings. But a problem occurs: we can't be picky about which emotions we suppress. We can't stifle the bad feelings and enjoy the good ones. When we repress the painful feelings, we block the enjoyable ones, too.

Staying busy probably is the most effective way to avoid feeling. Perhaps you've used this "drug." Each activity becomes like a deadening shot which desensitizes us to our hurts. Our theme song is Carly Simon's, *I Haven't Got Time for the Pain*. When we fill our lives with activities and superficial relationships, we don't have time to feel pain.

 What activities do you use—to avoid difficult people, to keep your mind off troubling situations, to avoid feeling hurt or admitting anger?

_____

_____

2. Pain Without Gain

Some of us may wish we were numb, but we aren't. We hurt. We hurt so badly we can hardly stand it; we experience a feeling of being hopelessly crushed. An intense feeling of loss with no hope of gain consumes us. We feel as though we've been broken into a million pieces, and no glue can fix us. We find no mending; only hurting.

Because we can't go through life admitting this kind of hurt to others, we put up a front of competence and happiness. Few people ever realize the blackness that lurks beneath the brightness outside.

Connie's story

Most people would describe Connie as healthy and mature. When she came to see me she said she had to talk to somebody; she thought she was losing her mind. Though she had many friends and was considered a successful mother, business woman, and church member, she was dying inside. She described the home of her childhood. On the surface it seemed normal enough: no alcoholism, no divorce, no addictions. Yet, she remembered her parents' relationship as being cool and aloof, like an armed truce. Their relationship with each other was duplicated in their relationship with her. Though no outward signs of a dysfunctional family existed, the family was, in fact, quite dysfunctional. She had been left an emotional orphan, fending for herself and lacking the love, protection, and support every child needs.

"I wanted to be loved so much, but no matter what I did to please him, I never felt he loved me."

She wept, "My father never held me. He never told me I was his special little girl or anything. I wanted to be loved so much, but no matter what I did to please him, I never felt he loved me." This dear woman is afraid to be loved. She is afraid that if she experiences someone's affection, it may be taken away from her, and the pain would be unbearable. She wants to be loved so badly; she needs it so desperately, but she's afraid of being hurt even worse than she hurts now. That is hurt with no hope, hurt with no healing, pain with no gain.

A sense of doom

Many of us live with a continual sense of impending doom. We believe we don't deserve for good things to happen to us or for people to love us. When good things *do* happen, we may assume something bad will occur to balance the good. One college student explained to me that he really had enjoyed his spring break vacation, but his enjoyment was tempered by his belief something bad would happen as soon as the break was over. That gloomy assumption stole his joy from a delightful situation.

Believing we are inherently bad people who are unworthy of love leads to self-condemnation and self-hatred. Some of us think and say terrible things about ourselves. We call ourselves horrible degrading names. If someone said those same things to another person, we would call that type of behavior hatred and abuse. We don't see the abuse when we call ourselves these names, however, because we believe we deserve that kind of treatment.

 Below I've rewritten the definition of abuse that you read in day 1 of this unit. I've changed its focus from behaviors directed toward another person to behaviors directed toward self. Read carefully and underline any words or actions you use against yourself.

> Abuse is defined as any behavior I use to control and subjugate myself through the use of fear, humiliation, and verbal or physical assaults. . . . (It is) the systematic persecution and wearing down of myself through my unrelenting criticism and fault-finding of myself. I do this to convince myself to be a better person.

 Circle how you feel right now after you have read this reworked definition, then fill in the blank below to explain why you feel this way.

Sad	Angry	Lonely	Ashamed
Guilty	Confused	Afraid	No feelings

"I'm feeling this because _____."

Flat affect–describes the lack of any range in emotions; a person with a flat affect rarely cries, rarely feels anger—in fact, rarely feels anything at all.

Years of numbing feelings produce something in people called a **flat affect**. Sadly, many codependents have a **flat affect** but do not recognize that their lives are emotionally sterile.

✎ **Read the definition in the margin. What are three things a person with a flat affect usually will be unable to do?**

1. _____

2. _____

3. _____

I have felt—

joy _____

_____

_____

sadness _____

_____

Take time now to review the highs and lows of your emotional range. Thinking back over your past two days, describe a moment of joy and a moment of sadness. In the margin box write your response.

A person with a flat affect is generally unable to cry, to feel anger, or to feel anything at all.

✎ **Read the verses from Psalm 139 in the margin. What wonderful truth do they teach you about God's presence?**

_____

The psalmist, singing his praise to God, said: "Where can I run from you? If I go up to the skies, you are there. If I lie down where the dead are, you are there."

–Psalm 139:7-8, ICB

Like the psalmist, we also can praise God for being everywhere we ever go— in the high places and the low places. I don't think we'd be stretching this truth to say also that God is with us when we feel lofty emotions like joy, and when our feelings weigh us down terribly as grief sometimes does.

✎ **Write a prayer of praise to God. Thank Him for caring about and being with you in the moment of joy and the time of sorrow you just described.**

_____

_____

_____

_____

Consider sharing this prayer experience with someone you trust.

Most codependents, and many other people as well, experience tremendous pain but very little comfort. This pain is like the pain you would feel from ripping off a bandage before a wound heals or tearing off a scab before the scar forms.

✎ **Do you have any emotional hurts that are not healing?** ❏ Yes ❏ No

If so, describe one here. _____

_____

Think about the self-abuse you read about in today's lesson. Are you doing or saying anything in this situation that keeps this wound raw and sore? Below explain your thoughts.

_____

_____

I could say, "The darkness will hide me. The light around me will turn into night." But even the darkness is not dark to you. The night is as light as the day. Darkness and light are the same to you.

–Psalm 139:11-12, ICB

◆ You may have felt some troubling emotions or some sad emotions as you've studied today's material and reflected on situations in your life. Pause now and pray that God will show you His viewpoint about these situations and about your feelings. Conclude your prayer by reading out loud Psalm 139:11-12, which appears in the margin. Thank God that "the darkness is not dark" to Him. He will not lose sight of you or your needs, no matter how dark you may feel your life is.

SUMMARY STATEMENTS

- When we repress painful feelings, we also block the enjoyable ones.
- Sometimes codependents conclude that since feelings are painful, feelings must be wrong.
- Believing we are inherently bad people who are unworthy of love leads to self-condemnation and ultimately to self-hatred.

DAY 3

Responding to Hurt and Anger (Part 2)

Today you'll explore two more defense mechanisms codependents often use to manage the pain of their hurt and anger. Remember, even if you are not a codependent person, you may find yourself described in these pages. Wider applications exist than simply to those in the codependent circle. So continue to read and reflect carefully.

3. Excusing the Offender/Blaming Themselves

Often, where no healing of the hurts of tangled relationships exists, codependents excuse the offenses of those who injure them. Instead of blaming the guilty person, they blame themselves. The desire to believe the best about the one who hurts them blocks their objectivity.

Thomas' story

Thomas' father was a workaholic who traveled several days a week and often worked on weekends. Thomas' mother had difficulty coping with her husband's neglect, so she ate to soothe her pain. A lot of pain called for a lot of eating; she weighed almost 300 pounds. She tried to love Thomas enough for both herself and his absent father, but her good intentions led her to smother him. She told him what to wear, where to go, which friends to play with, what to think, and how to feel. Later, Thomas had great difficulty in college and in marriage. He never seemed to have an opinion of his own. Neglect by one parent and smothering attention by the other did not promote stability, confidence, or maturity in Thomas.

As Thomas described the details of his life, I asked how he felt about himself. "Terrible!" he snapped. "I can't do anything right. I don't know how I feel. I don't know what to do." I asked how he felt about his parents. "Oh, they did the best they knew how. It's not their fault. If I had been a better son, they wouldn't have had such trouble with me." When I asked what he meant by "such trouble," he said: "Well, I just didn't turn out the way they wanted me to. I wish my parents were proud of me, but they're not. And it's all my fault."

Thomas' mother internalized her anger and pain and comforted herself with food. Thomas also learned to internalize his anger and pain. He blamed himself for his father's neglect and for his mother's manipulation. He excused the offenders and blamed himself. Excusing the offender with self-blame is one of the most common responses to hurt and anger in the family. No one wants to believe parents, spouses, or children would hurt them, so they take the responsibility for their own pain and blame themselves.

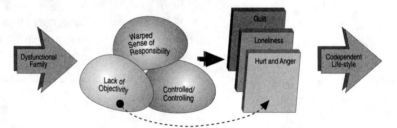

✎ **You see in the course map above the connection between lack of objectivity and hurt and anger. Describe below how Thomas' lack of objectivity fuels his hurt and anger.**

_____

_____

To whom did Thomas direct his anger? _____

Thomas' story illustrates a cycle one frequently finds in tangled codependent relationships. Codependents blame themselves for someone else's actions. Then they feel the other person's guilt, which leads them to ask forgiveness for the offender's sin and excuse the offender. All of this leads to more self-blame. Thomas' lack of objectivity led him to blame himself for his parents' behavior. He then felt pain and shame which were not his own. He directed the resulting anger toward himself.

This cycle operates because codependents feel remorse for someone else's offense. They fail to acknowledge the deep-seated hurt and anger they feel, and they refuse to acknowledge the source of these painful emotions. Instead, codependents who someone else wounds feel sorrow that the words, the acts, and the neglect which caused them pain ever happened. Persons who are deep in a situation may not see that they are the victims both of another's meanness and another's guilt. No wonder people deny these painful feelings.

Happy is the person whose sins are forgiven, whose wrongs are pardoned. Happy is the person whom the Lord does not consider guilty and in whom there is nothing false. When I kept things to myself, I felt weak deep inside me. I moaned all day long. Then I confessed my sins to you and didn't hide my guilt. I said, "I will confess my sins to the Lord," and you forgave my guilt.

—Psalm 32:1-3,5, ICB

Don's story

Don felt anger toward his father, but he never said anything to him about how he felt.

 Read the psalmist's words printed in the margin. Read them out loud as if these were *your* words. Circle or highlight the personal pronouns (*I, my, me*) in these verses. Read the words out loud a second time. Stop and pray; ask the Lord for courage to admit your sins to Him, and ask Him for courage not to take on the guilt of someone else's sin.

4. Displaced Anger

Codependents often express repressed anger at people or things that have nothing to do with the cause of their anger. The anger surfaces at odd times and in odd ways.

Don's garbage disposal broke. Being a frugal homeowner, he went to an appliance store and bought a new disposal. When he got home, he rolled up his sleeves, got out his tools, and plunged into the black hole under the sink. The old disposal came off easily. But when he tried to put the new one on, Don found the intake and outlet holes were in different places than on his old one. This called for some creative plumbing! The tube from the dishwasher to the disposal wasn't quite long enough, but if the disposal could be pushed over just a little, then clamped . . . there! So what if it slanted to the right a little? The rubber seal at the top would keep it from leaking. But with it leaning that way, the pipe coming out of the bottom on the left wasn't long enough. If the clamp could be put on really tight it would work. A tug on the pipe to pull it as close as possible, then tighten the clamp . . . one more turn to make it really tight and . . . crunch! The pipe split! Don took his wrench and beat the stuffing out of the pipe! It wasn't split anymore; it was pulverized! After spewing out a few curse words, he threw his wrench into the tool box and stomped off to buy more pipe.

Now why did Don get mad at that pipe? Did it call him dirty names? Did it say ugly things about his wife or push his little girl down on the playground? It was simple physics. The pipe is a thing and had no personal vendetta against Don. Why was he so mad? When he was growing up, Don's father never had been very handy around the house. He typically failed trying to do anything mechanical. When Don tried to work on things, his father often stood nearby and said, "You'll mess it up. You're gonna break it. You can't do it." Hearing those words once would be painful, but hearing them often hurt him deeply. Don felt anger toward his father, but he never said anything to him about how he felt.

So years into his own adulthood, Don wasn't angry at the pipe. He was angry with his father. His anger at the pipe was displaced anger. His situation was the domino effect in action.

The classic domino effect is like this.

| Boss yells at employee | Employee goes home and screams at child | child runs outside and kicks the dog |

Each person in the situation experiences anger from another. Victims don't deal directly with their persecutors. Instead the victims spend their fury on someone weaker, smaller, or more helpless than they are. One act of anger reproduces itself over and over!

Where are you typically standing when the anger dominoes start to fall? Are you the first domino, feeling anger in some situation and venting it on someone else? Are you the middle or last domino, trying to find someone on whom to dump your angry feelings other than toward the person who dumped on you?

 What are the kinds of people or things at which you tend to get angry? With whom do you get really angry?

_____

_____

 Practice the unit memory verse by writing it in separate phrases. Practice repeating each phrase from memory.

SUMMARY STATEMENTS

- Compulsive fixers often excuse those who have injured them and take the blame upon themselves.
- Codependents may not see that they are the victims of both another's meanness and another's guilt.
- Codependents often express repressed anger at people or things that have nothing to do with the original cause of their anger.

Responding to Hurt and Anger (Part 3)

DAY 4

Today you will finish studying defense mechanisms codependents use to cope with their hurt and anger. Outbursts of anger and using self-pity and anger to manipulate others are the last two defense mechanisms you will study.

5. Outbursts of Anger

Codependents not only displace their anger by venting it at the wrong thing or person, they also may become disproportionately angry. Their suppressed anger may explode like a tube of toothpaste that is squeezed until it pops and toothpaste squirts in all directions.

Debbie's story

Debbie's father was an alcoholic. He occasionally beat his wife and children. As the youngest of six, Debbie was terrified of him. The one stabilizing force in the family was her mother, but after years of neglect and abuse, Debbie's mother couldn't take any more punishment. She committed suicide when Debbie was 12.

As a child, Debbie never was able to distinguish between her father's angry threats and her mother's quiet defense of the children; so, when Debbie grew up and had her own family, she treated her three children both ways. She wanted to protect them and care for them, but when they disobeyed, she flew into a rage. She threatened them with brutal beatings. "I'll whip you with the buckle end of a belt if you do that again!" she screamed. But she seldom followed through on her threats. She wanted to be gentle, yet she found herself yelling at her children even for insignificant things. Then she felt deep pangs of guilt.

🖉 **Based on Debbie's story, respond to these statements by circling the response that best represents your ideas.** *SD* **means strongly disagree;** *D* **means disagree;** *A* **means agree;** *SA* **means strongly agree.**

- Debbie's anger is harmless to her children.   SD   D   A   SA
- Debbie's threats of punishment are scarier   SD   D   A   SA
  to her children than actual physical
  punishment would be.
- When Debbie's children learn they are receiving   SD   D   A   SA
  displaced anger, Debbie's threats and fury
  won't matter to them.

6. Using Self-Pity and Anger to Manipulate Others

Hurt and anger are powerful emotions. They affect us deeply and can be used to affect others, too. They can be powerful forces to manipulate others into caring about us and "dancing to our tune."

Ken's story   Ken's mother abandoned the family when Ken was six years old, leaving Ken and his brother with their father who didn't want them to bother him. He sent the boys to stay with various aunts and uncles. Ken grew up to be very popular, especially with women. To win their affection, he often described in detail his horrible childhood. His story of painful neglect, occasional abuse, abandonment, and heartache won the hearts of many. But when he began a deep, absorbing relationship, he tended only to end it and start another one. When a friend asked him why he stopped dating someone, Ken would snap, "That's none of your business! You don't understand me! Stay out of my life!"

Ken was a good athlete who loved to play softball. But he had to get hits; he had to make every play on the field; he had to win. When he made errors or outs, doing so seemed to flip a switch inside him. He threw his bat, kicked the ground, and cursed. He was the same in conversation. Ken always had an opinion—the right opinion. If people disagreed with him, even in the most polite or abstract terms, he took their comments as a personal offense. In his mind, people either were for him or against him.

When his uncontrolled, violent outbursts of anger threatened to shatter the heroic image he portrayed to others, he said sadly, "You just don't understand. If you had parents like mine, you wouldn't be nearly as mature and stable as I am." Self-pity usually restored his place of esteem in other's eyes. Ken also used anger as a means of manipulation. People became afraid of him. A raised eyebrow or a raised tone of voice meant you were treading on thin ice, and you'd better agree with him—or else! Ken got what he wanted: self-pity, respect (or was it only fear?), and surrender to his demands.

 You probably know several people like Ken. What do you do to soften their anger? How do you respond to their sense of always being right?

_____

_____

Ken used the phrase, "You just don't understand" to manipulate his friends' pity and concern. Suppose Ken attempted, like you are in this unit, to memorize Hebrews 4:15-16. Why might it be difficult for him to remember this verse?

_____

_____

Remember Ken's need always to be right? Can you imagine an argument he might have with God about the main point of these verses? In the margin box describe what you think Ken would say in such an argument.

Ken's prevailing belief that his suffering is unique and beyond others' ability to understand might make it difficult for him to "hide in his heart" Scripture verses reassuring him that Jesus understands every aspect of his life. Perhaps his argument with God would state: "Jesus had You for a Father and had a really spiritual mother. There's no way He experienced anything like what I did growing up. Maybe He is powerful enough to save me, but He won't understand what He's saved me from." Some people like Ken memorize Scripture about comfort, but it never seems to penetrate deeply in their lives.

Codependents are the products of manipulation, neglect, and abuse, but they can use these powerful forces on others as well. Not all of these forces are so blatant as they are in Ken's life. Most are more subtle but are just as effective in bringing out the responses of pity and fear—poor counterfeits for the love and respect they really want and need.

 Finish memorizing the unit memory verses. Write them in the margin. Look them up in your Bible to check your memory. Pause to praise God for sending His Son to people on earth "just as we are."

Ken's argument with God—

_____

_____

_____

_____

_____

SUMMARY STATEMENTS

- Codependents' built-up anger sometimes explodes and injures innocent persons.
- Some persons use the combination of anger and self-pity to control others.
- Codependents are the products of manipulation, neglect, and abuse, but they can use these powerful forces on others as well.

Memories

✎ Spend a moment reviewing the six defense mechanisms. Below, list those defense mechanisms. List as number 1 the one you believe you use most often to manage your own hurt and anger, list as number 2 the one you use second-most often, and so on. If you never use some of these, then leave them off of your list. Remember, you learned on day 2 that you do not have to be codependent to find evidence of these defense mechanisms in your life. Surely if you're honest you'll recognize several you have used.

1. _____

2. _____

3. _____

4. _____

5. _____

6. _____

✎ List here something you need to do so you can stop burying your hurt and anger beneath these defense mechanisms and begin dealing with them honestly as they occur in your life.

_____

_____

If I stop burying my hurt and anger—

_____

_____

_____

_____

What fears or concerns do you have about uncovering and dealing honestly with hurt or anger that began many years ago? In the margin box describe your fears.

Personal pain is one result of dealing honestly with hurt and anger. Remembering people, situations, fears, and hurts you've consciously worked to forget is another result. These results are the price of recovery. Not everyone is willing to pay the price. When persons begin to get in touch with the pain of the past, they often remember events long buried in the mind and heart. The hurt and anger these memories evoke are painful, and some people may feel that this pain amounts to going backward. But it is progress. Maybe Carl's story will help illustrate this.

Carl's story

I was riding in my car with Carl, a longtime friend. We were discussing codependency and the events in our lives that had caused us pain. A short lull occurred in our conversation; then, Carl groaned.

I wondered what was wrong. "I just remembered something that I haven't thought of in 30 years," he said. "When I was 7 years old, my older brother got in a habit of stealing money from me. I told my folks, but I guess they just didn't want to be bothered with it. Anyway, they didn't do anything. I was pretty good with money. I saved my allowance and earned extra money. My brother wasn't so responsible. He wanted his allowance, my allowance, and any other money I made, so he just took it. After a few weeks of having money mysteriously disappear (I knew where it went, but he would just laugh at me when I accused him), I realized I had to do something. So I got my Bible and opened it to Exodus 20 and the Ten Commandments. I underlined verse 15, 'You shall not steal,' and put my money jar next to it.

"I felt really good. Surely nobody would steal money from a jar next to a Bible open to the Commandment not to steal! But you know what? That jerk took my money anyway! I couldn't believe he would do that to me! It makes me mad to think about it now—and that was 30 years ago." We rode down the highway. The memory of his brother's stealing from him and laughing about it was painful, but it was a part of the healing process for Carl. As an adult, he was free to admit to and feel the anger stuffed inside 30 years ago when he was helpless to stop an older brother's actions.

A common response

Fear is a very common response to the reality of repressed emotions. We don't know how much is buried. We don't know how much we can take. We don't know how our relationships might change. Hopefully, your discovery group is promoting a safe environment in which you can express your hurt and anger honestly. If you need more help, ask your group leader or pastor for the name of a competent Christian counselor who can help you.

Remembering My Family

The inventory which follows may not be pleasant work for you; however, if it helps you to admit honestly and face long-buried feelings, then it is important work. As you answer the questions, work slowly. At any moment you become aware of some feeling stirring inside you or surfacing, pause and write that feeling beside the question you are answering. Remember, healing begins when you honestly face what you feel, not when you deny what you feel.

My parents

1. Today I would describe my father as (circle any that apply):

Passive	Gregarious	Angry	Sad	Manipulative
Harsh	Loving	Quiet	Gentle	Protective
Involved	Unpredictable	Tender	Strong	Dictatorial

As a child, I would have described my father as (circle any that apply):

Passive	Gregarious	Angry	Sad	Manipulative
Harsh	Loving	Quiet	Gentle	Protective
Involved	Unpredictable	Tender	Strong	Dictatorial

I am/am not afraid of becoming like my father because _____

_____

2. The phrase below which best describes the importance of television in my father's life is—

❑ Addicted to it   ❑ Occasionally watched it   ❑ Seldom watched it

3. Today I would describe my mother as (circle any that apply):

Passive	Gregarious	Angry	Sad	Manipulative
Harsh	Loving	Quiet	Gentle	Protective
Involved	Unpredictable	Tender	Strong	Dictatorial

As a child, I would have described my mother as (circle any that apply):

Passive	Gregarious	Angry	Sad	Manipulative
Harsh	Loving	Quiet	Gentle	Protective
Involved	Unpredictable	Tender	Strong	Dictatorial

I am/am not afraid of becoming like my mother because _____

_____

4. The phrase below which best describes the importance of television in my mother's life is—

❑ Addicted to it   ❑ Occasionally watched it   ❑ Seldom watched it

5. My parents' marriage typically was (check one):

❑ Unhappy   ❑ Routine   ❑ Good   ❑ Happy

6. My parents argued:

❑ Frequently   ❑ Occasionally   ❑ Seldom   ❑ Never

7. My father demonstrated affection for my mother:

❑ Frequently   ❑ Occasionally   ❑ Seldom   ❑ Never

My mother demonstrated affection for my father:

❑ Frequently   ❑ Occasionally   ❑ Seldom   ❑ Never

8. My parents' economic status was:

❑ Upper class   ❑ Middle class   ❑ Lower class

The effect of this economic status on them was _____

_____

The effect of this economic status on me was _____

_____

My relationship with my parents

1. My parents agreed with each other about how to discipline me:

❑ Frequently   ❑ Occasionally   ❑ Seldom   ❑ Never

Their usual methods of discipline were (circle any that apply):

spanking	extra chores	long lectures
sitting me in a corner	Bible reading	stern looks
silence	working with me to	withholding privileges
yelling and shouting	learn new behaviors	requiring restitution
beatings with an object	sending me to another	
	adult to punish me	

2. The things about me they consistently approved of were

_____

The things about me they consistently disapproved of were

_____

_____

3. As a preschooler, I most enjoyed being with: ❑ Father ❑ Mother

As a child, I most enjoyed being with: ❑ Father ❑ Mother

As a teenager, I most enjoyed being with: ❑ Father ❑ Mother

4. My father took time regularly to play with me and my siblings:

❑ Frequently ❑ Occasionally ❑ Seldom ❑ Never

My mother took time regularly to play with me and my siblings:

❑ Frequently ❑ Occasionally ❑ Seldom ❑ Never

5. To my knowledge, one or both of my parents was . . .

. . . physically abused	❑ Yes	❑ No
. . . verbally abused	❑ Yes	❑ No
. . . emotionally abused	❑ Yes	❑ No
. . . sexually abused	❑ Yes	❑ No

As a child, this affected my relationship with them by _____

_____

It also affected my relationship with God by _____

_____

My home life

1. I would describe my childhood home life as:

❑ Unhappy ❑ Routine ❑ Good ❑ Happy

2. The things I most enjoyed doing as a preschooler with my family were

_____

The things I most enjoyed doing as a child with my family were

_____

The things I most enjoyed doing as a teenager with my family were

_____

3. I have felt close to my siblings:

❑ Frequently   ❑ Occasionally   ❑ Seldom   ❑ Never

4. I was teased as a child.   ❑ Yes   ❑ No

(If yes) I was teased by _____

about such things as _____.

My typical response was _____.

5. As a child, I was . . .

. . . physically abused   ❑ Yes   ❑ No
. . . verbally abused   ❑ Yes   ❑ No
. . . emotionally abused   ❑ Yes   ❑ No
. . . sexually abused   ❑ Yes   ❑ No

This affected my relationships with adults by _____

_____

It also affected my relationship with God by _____

_____

6. I had a serious illness as a child.   ❑ Yes   ❑ No

This affected my relationships with my family by _____

7. I would try to manipulate my parents to get attention or special treatment:

❑ Frequently   ❑ Occasionally   ❑ Seldom   ❑ Never

Reflection

1. List all the feelings you've written in the margins as you completed this inventory.

_____

If you did not write any feelings in the margin, pause now and record on the line on the previous page how you feel after completing this inventory.

What insights about yourself do you gain from identifying these feelings?

_____

_____

2. Review your answers for the inventory. Describe the source of any hurt you remembered as you were answering it.

_____

_____

Describe the source of any anger you remembered as you were answering it.

_____

_____

3. What response do you need to make, or what steps do you need to take, to better manage your hurt and anger today?

_____

_____

✎ **Review this unit. Find one statement in the text that helped you to understand better the codependent person(s) you love.**

Below rewrite that statement in your own words.

_____

Now, find one statement or insight you wrote that helped you to understand yourself better, whether or not you identify yourself as a codependent. Below write it again, and describe how this new insight benefits you.

_____

Review the memory passage. Look it up and check your memory. Then close your Bible and write the passage in the margin. How have you made application of this passage during your study? Below record your thoughts.

_____

_____

Notes

[1]Susan Forward and Joan Torres, *Men Who Hate Women and the Women Who Love Them* (New York: Bantam Books, 1986), 43, 46.

Guilt and Shame

TRYING TO BUY LOVE

Emma grew up in a dysfunctional family. Her mother was an alcoholic; her father was a passive participant in family matters. Emma knew something was wrong, and she concluded that the problem certainly was her fault.

Emma desperately wanted to be loved. When she was eight or nine years old, she often saved enough money to buy gifts for her family. She got on her bike and pedaled to town. There she spent her carefully-saved money to buy baseball cards for her father, a cheap necklace or handkerchief for her mother, and a toy for her sister. She rode back home with great hope in her heart and presented these gifts at supper. Each time her father, mother, and sister would politely respond, "Thanks."

One night after a gift-giving session, Emma heard her mother ask her father, "I wonder why Emma keeps buying us these silly little things? Why do you think she wastes her money like that?" (Read more about Emma on page 113.)

What you'll learn

This week you will learn—

- the difference between the objective guilt God sends and the shame-filled guilt which codependents often feel;
- the destructive effects of guilt motivation;
- the dangerous pattern of self-examination that shame produces;
- how guilt becomes a form of self-inflicted punishment;
- how codependents, by using guilt on others, continue the cycle.

What you'll study

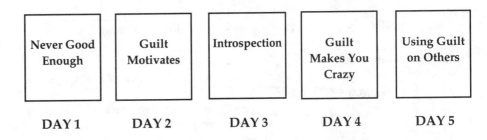

Never Good Enough	Guilt Motivates	Introspection	Guilt Makes You Crazy	Using Guilt on Others
DAY 1	DAY 2	DAY 3	DAY 4	DAY 5

Memory verse

This week's passage of Scripture to memorize

I sought the LORD, and He answered me, and delivered me from all my fears. They looked to Him and were radiant, and their faces shall never be ashamed.
–Psalm 34:4-5

Never Good Enough

Codependents often feel guilty. They feel guilty for what they've done and haven't done, for what they've said and haven't said, for what they've felt and haven't felt. They feel guilty for *just about everything*. Such guilt produces feelings in them of worthlessness and **shame**.

shame–n. a painful emotion caused by awareness of guilt, shortcomings, or improper behavior, a condition of humiliating disgrace[1]

Codependents find their worth—their identity—in what they do for other people. Rescuing . . . helping . . . enabling. But no matter how much they do for others, it's never enough. It's never enough for the significant people in their lives who reject or belittle their efforts, or it's never enough for codependents personally. When people tell a codependent, "You've done a good job" the codependent replies, "Oh, I should have done better," or "I ought to have done more." Feeling worthless is a learned and practiced habit. If others aren't contributing to this well of worthlessness, codependents will be sure to fill it themselves. Codependents are caught in a no-win situation that feeds their conviction that they are inadequate and worthless. Those convictions lead to feelings of guilt and shame.

Objective guilt

Guilt, and the accompanying feeling called shame, comes in two varieties. Objective guilt is important and valuable. Objective guilt shows us that we are human, and it points us to our need for God. But when false or codependent guilt becomes a habit based on painful life experiences rather than an experience based on reality, shame becomes our way of life.

If you are caught speeding down the highway at 85 miles per hour, and the judge's ruling is "guilty as charged," that is objective guilt. The guilt is real, earned, and deserved. In this sense, all humanity is guilty and stands before God needing forgiveness and a relationship of acceptance and love.

Let's look at God's solution to the problem of objective guilt.

✎ **Read the two Scriptures in the margin, and complete the statements below.**

There is no one righteous, not even one; there is no one who understands, no one who seeks God.
–Romans 3:10–11, NIV

1. No one is _____ (Romans 3:10). (This means rightly related to God), and

For all have sinned and fall short of the glory of God.
–Romans 3:23, NIV

2. Everyone has _____ (Romans 3:23). (This means they have fallen short of being and doing what pleases God.)

The Bible is clear. No one is righteous, and everyone has sinned. Therefore, we all are separated from God and His loving plan for our lives. We experience this separation, and we feel objective guilt.

If we claim to be without sin, we deceive ourselves and the truth is not in us. If we confess our sins, he is faithful and just and will forgive us our sins and purify us from all unrighteousness.
–1 John 1:8-9, NIV

✎ **From the verses from 1 John in the margin, we learn about the solution to the terrible guilt of sin. What is your part in the solution?**

_____

What is God's part in the solution? _____

_____

God is the one who paid for our sin by giving Jesus to die in our place. He has the ability to forgive us and cleanse or purify us from all sin. Our responsibility is to confess our sin to Him.

The cleansing of sin comes in two varieties. The first time we receive God's forgiveness of sin is called the new birth. We confess that we are sinners (Romans 10:9-10). We believe that Jesus died to pay the penalty for our sin (Romans 8:1). We receive the gift of salvation God has provided (John 1:12). At that time we are born into God's family (John 3:1-16). God gives to us the gift of eternal life as His child (1 John 3:1).

✎ **Read 1 Peter 2:10 in the margin. How does this verse describe these people before they trusted Christ?**

_____

What does the verse say about them now that they have trusted Christ?

_____

Until they trusted Christ they were not a people—not members of the family of God, and they had not received **mercy**. Now they have received mercy and are God's people.

Because we are all sinners by nature and choice, everybody has a before. Everybody also needs to have an after meeting Christ. Have you received God's mercy? Have you come to the place in your life that you have received God's gift of forgiveness of sin? God loves you and wants to have a love relationship with you; however, He will not force His way into your life. He waits for you to invite Him.

If you have not yet accepted God's gift of forgiveness by receiving Jesus Christ as your Savior and Lord, consider expressing this prayer to Him:

> Dear God, I know that Jesus is Your Son and that He died on the cross for me and that He was raised from the dead. I know that I have sinned and need forgiveness. I am willing to turn from my sins and receive Jesus as my Savior and Lord. Thank you for accepting me and giving me the gift of salvation. In Jesus' name. Amen.

If you have chosen to receive God's gift, congratulations! A whole new life begins with receiving Christ. The problems of life do not go away, but God can give you wisdom and strength so you can honor Him. As a next step we encourage you to call your discovery-group leader, your pastor, or a trusted Christian friend and tell them about this decision. The church is the family for believers. Your brothers and sisters in Christ will be excited to share of your joy as you make public your decision. They want to help you to grow.

Now, the second kind of cleansing from sin mentioned in 1 John 1:9 on the previous page is for believers. Salvation does not mean Christians never sin. When we sin God leads us to confess that sin. He cleanses us and forgives us. He cleanses us from our objective guilt. Unfortunately, another type of guilt also exists.

Codependent guilt

In the rest of this unit you will study a different kind of guilt. You will study guilt that does not promote objective judgment about mistakes or offenses. This guilt lacks objectivity about its causes and effects, and it is unforgiving. It promotes no love or acceptance. This guilt is a painful, gnawing perception that, "I am worthless, unacceptable, and never can do enough to be acceptable, no matter how hard I try. I am 'guilty' of being a terrible person."

This guilt comes from within and not from God. Codependents are particularly prone to experiencing such guilt and its accompanying shame. What a vast difference between these two kinds of guilt! Objective guilt produces sorrow that leads to the positive, refreshing change called **repentance**. Codependent guilt produces a sorrow that crushes a person.

When Paul wrote to the young church at Corinth, he described perfectly these two kinds of guilt. He wrote:

I now rejoice, not that you were made sorrowful, but that you were made sorrowful to the point of repentance; for you were made sorrowful according to the will of God, in order that you might not suffer loss in anything through us. For the sorrow that is according to the will of God produces a repentance without regret, leading to salvation; but the sorrow of the world produces death (2 Corinthians 7:9-10).

repentance–n. change of mind and purpose; repentance in the New Testament always means change for the better; this change of mind and purpose involves both turning from sin and turning toward God. (Vine's)

✎ **Draw an arrow next to each of the phrases in the center column pointing to the correct heading: "objective guilt" or "codependent guilt." Use the introductory paragraphs and the Scripture above to guide your choices.**

Objective Guilt		Codependent Guilt
	1. Leads to withdrawal	
	2. Leads to forgiveness	
	3. Promotes honorable behavior	
	4. Promotes bitterness and shame	
	5. Rooted in God's desire for our good	
	6. Rooted in Satan's desire to destroy and defame us	
	7. Produces sorrowful repentance without regret	
	8. Produces sorrowful shame and emotional death	

✎ **Recall the most recent time you felt guilty. Which phrases above best describe the experience? Place a check by those phrases.**

Which type of guilt do you feel most often? ❑ Objective ❑ Codependent

If you checked objective guilt, what sin do you need to confess to

experience God's forgiveness? _____

Numbers 1, 4, 6, and 8 are characteristics of codependent guilt. Numbers 2, 3, 5, and 7 are characteristics of objective guilt.

♦♦ **Pause now and pray about your need. If you circled codependent guilt, what responsibility were you trying to assume at the time you felt that guilt?**

_____

♦♦ **Pause now and pray for continued insight through this course. Pray that you may identify and lay aside any codependent behaviors.**

Realizing personal wrong coupled with forgiveness brings hope and change.

Realizing personal wrong, coupled with a knowledge of forgiveness, brings hope and change, but the feeling of personal wrong without forgiveness brings condemnation and hopelessness. In dysfunctional families, family members magnify personal wrongs while they withhold forgiveness, love, and acceptance. Condemnation is a constant reality in the lives of codependents.

Guilt crushes

All of us do things that are wrong, but codependents attach greater weight to those wrongs than they do to forgiveness. They feel deeply ashamed and believe the terrible things they've done cannot possibly be forgiven. Harry described his constant pangs of guilt. When someone asked him, "Harry, when are you happy? When do you feel good?" he replied sadly, "I don't want to be happy. I'm not a good person, so I don't have any right to feel good." Harry, who excused and tolerated his lifetime of parental neglect, was completely intolerant of the slightest mistakes he made.

"If I were the kind of husband she needed, she'd be OK. It's all my fault!"

Anger compounds the guilt and reinforces the codependent's tragic sense of worthlessness. One friend explained about how he felt pushed to his limits to help his wife, who had an eating disorder. He'd become very angry, but then he'd think, "She can't help it." He was angry again, but this time, he was angry at himself for not supporting his "poor, helpless wife." He'd curse himself, calling himself vile and degrading names. He even considered punishing himself for being so selfish and callous.

The crushing effects of guilt—shame, worthlessness, self-hatred, and self-condemnation—take a heavy toll. Some people escape into a shell of numbness, passivity, or depression. Some develop psychosomatic illnesses. And some simply plod along, day after day, year after year, under the oppressive weight of guilt.

♦♦ **Read the unit memory passage. Mark these verses in your Bible and begin memorizing them.**

SUMMARY STATEMENTS

- Codependents feel guilty for just about everything. Codependent guilt produces feelings of worthlessness and shame.
- Objective guilt shows us that we are human and points us to our need for God.
- Codependents attach greater weight to the wrongs they do than they attach to the forgiveness of God.

Guilt Motivates

Guilt-riddled codependents assume that the only way to win at life is to earn the respect of others. Since they lack objectivity, that's their only choice. Feeling worthless and unloved, they decide something is wrong with them. Then they feel guilty and compelled to choose actions that hopefully will make up for their shortcomings.

The hope of gaining acceptance and the threat of losing it are powerful motivators. This hope and threat prompt codependents to rescue people who take advantage of them. Oh, they receive a bit of what they crave—some appreciation and respect—just enough to keep them "on the job," but not enough to satisfy them. So they continue their endless running on the treadmill of hope, guilt, and fear.

Codependents continue their endless running on the treadmill of hope, guilt, and fear.

 Begin today's study by reading the unit memory passage. This unit on guilt and shame may be very difficult for you at times. Do you have any fears about continuing this study? If so, list them in the margin now. Pause and confess these to God. Thank Him for "delivering you from all your fears."

Guilt motivation combines the desire to avoid condemnation with the desire to perform or to measure up to standards someone else sets. We perform with a sense of urgency and desperation because we think we have to, not because we want to. "I have to" and "I can't" statements like the ones below reveal our motivation:

I *have to*
- I *have to* accomplish this today!
- I *have to* go here!
- I *have to* help this person in this way at this time!
- I *have to* say yes!
- I *have to* control my anger and hurt!

I *can't*
- I *can't* fail this assignment!
- I *can't* let her down!
- I *can't* let my anger get out of control!
- I *can't* say no!

 Read one more time the above list of "have to" and "can't" statements. Check any you've thought or said in the past year.

Reread those statements. What do they have in common?

_____

You may be able to identify several common guilt motivators in your life. We continue to respond to these because of our fear of rejection and of failure. You may be building such high standards of excellence, or you may be allowing others to impose them on your life. Either way, the message you hear, no matter what's said, is clear: *Respond or else!* The ability to say no, to make our own decisions, to relax, and to enjoy life are foreign to us because they don't contribute to our consuming goal in life: the drive to gain a sense of self-worth.

The ability to say no, to make our own decisions, to relax, and to enjoy life are foreign to us.

Trying to Buy Love

Using guilt to motivate others simply is another form of manipulation. All persons need to win love and affection. People attempt to gain love in many ways.

Emma's story

Emma grew up in a dysfunctional family. Her mother was an alcoholic; her father was a passive participant in family matters. Emma knew something was wrong, and she concluded that the problem certainly was her fault. She desperately wanted to be loved. When she was eight or nine years old, she often saved enough money to buy gifts for her family. She would get on her bike and pedal to town. There she spent her carefully saved money to buy baseball cards for her father, a cheap necklace or handkerchief for her mother, and a toy for her sister. She rode back home with great hope in her heart and presented these gifts at supper. Her father, mother, and sister would politely respond, "Thanks."

One night after a gift-giving session Emma even heard her mother ask her father, "I wonder why Emma keeps buying us these silly little things? Why do you think she wastes her money like that?"

Suppose you had wandered in at just the moment Emma's mother spoke. What explanation would you give the mother about Emma's behavior? In the margin box write your response. What would you like to be able to explain to Emma about the situation? In the margin box describe what you would say.

Clearly Emma's mother was unaware of the needs of her daughter. She had no idea Emma was trying to buy love. Emma needs to feel love and acceptance from God and from some emotionally healthy people. I would like to help Emma understand that she cannot get love from parents who simply do not have it to give. The issue is not Emma or her performance; the point is that her parents are unable to give her what she needs.

> **To Emma's mother I would explain—**
>
> _____
>
> _____
>
> _____
>
> **To Emma I would like to say—**
>
> _____
>
> _____
>
> _____

Shoulds and Oughts

Codependents live by shoulds and oughts and not by the confidence of security and significance. They are driven to have more, to be more, to say more, and to do more. No matter how much they do, no matter how much they have, no matter how clever or successful they are, codependents almost always have the nagging thought, "I *should have* done more," or "I *ought to have* said it differently," or "I *should have* been better."

Glenn and Lucy's story

Glenn tried everything to please his demanding wife Lucy. He worked long hours to provide extra money so she could have nicer clothes and furniture. He kept the yard immaculate, and he heard her say, "You ought to trim that bush more often. What will the neighbors say?" "OK, honey," was his passive reply. He brought her breakfast in bed almost every day. In spite of this, Lucy seemed to have a mental list of everything husbands have done for wives since the beginning of time, and she expected Glenn to do them all. In short, he was her slave—a slave to her "shoulds" and "oughts."

In this codependent relationship, Lucy believes she's suffering from Glenn's bungling attempts to please her. Glenn probably is numbed to his own pain for "failing" Lucy so often.

✎ Be objective about Lucy and Glenn. What is the *real* problem in their lives and in their marriage?

Lucy? _____

Glenn? _____

Could it be that both Lucy and Glen suffer from a lack of healthy self-worth? Each of them looks to the other to provide a sense of purpose to life and make them happy. Neither of them has the skills to build a healthy relationship.

True Commitment?

Codependents usually use the word commitment to refer to their guilt-motivated drive. They may work extremely hard in businesses, churches, and community organizations but with what purpose? Often, they do this to earn the respect they want and to avoid the rejection they fear. The motivation is selfish. They serve others so they will look good. Try to answer the questions in the margin box about this paragraph.

These are not easy questions to answer. But consider this: if a large group of people fear failure or rejection, then the system itself probably is guilt-inducing. Guilt-motivated people, however, are attracted to the rigidity and demanding environment of guilt-producing organizations. They feel more comfortable with rules, formulas, high expectations, shoulds, and oughts. They probably don't feel loved or valued there, but at least they know where they stand in expected behaviors and activities. Some codependents who are crushed by guilt and have retreated to passivity are poor workers. But most are the best workers businesses and churches have because the stakes are so high. They work to avoid condemnation and to gain a sense of worth.

NOTE: I'm not saying a person who overcomes codependency will become a lazy slob. Secure, stable people usually are hardworking people, but they work hard for a different reason—to help people, not to gain a sense of worth.

✎ **Try to write from memory the unit memory passage. Use the space in the left margin below to write this passage.**

◆ **Do you recognize any sin or fear you need to confess to God? Take time now to pray. Acknowledge before Him your sins and fears. Thank Him for providing a refuge—a safe place—for you.**

<aside>

Commitment or codependency—

Is this guilt-motivated drive the fault of the codependent or the boss? In a church, is this the fault of the codependent or the pastor?

_____

Do codependents interpret normal life through their own distorted guilt filter yet think the system is at fault? ❑ Yes ❑ No

Does the boss or pastor induce guilt motivation by a manipulative use of praise and condemnation?

_____

Is it possible some codependents have bosses and/or pastors who also are codependents? ❑ Yes ❑ No

</aside>

SUMMARY STATEMENTS

- Guilt-riddled codependents try to succeed in life by earning the love and respect of others.
- We perform with a sense of urgency and desperation because we think we have to, not because we want to.
- No matter how successful they are, codependents almost always have the nagging thought, "I should have done more," or "I should have been better."

Introspection

introspection–n. the examination of one's own thought and feeling: self-examination. (Webster's)

What they seek to gain from helping—

_____

_____

_____

---

morbid–adj. characterized by gloomy or unwholesome feelings. (Webster's)

Codependents try to stifle their pain either by putting up a wall and refusing to think about life, or by thinking about themselves, all day. . . every day. In this **introspective** mode, they analyze every word, conversation, action, and thought. This seems paradoxical. They devote their lives to rescuing and helping others, but they think about themselves all the time.

The motivation behind the codependent's actions is the key to this odd combination of serving and selfishness. Do you remember the reasons for the rescuing and helping behaviors of codependency?

What are some common motivations for codependents' compulsion to rescue? What do they expect to gain from helping others? In the margin box write your response.

Did you write something like—*Codependents serve others in an attempt to gain a sense of worth, to be loved*, and *to achieve the respect and appreciation they so desperately want?* These are some of the reasons we've noted in past units for rescuing and helping behaviors of codependents.

Reflection or Morbid Introspection?

Healthy reflection and morbid introspection are vastly different mental activities. Reflection involves looking at ourselves honestly, based on reality. It is objective, healthy, and not predisposed to condemn. Healthy reflection builds on a positive self-image.

Morbid introspection occurs when a person with a negative self-concept digs through thoughts, motives, and actions with two hopes—to find the wrong in life and change it, or to find what's right about life and therefore feel good about himself or herself. This interior digging is not objective. It does not begin with a sense of value and worth. Rather, it begins and continues with the underlying pessimistic assumption: "Something is very wrong with me, and I've got to make it right." With that assumption, self-condemnation dominates thinking. Hurt and anger are not permitted—they are considered wrong—and so such painful feelings are kept inside.

✎ **Read the statements below. They are examples either of objective reflection or morbid introspection. Decide which they represent, and mark the examples of objective reflection with a plus sign (+) and the examples of morbid introspection with a minus sign (-).**

_____ 1. Why is he staring at me? What's wrong with my hair, or clothes, or what I'm doing, or what I've just said?

_____ 2. It wasn't my best day, but it wasn't my worst one either.

_____ 3. A C minus on my test—pretty lucky since I forgot to study for it.

_____ 4. A C minus on my test—the teacher obviously hates me and wants me to fail.

_____ 5. If I were any kind of a parent, I'd have freshly baked cookies for my kids everyday.

_____ 6. I ought to pray more and give more to the church; God's going to give up on me.

Healthy reflection is not self-centered. Examples 2 and 3 are the examples of reflection. The other responses are morbid introspection.

In a relationship with a compulsive person, introspective codependents try to rescue and enable. They feel angry about being used. Codependents then justify the behavior of the compulsive person and blame themselves for being so selfish as to get angry.

Codependents justify the behavior of the compulsive person and blame themselves for being so selfish.

 Review the people's stories listed below. Which one (or ones) is an example of the behaviors the previous paragraph described? Circle your answer(s).

Susan's story, page 52, (unit story, unit 3)
Marianne's story, page 89, (unit 5, day 1)
Thomas' story, page 95, (unit 5, day 3)

You may have drawn one, two, or three circles above. Any or all of these stories illustrate the anger codependents feel toward those who manipulate them and toward themselves for being manipulated.

Choose one of the three stories to reread. Then, record in the margin box some of the "morbidly introspective" thoughts you believe the character in the story might think about himself or herself.

Morbid introspection is not confined to relationships with compulsive people; it's only at its worst in those relationships. Codependents can be introspective about all parts of their lives. They analyze everything and everyone in hopes of discovering the wrongs in their lives and finding something—anything—good enough to produce a sense of worth. This inner search is all-consuming; it is deadly because nothing is ever "good enough."

Morbidly introspective thoughts—

_____

_____

_____

_____

The words in the margin came through the prophet Zechariah to people needing to rebuild the Jewish temple and needing to rebuild their spiritual hope in a coming Messiah. This verse emphasizes the truth that the people never would be strong enough or powerful enough to rebuild their temple or their hope—only the Spirit of God in them would accomplish these important tasks. The codependent who never feels good enough needs the message of this verse to rebuild a life which seems to be broken and in disrepair.

"Not by might nor by power; but by my Spirit," says the LORD Almighty.
                    –Zechariah 4:6, NIV

 Personalize this verse of Scripture by rewriting it as it applies to your greatest area of struggle in life. For example you might say, "I have tried to . . . but I realize that only God can . . ."

_____

_____

For example, I might write that I have tried to work hard enough and impress enough people to make me feel good about myself. I now realize that it is not by my efforts but through God's Spirit, knowing that He loves and accepts me, that I may come to feel secure.

Comparison

One of the prime ingredients of introspection is comparison. Persons who lack security and significance need some means of determining where they stand. Comparison is the perfect solution! These persons need to be one step further, one notch higher, one quip wittier, or a bit better looking than everyone else. If codependents cannot think of enough standards by which to compare themselves, their dysfunctional relatives usually will help them by comparing the codependent's clothes, hair, job, children, intellect, or athletic ability to their own and to others. As if codependents needed any help!

Feeding the fantasies

Constant comparison feeds the fantasies of introspective codependents. They imagine themselves getting praise and promotions, having beautiful things, and accomplishing great feats of daring—all just a little bigger and better than someone else.

You shall not covet your neighbor's house. You shall not covet your neighbor's wife, or his manservant or maidservant, his ox or donkey, or anything that belongs to your neighbor.
    –Exodus 20:17, NIV

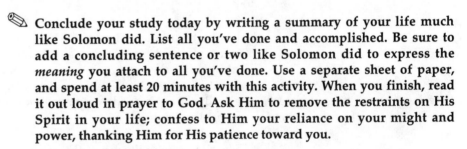 **Read the verse printed in the margin. What does the Bible call this continual comparing of self to others?**

_____

Let's be very honest. Whether or not we are codependent, we all struggle in life to have more, to accomplish more, to be better than this person, to be more sought after than that person, to be needed more than any person alive. The word in Exodus 20:17 is covet, meaning to envy and desire that which is another's.

Solomon described his search for meaning in the Scripture in the margin. His key word was *vanity* or *meaninglessness*. When you take time for self-examination, do you find meaning in the midst of life's storms, or do you only feel the storm?

I thought in my heart, "Come now, I will test you with pleasure to find out what is good." But that also proved to be meaningless.

I undertook great projects: I built houses for myself and planted vineyards. . . . I also owned more herds and flocks than anyone in Jerusalem before me. I amassed silver and gold for myself, and the treasure of kings and provinces . . . I became greater by far than anyone in Jerusalem before me.

Yet when I surveyed all that my hands had done and what I had toiled to achieve, everything was meaningless, a chasing after the wind; nothing was gained under the sun
    –Ecclesiastes 2:1,4,7-9,11, NIV

✎ **Conclude your study today by writing a summary of your life much like Solomon did. List all you've done and accomplished. Be sure to add a concluding sentence or two like Solomon did to express the *meaning* you attach to all you've done. Use a separate sheet of paper, and spend at least 20 minutes with this activity. When you finish, read it out loud in prayer to God. Ask Him to remove the restraints on His Spirit in your life; confess to Him your reliance on your might and power, thanking Him for His patience toward you.**

➥ **Review your memory passage for the week by repeating it three times and then copying it from memory. Use the space in the left margin below to copy the verse.**

_____

_____

SUMMARY STATEMENTS

- The paradox of codependency is that people seek a sense of self-worth by selfishly serving others.
- Codependents devote their lives to helping others, but they think about themselves all the time.
- Reflection is healthy and honest self-examination.
- Introspection is unhealthy obsession with one's self.

Guilt Makes You Crazy!

DAY

4

Deep within our minds and hearts, we sometimes ask ourselves, "What's wrong with me? Am I crazy? Life is *so* difficult." Even the fun things—things we hope and dream will bring satisfaction and relief—turn out to be difficult. The people who are supposed to be supportive and affirming often prove to be critical and distant. Were they like that already, or did we somehow make them that way? Why is *everything* so hard?

A squeeze play is at work. On one side, pressing against you are all your desires, hopes, and dreams—to assert yourself, to be creative, and to have a sense of worth. On the other side is guilt for being so selfish in wanting those things. If you enjoy life you are stuck feeling guilty.

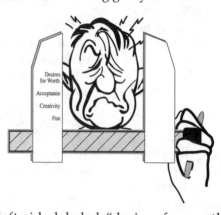

Look at the vise. The left side labeled "desires for worth, acceptance, creativity, and fun" has no apparatus manipulating it. It is stationary. The right side moves toward or away from it, but the left side doesn't move. Symbolically, the picture is affirming important truths we've studied already—people need acceptance and worth, and their desires for these are normal and natural.

The desire for acceptance and worth is normal and natural.

The right side of the vise is the introspective, codependent, self-imposed guilt. It's the side *with* a handle. Only human hands—our own hands or someone else's—turn that handle and squeeze life from us. This is not God's doing.

✎ We all sabotage God's work in our lives and take over control. How do you do this? List at least three ways you turn the guilt handle and override God's love and acceptance of you.

1. _____

2. _____

3. _____

Now in the margin box write at least three ways you turn the guilt handle of someone else's life and override God's love and acceptance of them.

❧ **Pause now and pray about all you've just read, felt, and written. Confess to God your hurts, fears, and sins, and place your worth firmly in His hands.**

How I "guilt" others—

1. _____

_____

2. _____

_____

3. _____

_____

Jenny's story

Jenny wanted to do some creative things for Christmas—decorate her house, fix special presents, bake, and make the holiday a meaningful, festive, and colorful season. "But these things take so much time," she lamented to me. "And I could probably use my time more effectively doing other things." I asked her what kind of things she would do. "Oh, I don't know. Like helping out at church, or doing things for my neighbors, or cleaning the garage. It's a mess."

She felt guilty and selfish because she wanted to do her projects.

She seemed to have an almost endless list of "good things" to do, but she didn't want to do those. She wanted to do special Christmas tasks and projects, but she felt guilty even for considering those. "I'm so selfish," she said.

We went through the list of questions below to help her analyze her situation.

- Which of my desires are OK and which aren't?
- What is the wise thing to do?
- What is most productive?
- Why do I feel so guilty when I want to do something creative and fun?

"If I do the things I want to do, I feel guilty, but if I don't do them, I get angry. What's wrong with me?"

Jenny condemned herself for not living up to her expectations and yet was angry she might not get to do what she wanted to do. Her sense of always having to do things that appeared more productive to help others was driving her into despair and confusion. "If I do the things I want to do, I feel guilty, but if I don't do them, I get angry. What's wrong with me?" she asked sadly.

"Nothing is wrong with you," I assured her, "except you won't relax and be yourself. You're asking the wrong questions. The question is not, 'How can I get more done?' The question is, 'How do I get my worth?' As long as you try to get your worth from being productive and constantly serving others, you will feel pressured, condemned, and confused for having any desires and dreams of your own.

Because you want to

"You already have worth! You already have value! You can be yourself. Everything you do doesn't have to be productive. You don't have to serve others all the time. As you express yourself and gain a sense of confidence, you'll feel the freedom to be yourself more often. And you'll do things that are productive and helpful to others because you *want* to, not because you think you *have* to!"

One conversation didn't change years of repressed desires and guilt motivators squeezing the life out of Jenny, making her feel she was going crazy. But it was a start.

✎ **Answer for yourself the question that was asked of Jenny: "How do I get my worth?"**

_____

_____

Because of today's study, is your answer different than it would have been several weeks ago?   Yes   No   Circle one.

A beautiful affirmation based on biblical truth is found in *Search for Significance* LIFE Support Edition. You will read it on the next page.

Because of Christ's redemption,
I am a new creation of infinite worth.

I am deeply loved,
I am completely forgiven,
I am fully pleasing,
I am totally accepted by God.
I am absolutely complete in Christ.

When my performance
reflects my new identity in Christ,
that reflection is dynamically unique.

There has never been another person like me
in the history of mankind,
nor will there ever be.
God has made me an original,
one of a kind, really somebody![2]

✎ **Before your next group session talk to three people not in your discovery group. Read "My Identity in Christ" to them; ask them to respond and react to it. In the margin record their ideas.**

◆ **Ask one of the people with whom you share the affirmation to help you with your Scripture memory. Review your memory verses by repeating them to that person.**

SUMMARY STATEMENTS

- The need and desire for acceptance and worth is normal and natural.
- Our own hands are most often the ones tightening the vise of guilt in our lives.
- As long as you try to get your worth from being productive and constantly serving others, you will feel pressured, condemned, and confused for having any desires and dreams of your own.

DAY 5

Using Guilt on Others

The law of sowing and reaping takes effect in the area of guilt just as it does in every other part of life. Like begets like, and if others have used guilt to motivate and manipulate you, you will probably use it on others. It is a strange fact that even if you detest the way others have treated you, that model is so strong you may find yourself treating others the same way.

✎ **Reflect for a moment on that paragraph. On the top of the next page, fill in the statements with personal examples.**

I have said, "I will never say '_____' to my children," but I hear myself saying it to them.

I have said, "I will never do _____ to a friend," but I find myself doing it to my friends.

I have said, "I will never expect _____ of my spouse," but I now realize I do expect it of him/her.

I have said, "I will never be hurt by _____ again," but I do hurt when it happens again.

A father hated himself, but it was the way his parents had treated him and it was all he knew.

One father realized he both condemned his children and withdrew his affection from them to manipulate their obedience. He felt terrible about it. He hated and despised himself when he did it, but this was how his parents had treated him. He knew only this way to respond, even though he realized it was wrong and knew how much it had hurt him.

Out of Balance

A poor parental model produces poorly functioning adults.

The same words of praise and condemnation, the same actions, tone of voice and expression, the same aggressive, angry behavior, and the same withdrawal and passivity used to manipulate us are the behaviors we tend to use on others. Or, we may make a totally opposite choice. Instead of harshly condemning, we may withdraw; instead of being passive and neglectful, we may smother. A poor parental model will produce from its offspring poorly functioning and poorly relating adults. They may be duplicates or opposites, but either way they will be out of balance.

The Grip of Addiction

Bluntly stated, the struggle with codependency is a struggle with addiction. The manipulation, guilt, shame, and control imposed on the codependent, often from childhood, causes the codependent to become just as manipulative, guilt-inducing, shame-filled, controlled or controlling, and relationally handicapped as the original abuser. Codependents are just as addicted to their way of living life as is an addict to a substance or behavior.

 Read carefully the following story about Keith. Whether you are in this discovery group to understand codependency better or to understand a codependent better, you will find a point of identification with Keith. When you do, circle the portion(s) of his story which is similar to your own or that of the codependent you know.

Keith's story

Keith recalls: "I saw that crouching behind my compulsive religious working and overachieving was a lonely and starved self, like a lost child—which in one sense I'd felt like all my life . . . even though I had caring parents and a brother and we lived in a 'Christian home.' I saw that I was almost completely focused on getting love and attention. I used everything I had—all my talent and energy—to manipulate the people and things around me, often 'for their own good,' but really so they would love me and think I was a great person. I saw, in short, that I am an almost completely self-centered person, one who puts himself in the center and tries desperately to control his world and the

"I built a life and a ministry trying to feel good about myself."

people in it—traits I have always abhorred in other people. Since this had not been conscious, I'd never faced these behaviors and had built a life and a ministry trying to solve this need for feeling OK about me.

"As I began to face myself at this new level I was horrified to see that this self-centered grandiosity, this playing God I'd been involved in was 'addictive.' I could somehow hide it from myself, but despite all my resolve, I couldn't *stop* it. I realized that this compulsive, driving busyness to be enough, do enough, to please people (to get their attention, approval, or love), to fix *them* up in order to become OK myself, operated like any other addiction. There was in me an uncontrollable compulsion to repeat these self-defeating behaviors. Sometimes I felt as though I must be crazy not to be able to change simple habits I wanted to be rid of.

"I had an uncontrollable compulsion to repeat these self-defeating behaviors."

A spiritual disease

"It dawned on me with an awesome certainty that when people speak of themselves as being 'sinners in need of God's healing' they are actually talking about being in the grips of the addictive spiritual disease the Bible portrays in connection with 'sin.' I realized that this disease can disrupt our everyday lives and relationships and *never be seen to even be connected to sin*. And I saw that this Sin-disease may well be the matrix for all compulsive, manipulative, and controlling behavior . . . the source, the breeding ground, of all other addictions and for the irrational destructive and addictive behaviors that are destroying our lives . . . ."[3]

 No doubt, Keith tells part of my story and part of yours, too. Once again, circle what you are feeling right now after reading Keith's story.

Sad   Angry   Lonely   Ashamed   Guilty   Confused

Afraid   No feelings   Other: _____

I am feeling this way because _____

You're halfway through *Untangling Relationships*. When you complete the next unit, you will have a very complete understanding of codependency. Its roots are deep and stubborn, its behavioral patterns difficult to change, and its fears and guilt and shame very real.

Attitude of selfishness

But if Keith's insights are to help us at all, they will help us confess that, in the midst of all the explanations for and insights into the tragedy of codependency, it is at its core a behavior and attitude of *selfishness*. Codependency is the opposite of lordship. To honor God is the motive of lordship. To avoid pain and to build up self are the motives of codependency. The blindness of denial complicates but does not excuse the problem. The intentional choice to live for our own purposes and refuse to serve and honor God is *sin*. We need God's forgiveness and courage to make better choices.

A doctor who treats people with addictions once told me what he tells patients in his recovery center: Your addiction is not your fault. Your response to it is.

 Each day in this unit you paused for moments of confession. As you conclude this unit, look on the top of the next page and write a prayer to God. In the prayer confess to Him your response to your codependent addiction and to your sin addiction. Claim again the promise of 1 John 1:9—God's faithfulness to forgive what we confess.

_____

_____

_____

_____

✎ **Review this unit. Find one statement in the text that helped you to understand better the codependent person(s) you love.**

Below rewrite that statement in your own words.

_____

_____

_____

Now, find one statement or insight you wrote that helped you to understand yourself better, whether or not you identify yourself as a codependent.

Below write it again, and describe how this new insight benefits you.

_____

_____

_____

Review the memory passage. Look it up and check your memory. Then close your Bible and write the passage below. How have you made application of this passage during your study of this unit? Below record your thoughts.

_____

_____

_____

_____

Notes

[1]Robert S. McGee, _Search for Significance_ LIFE Support Edition (Houston: Rapha Publishing, 1992), 148.
[2]McGee, 224.
[3]J. Keith Miller, _Hope in the Fast Lane: A New Look at Faith in a Compulsive World_ (San Francisco: Harper & Row, Publishers, 1987, originally published as _Sin: Overcoming the Ultimate Deadly Addiction_), 16-18.

Lonely and Pressured

> ### FEELING REJECTED BY GOD
>
> Jeff's mother was harsh and demanding. His father escaped her demands by working long hours, developing friends outside the neighborhood, and being passive at home. When Jeff, in his early 20s, became a Christian, he felt the love and acceptance he had always wanted both from his relationship with the Lord and his relationship with other Christians.
>
> But after a few months, Jeff's warm feelings about God began to fade. His old learned feelings began to shape his new relationship with God. He had learned to cope at home by doing everything his mother wanted, but nothing could please her. Jeff began to feel the Lord didn't quite accept and love him, so he began to act toward God the same way he had acted toward his mother.
>
> Trying to please his mother had led Jeff to empty perfectionism; trying to please God led him to strict legalism. (Read more about Jeff on page 127.)

What you'll learn

This week you'll learn—

- how feelings of loneliness result when codependents feel God and people have abandoned them;
- about the paradox of wanting the approval of those in authority while resenting and fighting the control of authority figures;
- to define the particular struggles of codependent Christians;
- why codependent Christians have difficulty in understanding and applying the Scriptures;
- the reasons why superficial solutions do not automatically solve the problems of codependency for Christians.

What you'll study

Feeling Lonely	The Paradox of Loneliness	The Codependent Christian	The Scriptures and Codependency	Superficial Solutions
DAY 1	DAY 2	DAY 3	DAY 4	DAY 5

Memory verse

This week's passage of Scripture to memorize

Be strong and courageous, do not be afraid or tremble at them, for the LORD your God is the one who goes with you. He will not fail you or forsake you.
–Deuteronomy 31:6

DAY 1

Feeling Lonely

Codependents spend their lives giving, helping, and serving others. From the outside, they appear to be the most sociable people in the world, but inside they are lonely. They attempt to win the affection of others by helping and serving. Though codependents occasionally get a taste of love and respect, the taste fades all too quickly. Then, thinking that people and God have deserted them, they feel empty and abandoned. They distrust authority. They fear that anyone above them is against them, and they build elaborate **facades** to hide their painful feelings of loneliness.

facade–n. a false, superficial, or artificial appearance. (Webster's) A facade is a "false front."

✎ The five statements below describe the feelings of many people. On a scale where one means seldom and five means almost always, rate each statement on a scale of one to five how often the statement reflects your feelings and actions. Write your answer beside each statement.

_____ 1. "I'm OK. No, nothing is bothering me." Codependents are afraid of their emotions, so they pretend to themselves that nothing is wrong.

_____ 2. "I could never tell her I'm angry about that; what if she never spoke to me again?" Codependents are unwilling to speak honestly about their hurt and anger because they are afraid people will abandon them.

_____ 3. "I'm lost and lonely without my friends." Rescuers are controlled by fear that others will go away and that this will leave them more lonely.

Rescuers are controlled by fear that others will go away.

_____ 4. "If I don't say I appreciate his taking the kids to the park, he'll blow up at me and call me ungrateful." Codependents use their gratitude, or their pretend gratitude, as a means to avoid others' anger and abandonment.

_____ 5. "After all, he's all I've got." Codependents feel lonely so often, they simply don't want to feel more loneliness and rejection. They accept abusive behavior from others rather than face loneliness.

Abusive or addicted people usually give a little and take a lot. In contrast, codependents give a lot but feel they receive very little. A codependent is like a tank of water with a slow drip coming in and a stream going out. For a while, the tank will flow, but eventually it will run dry. The trickle never can fill the tank as long as the hole in the bottom exists. Codependents may get a little encouragement, but they spend so much more time and emotional energy that they literally are "running on empty."

entitlement–n. a right to benefits. (Webster's) A sense of entitlement is the belief that I am "owed" a debt because of my self-sacrificing service.

As codependents give and give, a destructive sense of **entitlement** grows within them. They feel that others owe them the appreciation and respect they desire. Receiving strokes—being told they are appreciated—becomes a compulsion. When they do get recognition, they temporarily are satisfied—much like an alcoholic taking a drink. What an irony that the codependent responds and acts just like the addict!

When they don't get the positive feedback—their strokes—codependents begin to feel abandoned, condemned, controlled, confused, and lonely. And, codependents feel angry but believe they can't say anything about their anger.

They fear that if they do, they may experience even more condemnation, manipulation, and loneliness. They feel hopelessly trapped.

Desperate for intimacy

Although they are desperate for intimacy, codependents don't feel lovable and are afraid of losing what little warmth they already have. The combination of these factors paralyzes and confuses them.

✎ **Review the five numbered statements on the previous page. Then match the following summary statements to the numbered statements by placing a number from 1–5 in the blanks. Codependents—**

_____ a. deny to others their emotions and problems.
_____ b. accept anyone and do anything to prevent lonely feelings.
_____ c. deny to themselves their emotions and problems.
_____ d. use being grateful or pretending to be grateful for what others do as a way to prevent experiencing the other person's anger.
_____ e. are controlled by the fear that their friends and family will leave them and they'll be lonely.

Many of us are so crushed and have such a low sense of our own worth, we can't even accept genuine love and affirmation. The answers to the exercise are 2-a; 5-b; 1-c; 4-d; 3-e.

Rhonda's story

I encouraged Rhonda, a woman with a very painful family background, to find a friend who would share her hurts and joys. I knew of a mutual friend, Sandy, who really loved Rhonda and wanted to build a friendship with her. The situation looked perfect for Rhonda. Month after month passed, but Rhonda only developed a superficial relationship with Sandy.

"I'm afraid if she really knew me, she wouldn't like me."

My encouragement didn't seem to help the situation. After a long time, I decided to ask the hard question. I said, "Rhonda, Sandy really loves you. She wants to be the kind of friend to you that we've talked about. Why don't you open up to her and let her be your friend?" Rhonda looked very sad. "I can't; I just can't," she said. "I'm afraid if she really knew me, she wouldn't like me."

✎ **Rhonda's story is a good example of someone who desperately wants and needs intimacy but is unable to accept love. Write what you suppose Rhonda would say or do in the following situations.**

Sandy compliments Rhonda's dish at the pot-luck dinner. Rhonda says . .

_____

Sandy thanks Rhonda for remembering her birthday. Rhonda says . . .

_____

Sandy and Rhonda spend time together three or four times a week, but . .

_____

Codependents have difficulty accepting compliments.

Codependents have difficulty accepting compliments. They don't believe they deserve praise (even though they desperately want to be affirmed), so they explain away their successes, shift the compliment to someone else, or in some other way discount what they have done. They long for appreciation, but when they receive it, they feel they are unworthy of being appreciated. They remain lonely and feel abandoned and empty.

Feeling Abandoned by God

Codependents need the message of the unconditional love, forgiveness, and acceptance of God. Instead, most feel distant from Him. They feel that He disapproves of them and that they can't do enough to please Him—no matter how hard they try.

In the margin box, describe a time you felt God was not pleased with you and a time when you felt distant from God.

Everyone has experienced times of feeling that God is distant or displeased. Times such as the ones you've just described complicate codependents' feelings of hopelessness, pain, and loneliness. Why? Because they see God as their last hope. They think, "If He doesn't love me, who will?" Codependents almost always view God in the same way they view their parents. If their parents neglected them, they will feel God couldn't care about them. If their parents condemned them, they will experience God as harsh and demanding. The way their parents treated them is the way they perceive God. They see God as part of their problem rather than as the solution.

✎ **Many "feeling" words appear in the paragraph above. In the two situations you just described in the box did you find yourself writing any of those feeling words? If so, write those feeling words here.**

_____

Codependent Christians tend—as usual—to go to one of two extremes. Sometimes codependents view God as distant and harsh, and this keeps them from feeling as close to God as they desire to do. Other codependents sense God's love to such an extreme depth, they become hyper-mystical. They lose their own identity in their imagined relationship with God.

Jeff's story Jeff's mother was harsh and demanding. His father escaped by working long hours, developing friends outside the neighborhood, and being passive at home. Jeff became a Christian when he was in his early 20s. At first he felt the love and acceptance he had always wanted from his relationship with the Lord and his relationship with other Christians. But after a few months, Jeff's warm feelings about God began to fade. His old learned feelings began to shape his new relationship with God. He had learned to cope at home by doing everything his mother wanted, but nothing could please her. Jeff began to feel the Lord didn't quite accept and love him, so he began to act toward God the same way he had acted toward his mother.

Jeff began to feel the Lord didn't quite accept and love him.

Trying to please his mother had led him to empty perfectionism; trying to please God led him to strict legalism. Jeff thought of plenty of things he felt he ought to do to please God, so he tried to do them all. He attended every meeting, read the Bible religiously, and gave away lots of money. Instead of feeling closer to God, however, Jeff increasingly grew to feel that God was distant, harsh, and demanding. Guilt replaced his feeling of acceptance and joy. His "I-want-to" freshness in those first months as a Christian had become a stifling, condemning, "I-have-to" burden.

> ## I remember—
>
> A time when I felt God was displeased with me . . .
>
> _____
>
> _____
>
> _____
>
> A time when I felt distant from God . . .
>
> _____
>
> _____
>
> _____

✎ Suppose you were Jeff's Christian friend and knew his story. At this point in Jeff's life, how would you pray for him? Write a prayer interceding for Jeff.

_____

_____

_____

◆✛ Mark Deuteronomy 31:6, the unit memory verse, in your Bible. Spend five minutes beginning to memorize it.

SUMMARY STATEMENTS

- Many codependents appear very sociable but are lonely on the inside.
- Ironically the codependent responds and acts like an addict. The codependent is addicted to approval and affirmation.
- Codependents need the message of God's unconditional love, forgiveness, and acceptance.

DAY 2

The Paradox of Loneliness

The loneliness you feel in the presence of one with whom you are supposed to have a meaningful relationship can be devastating. As with every day's study, you need to study today's work in quiet and solitude. You need to be alone. But you don't need to feel lonely.

◆✛ Begin today praying for an awareness of God's presence. Thank Him for His promise never to leave you or forsake you. Ask Him for a clear mind to memorize the promise you find in the unit memory verse.

Feeling Abandoned by Authority

Codependents view authority the same way they view the addicted or abusive people in their lives.

Codependents tend to view authority the same way they view the addicted or abusive people in their lives, especially if those people are their parents. Codependents often are intensely loyal to their parents, bosses, pastors, or other leaders. They may believe those in authority can do no wrong. They believe others are all-powerful because they themselves feel so inadequate. They will ignore all kinds of mistakes until, at last, the pendulum swings. Then the authority figure who could do no wrong suddenly can do no right.

paradox–n. a statement that seems contradictory, unbelievable, or absurd but that actually may be true in fact. (Webster's)

Beneath these feelings is this **paradox**: Codependents want those who are in positions of importance and respect to appreciate them, so they value the opinions of authority figures too highly, but they also feel that those in authority are out to get them, to use them, and to manipulate them. Depending on which direction the pendulum has swung, they see authority as either for them or against them.

- When they are suspicious of authority, rescuers feel misunderstood, abused, and abandoned. They interpret even the slightest disagreement as, "They just don't understand me! They don't care about me at all! They're taking advantage of me!"

- When people with a compulsion to fix others feel that authority figures are perfect, they feel unworthy and unsuitable for anyone's appreciation or affection. They discount positive gestures with, "If they really knew me, they wouldn't be saying or doing those kind things."

Below are some descriptive words and phrases describing the extremes of black-and-white thinking. As you answer the questions in the margin box, you may want to use some of these words or phrases or add your own.

misunderstood	I'm not worthy	I need to be accepted
abandoned	undeserving	I need to be appreciated
loyal	abused	awed someone so important notices me

Steve was a loyal, hardworking agent in a real estate company. He sold many homes. He usually had good insights at sales meetings, and people respected his opinions. But after three years, the brokers made a series of decisions he disliked. Steve interpreted these disagreements as personal attacks against him. Casual friendships he had enjoyed with the brokers evaporated as Steve withdrew from them. He became more intense. As he talked to other agents, he began making subtle jabs at his bosses. A few weeks of Steve's lobbying and smear campaign resulted in an revolt at the office. A sales meeting turned into an "us-against-them" fight as Steve and the people he had won to his side argued against people who had been their friends and co-workers. Steve demanded the brokers take his advice. They didn't. Instead, they fired him.

Whether or not Steve was right about the issues was not the problem. He had interpreted disagreement as a personal attack. Disagreement made him feel misunderstood, used, and abandoned by those in authority.

✎ **Choose two of the words you placed in the margin box above that best describe Steve's feelings and place the word or phrase in the blanks below. Then complete the statements. I have completed one as an example for you.**

Steve felt _a need to be accepted_ when . . . _he worked so hard convincing others to accept his version of the office situation._

Steve felt _____ when _____

_____

Steve felt _____ when _____

_____

Interesting, isn't it, how feelings find a way into our actions? Steve's feelings of being misunderstood, abused, and manipulated were evident in his actions at the office. Denying feelings does not work, because one way or another our feelings will find expression in our attitudes and actions.

The paradox of codependency—

When I am feeling positive toward authority I feel . . .

_____

_____

_____

When I'm feeling negative toward authority I feel . . .

_____

_____

_____

Feelings find a way into our actions. Our feelings will find expression in our attitudes and actions.

You may have observed that Steve felt abandoned or abused when his bosses made decisions he did not like. He felt a need to be appreciated when he perceived his ideas were not being recognized.

Hiding Behind Facades

Hiding from love

During childhood people often learn to put up false fronts as a survival technique. Looking calm, cheerful, or tough enabled them to shield their feelings. Although these facades protected them in the past, they are damaging because they prevent people from developing honest and genuine relationships. Codependents desperately want to be understood and to feel close to others, but they are afraid to take the risk of involving themselves in relationships because they might be rejected. To avoid this risk, to avoid more pain, they protect themselves by appearing to be happy and well adjusted even when they are dying inside. They build facades. Hiding behind these facades, they don't say what they mean, and they don't mean what they say. **To put it bluntly, they lie a lot.** Here are some examples. Perhaps you've said some things like these, too.

- They say yes when they want to say no.
- They say "I'm just fine" when they feel just a step or two away from suicide.
- They say "I'd love to go" when someone invites them to an event because they think going will make someone else happy enough to like them.
- They get so wrapped up in other people's desires and making other people happy, they are confused about their own desires and numb to their own feelings.
- They exaggerate, making good things a little better so people will be more impressed with them and making bad things a little worse so people will feel sorry for them.
- They smile and offer to help even when they're so angry they could "spit nails."
- If their facial expression slips and someone asks, "Anything wrong?" they give a partially true excuse which keeps others at arms' length. For example they may say, "I have a headache today," or "I'm just not having a good day, but I'm all right."

 What other examples can you give of not saying what you mean?

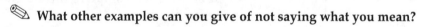

 Now reread all the above examples of not speaking the truth. Draw a star beside those behaviors and words you sometimes use.

In day 1, you read about feelings codependents often experience when they do not receive the appreciation or respect they desire. Those feelings were: *abandoned, condemned, controlled, confused, lonely, angry,* and *trapped.* Did you feel such feelings in the situations you starred just now? Beside the star record those feelings.

People become masterful at selling themselves. They act as if they are enthusiastic about jobs, families, accomplishments, new hairstyles and clothes. They find something good and use it so that others will believe they really are doing well, but in reflective moments they realize their words are lies. The prophet Isaiah records the words of people who had turned their backs on God and on His claim on their lives.

We have entered into a covenant with death, with the grave we have made an agreement. When an over-whelming scourge sweeps by, it cannot touch us, for we have made a lie our refuge and falsehood our hiding place.
–Isaiah 28:15, NIV

✎ **Read the words in the margin from Isaiah. Below describe how the codependent practice of hiding behind facades is similar to the actions of the people of Isaiah's day.**

_____

_____

The people of Isaiah's day hid behind a kind of denial. In the same way codependents often hide from painful reality by pretending things are different than they really are. Hiding from painful reality makes matters worse. Denial prevents cleansing and healing.

✎ **Spend five minutes practicing the unit memory verse. Below write what you feel God says to you in this verse.**

_____

_____

◆✦ **Complete your study today by thanking God for saying clearly what He means.**

SUMMARY STATEMENTS

- Individuals with a compulsion to rescue often are intensely and inappropriately loyal to their parents, bosses, pastors, or other leaders and often are bitterly disappointed.
- Codependents desperately want to be understood and to feel close to others, but they are afraid to take the risk of involving themselves in relationships because they might be rejected.
- Persons with a compulsion to please others often fail to tell the truth because they fear others' disapproval.

DAY 3

The Codependent Christian

"For I am not ashamed of the gospel, for it is the power of God for salvation to everyone who believes" (Romans 1:16).

"If therefore the Son shall make you free, you shall be free indeed" (John 8:36).

The gospel of Jesus Christ is a message of freedom, forgiveness, hope, love, joy, and strength. The *good news* is the most liberating and energizing message humankind has ever or will ever hear! Through the distorted glasses of codependency, however, this wonderful message appears oppressive, condemning, and guilt-inducing. Freedom is turned to bondage, forgiveness to guilt, hope to despair, love to condemnation, joy to pessimism, and divine grace–n. God's freely choosing to favor people with His graciousness, lovingkindness, and redemptive mercy in order to produce freedom and joy in them. An informal definition of grace is "receiving a gift from God we don't deserve." When the New Testament speaks of grace, it almost always means "salvation offered in Christ Jesus."

strength to self-sufficiency. Why is it so difficult for the codependent Christian to understand and apply God's **grace**?

✎ In each unit you have identified insights about codependency. Pause now and reread each key statement you identified in the unit reviews of units 1–6. Reflect on each review statement and consider the definition of grace in this margin; then, as you think about your insight from each unit, describe in the spaces below why you think codependent Christians have trouble understanding and applying God's grace. I have given you an example.

Unit 1: *because we feel responsible for everything and everybody.*

Unit 2: _____

_____

Unit 3: _____

_____

Unit 4: _____

_____

Unit 5: _____

_____

Unit 6: _____

_____

In your discovery group this week be ready to discuss some of your insights.

Oughts and Shoulds

As we have seen, codependents have a warped sense of responsibility. They perceive that their worth comes from their ability to perform. How do persons measure their performance so they can see if they have achieved value and worth? They do what they *should* do. They do what they *ought* to do, and they divide life into distinct categories: the "have-to's" and the "can't's." This black-and-white definition steals the fun and spontaneity from life and produces an overactive conscience in codependents. Inside, they feel pride if they have done well, despair if they haven't, and a fear of failure and rejection no matter how well they have done.

This steals the fun and spontaneity from life.

Codependent Christians carry not only society's oughts and shoulds, they add the oughts and shoulds of Christianity to their already oppressive load. Instead of overcoming the oppression of codependency, this distorted perspective of Christ and the Christian life oppresses even more. Instead of experiencing grace they feel guilt. Only fully experienced grace ultimately produces a "want-to" motivation. Even then it may take a long time to develop the desire to obey God.

Oppresses even more

✎ **Read the familiar words below from the hymn, "Grace Greater Than Our Sin." Underline the three phrases which apply most to your life.**

Marvelous grace of our loving Lord,
Grace that exceeds our sin and our guilt,
Yonder on Calvary's mount outpoured,
There where the blood of the Lamb was spilt.

Marvelous, infinite, matchless grace,
Freely bestowed on all who believe;
All who are longing to see his face,
Will you this moment his grace receive?

(Refrain) Grace, grace, God's grace,
Grace that will pardon and cleanse within;
Grace, grace, God's grace,
Grace that is greater than all our sin.[1]

In the margin box describe to God how you feel about His marvelous grace.

Three dominant emotions commonly surface in an exercise like you have just done. Some people feel thankfulness or relief over God's grace. Others feel anger, and some persons feel confusion. Feeling your true feelings is OK.

A pastor friend of mine sorrowfully explained that he could teach for 29 minutes on the love and grace of God, finishing with only one minute of application stressing obedience in light of that grace, and some people would leave having heard only the last minute. They completely miss the message of grace behind the call to obedience. Instead of grace, they hear guilt and condemnation. My friend was saddened deeply that people miss the motivation for obedience. Another friend presented a Sunday School class series on *Search for Significance.* He explained the love, forgiveness, acceptance, and grace of God. His talks and discussions encouraged and motivated most of the people in the class, but several had the opposite response. They somehow couldn't hear the liberating message of the material. They only heard "do more" and "do better" to be accepted by God. This was the exact opposite of what the material intended!

✎ **Take a moment to reflect on the reaction you're having to *this* material. Finish the sentence: The more I understand about codependency, the more I . . .**

. . . think_____

. . . feel _____

. . . want _____

Codependent Christians separate grace—the source of perspective and power—from the high moral and ethical expectations of the Bible. They feel obliged to meet these higher expectations with only the motivation of guilt and their own wills to do so. The more they read the Bible, the clearer these expectations become. The sense of guilt increases, the mercy of grace decreases. Above, did you respond that learning more about codependency makes you feel more of God's grace or more guilt?

When I consider your grace I feel—

_____

_____

_____

_____

_____

They only heard "do more" and "do better" to be accepted by God.

Codependent Christians separate grace from the high moral and ethical expectations of the Bible.

Misinterpreting the Scriptures

They attempt to turn the commands into works to gain a sense of worth.

Codependents misinterpret many commands in the Scriptures. They attempt to turn the commands into works to gain a sense of worth. Some of these commands which can be misapplied include—

- going the second mile to help someone (Matthew 5:41);
- turning the other cheek when someone hurts you (Matthew 5:39);
- loving those who don't love you (Matthew 5:43-46);
- giving cheerfully (2 Corinthians 9:7);
- denying your own desires for the sake of others (Matthew 16:24);
- loving your neighbor as you love yourself (Matthew 7:12);
- having a disciplined life of prayer and Bible study (Ephesians 6:18);
- letting no unwholesome word proceed from your mouth (Ephesians 4:29);
- forgiving, loving, and accepting others as Christ does (Romans 15:7; Ephesians 4:32).

 Because codependent Christians give up God's grace to make room for their own feelings of guilt, they read such biblical standards as the above with an "or else" phrase attached to the end. Choose three of the statements above, and add the "or else" phrase codependents are likely to add. For example, "I must love those who don't love me, or else God won't love me anymore." Make your notes in the margins above.

Codependent Christians seem to believe they are expected to perform these commands perfectly.

Codependent Christians seem to believe they are expected to perform these commands (and all the others) perfectly, with feelings of love, peace, and joy at all times. They think that no room exists for hurt and anger in the Christian life—at least not in their lives.

Conclusion of Despair

Rescuers further complicate their plight by denying their emotions. They stuff away their hurt and anger with thoughts like, "A good Christian shouldn't feel this way, so I won't." As a result, they feel torn between what *should* be and what is. They find themselves thinking, "It is so wonderful to be a Christian, but I'm dying inside." Sooner or later, despair catches up with them, and their thoughts become something like this:

- "If I were walking with God, I wouldn't have these problems."
- "God has deserted me. Nobody cares about me. I'm all alone."
- "Maybe I'm not really a Christian after all. Surely nobody who feels this way can be a Christian."

Defend God

At the same time, they often defend God so that no one will think badly of Him. For example, a codependent would be horrified at someone's suggestion that he or she might be angry at God about the death of a loved one. Just as codependents deny their hurt and anger and excuse and defend the person in their lives who hurts them, they also deny the hurt and anger they believe God causes them. They try to make sure God doesn't get any blame for their calamities. In the rescuer's eyes, the Savior needs a savior.

 Isn't it tragic how the thoughts and feelings of Christian codependents lead them to despair in their relationship with God? You probably know some people who have made statements like the ones in this final section. Pause now and pray for them by name. Then, if you are

willing, write the unit memory verse on a card, include an encouraging note, and mail one to each person for whom you have just prayed.

SUMMARY STATEMENTS

- The wonderful message of grace may appear oppressive, condemning, and guilt-inducing to codependents.
- Only the experience of grace will produce a "want-to" motivation.
- Persons with a compulsion to rescue try to make sure God doesn't get any blame for their calamities.

DAY 4

Russ's story

The Scriptures and Codependency

Codependents have a strange view of the Scriptures. They tend to see the Scriptures as teaching codependent behavior. You began to see evidences of this as you read the day 3 material.

Russ's friend, Ben, called to ask a favor. "Russ, I'm in a real jam. I've had some unexpected expenses lately that just blindsided me. I haven't known what in the world to do, man, but I knew I could count on you." Russ snapped into his savior mode when he heard that last statement. "Can you let me have $700 until next week? I promise I'll pay you back next Friday. This would really help me out, and I don't have anybody else to count on." Russ quickly remembered passages of Scripture that said to give cheerfully (2 Corinthians 9:7), to give without asking anything in return (Luke 6:30-35), and to give liberally (Romans 12:8). He withdrew the money from his savings and delivered the check that night.

The next Friday, Ben didn't call. Russ was disappointed, but he remembered that Luke 6:30 says not to ask for the money back. A few days later, the phone rang again. It was Ben. "Russ, old buddy, I'm really in bad shape. Somebody in the church just beat me out of $500. That's the money I was going to use to pay you back, but now I'm in real trouble. I know I shouldn't ask you for it, but Russ, I'm desperate, and I know you're the only person I can turn to. Can you let me borrow another $500? I'll get it back to you next week for sure."

Russ thought, "Another $500 will put us in a shaky situation if anything should happen, but what can I do? I have to do what the Scriptures say." He replied, "Sure Ben, when do you need it?" After weeks, months, and now years, Russ hasn't been repaid. The loss put his family in a financial bind. "Didn't I follow the teaching of Scripture? Didn't I do what was right?" Russ often reasoned. In his desire to help, Russ fell into the trap of enabling.

 Ben obviously is behaving in an unhealthy way, and Russ is his codependent Christian friend. In the margin box describe first what Russ is tempted to do "for" Ben. Then describe what Ben really needs Russ to do for him.

Ben was addicted to prescription drugs and needed the money to keep up his habit. Russ didn't think to ask a couple of tough questions that would expose

Russ is tempted to—
_____
_____
_____
Ben really needs Russ to—
_____
_____
_____

reality. He would have helped Ben a lot more if he had asked those questions and then asked himself, "What will really help Ben?" His lack of objectivity, coupled with a habit of enabling as a savior, had led Russ to misinterpret and misapply the Scriptures. What Russ did was try to bail Ben out. He took responsibility which Ben needed to take for himself. He didn't make Ben stand on his own feet. What Ben needed was for Russ to say no and to force him to face the consequences of his own actions.

Russ didn't make Ben stand on his own feet.

We Need Perception

Abandon Scripture?

If codependency so distorts the Christian faith that freedom becomes slavery, should the codependent ignore Scripture? Is codependency an excuse to disobey the Lord?

God gives us the Word of God, the Spirit of God, and the people of God as the tools to change our behavior. But it takes perception and understanding to overcome our blindness and see our codependency clearly. Codependent Christians need the truth of the Word of God, energized by the Spirit of God, in the loving and affirming context of the people of God to be freed from this bondage.

When I first began to study codependency, I wondered, "If codependency is such a problem, why don't the Scriptures say anything about it?" Then I realized, they do! The main themes of the Bible speak directly to change warped, codependent perceptions.

 Below you will find five key themes of the Bible which speak powerfully to the issue of codependency. Select one of the themes from the list. Describe in your own words how this theme affects the issue of codependent behavior. In the margin box I have given you an example.

- The character of God
- The grace of God
- His unconditional love and acceptance
- Our worth and value based on our identity in Christ rather than on our performance
- Helping people for their sake, and God's sake, not our sake.

The theme I've chosen affects codependent behavior by _____

_____

_____

> *The character of God shows me that I cannot bribe Him with good behavior to make Him love me.*

Your answers to the activity are uniquely your own. These transforming truths speak powerfully to the root needs of codependents for love, acceptance, worth, and value.

Motivations for Obedience

The writers of the Scriptures taught about the character of God, our identity as His children, how we relate to others, and our motivations for obedience. In *Search for Significance*, Robert S. McGee outlines several of these motivations from the Scriptures.[2]

- The love of Christ motivates us to obey (2 Corinthians 5:14).
- Sin is destructive (Matthew 7:13).
- The Father will discipline us in love (Hebrews 12:7-11).
- His commands for us are good (John 15:11-14).
- We will receive rewards (Matthew 6:19-21).
- Obedience is our opportunity to honor God (1 Peter 1:14-16).

The Bible contains many good motives, but they are centered on a right view of God and a proper view of our identity.

As you can see, guilt is not one of these motivations! Neither is the desire to be accepted! Nor is the fear of punishment! The Bible contains many good motives, but they are centered on a right view of God and a proper view of our identity as His beloved children. This results in "I-want-to," not "I-have-to" motivations.

You may have concluded that the commands of Scripture are wrong and harmful for guilt-riddled codependents. As you change your view of God and the Scriptures, you will see that God is not like the harsh, manipulative, or neglectful person in your life. And you are not the terrible, worthless person who always has to be more, do more, and say more to be accepted.

Yes, you are a sinner, but you are a sinner who has been redeemed by Christ, adopted as a dearly beloved child of God, and given the incredible privilege of knowing, loving, and serving Him.

❧ **Briefly review the memory verses to this point in your study. Can you still say them all by memory? Which one was hardest for you to memorize because it was hardest for you to accept and believe? From studying this unit, do you have any new insights about that particular Scripture? In the margin box describe your insights.**

I have gained the insight that—

_____

_____

_____

_____

> **SUMMARY STATEMENTS**
>
> - Codependents tend to see the Scriptures as teaching and reinforcing codependent behavior.
> - The main themes of the Bible serve to change warped codependent perceptions.
> - The Scriptures give many positive motivations for obedience, but guilt is not one of them.

DAY 5

Superficial Solutions

The Quick Fix

Because they lack objectivity and are performance-oriented, codependents look for quick, simple solutions to fix themselves and other people. The problem is that simple solutions don't work! The compulsion to control does not lend itself to quick, simple solutions precisely because it is a deep, long-term problem. Codependency is not primarily a problem of wrong action. If it were it could be corrected relatively easily. But codependency is a problem of perception.

Instead of helping codependents with their warped perspectives, both secular society and the Christian culture reinforce codependency by valuing codependent behavior. Helping, fixing, enabling, being intense, being easily motivated or manipulated, being effective, being conscientious, and pleasing others are considered virtues! Codependents often make the best employees and church workers because they are effective, loyal, and committed. In some Christian circles, the obsessive-compulsive drive of codependency is equated with a deep commitment to Christ! That is why you began your discovery about codependency in unit 1 recognizing that many qualities of codependents are positive and valued. By now, you've gained a great deal of insight about the sources of those positive qualities and know they provide a false front behind which a lonely, hurting, manipulated, and controlling person hides.

The efforts of a codependent provide a facade behind which a lonely, hurting, manipulated, and controlling person hides.

We hear and read the biblical call to "deny self," but for a codependent with a broken identity, denying self just confirms the worst fears of being unloved and worthless and not having an identity. The Christian codependent who is told to deny self should also be told "you are greatly valued, deeply loved, and accepted."

I know a woman who is seen by most people as the highest example of Christian maturity. One day she confided to me that she feels driven to say, be, and do the right things to win the approval from others which she never received from her father. She is an outstanding Bible student, she is a gifted organizer, and an activist in evangelism and discipleship. She always is ready to help others, and she does an excellent job of it, too! But she has a nagging, gnawing emptiness in her heart which she tries to fill with all her activities.

Lacking Perception

Why do codependents remain this way? Why do they go from one quick, empty solution to the next, wondering why these solutions work for other people—or so the codependent person supposes—but not for them?

Use what you've learned in units 1–6 to write in the margin box at least two answers to the questions above.

Perhaps you wrote something like this: The lack of perception is one reason. Codependents don't see that they have other choices. Seen through the distorted glasses of codependency, their thoughts, feelings, and behaviors appear to be the only choices available to them. Fear of the unknown is another reason. They cling to painful, empty solutions because they fear that something else may be even more painful and more empty.

In this fear and denial, they believe others' promises and lies because they can't see the truth and are afraid the truth will hurt too much. They gloss over the offenses of others—even though others hurt them deeply. As they gloss over these offenses, they attempt to forgive and forget. These seemingly godly responses are actually codependent behaviors because they are designed to cover up pain and excuse the offenders. True forgiveness recognizes the truth in all of its pain and ugliness, seeks to help the person see the underlying problem that caused the offense, and then perseveres in the relationship. The quick-fix tendency of codependent forgiveness is very different than true forgiveness.

Why do codependents continue?—

_____

_____

_____

_____

_____

◆◆ You are on the brink of moving from understanding the problem of codependency to understanding solutions to codependency. That is where unit 8 begins. Pause now and pray. Confess to God your reliance on any godly responses to earn the acceptance of others and the acceptance of God. Confess your fears about losing God's love and the love of others. Conclude your prayer with the words of the unit memory verse.

Real answers needed

Superficial solutions sound so good. They seem to help so many people. But in the long run, quick and easy answers only make the problems of codependency worse. Real answers are needed to speak to the real issues of worth and identity. These solutions should be experienced in a long process so they will sink in deeply and profoundly. In the units which follow, we will explore our identity in Christ and the profound impact of healthy relationships in the healing process. We will also learn how to identify codependent behavior, how to detach and gain objectivity, and how to make good, healthy decisions.

✎ **Review this unit. Find one statement in the text that helped you to understand better the codependent person(s) you love.**

Below rewrite that statement in your own words.

_____

_____

Now, find one statement or insight you wrote that helped you to understand yourself better, whether or not you identify yourself as a codependent.

Below write it again, and describe how this new insight benefits you.

_____

_____

Review the memory passage. Look it up and check your memory. Then close your Bible and write the passage below. How have you made application of this passage during your study of this unit? Below record your thoughts.

_____

_____

Notes
[1]"Grace Greater Than Our Sin," *Baptist Hymnal*, 1975 edition. Words, Julia H. Johnston, 1910. Tune MOODY, Daniel B. Towner, 1910. Copyright 1910. Renewal 1936 extended. Hope Publishing Co., owner. All rights reserved. Used by permission.
[2]Robert S. McGee, *Search for Significance* LIFE Support Edition, (Houston: Rapha Publishing, 1992), 55.

Identity: A Sense of Worth

Case in point

> ### GETTING TO BE MYSELF
>
> Melanie approached Robert at a party. "What's new, Robert?" she asked. He replied with a smile, "If you really want to know, I'll tell you, but it will take a while to explain." Melanie was curious now. "What *is* going on with you?" she persisted.
>
> Robert leaned against a wall and began, "Over the past few months I've realized how my family has affected me. My mother is an alcoholic, and I've always felt responsible for making her happy. Nothing I did seemed good enough to please her. But, now I'm becoming a new person!"
>
> "What do you mean?" Melanie was confused. "You look the same to me."
>
> "I've been trying to help others so much all my life, I've been just like a puppet on a string. A couple of months ago I realized I've always tried to be the person others wanted me to be. I've never really been myself. In fact, I haven't been myself for 43 years—until lately! With the encouragement of a great support group, I've been me for about a month now, and I like it!" (Read more about Robert on page 141.)

What you'll learn

This week you'll learn—

- how the six characteristics of codependency influence your sense of worth;
- how to answer the question, "Who am I?" with biblical truth;
- the relationship between who God is and who you are;
- the importance of accurate, honest perception to your identity;
- when and how your perceptions about yourself and others become distorted from the truth.

What you'll study

The Code-pendent's Identity	Your Biblical Identity	The Character of God	Developing Perception	Identifying Distorted Perceptions
DAY 1	DAY 2	DAY 3	DAY 4	DAY 5

Memory verse

This week's passage of Scripture to memorize

Therefore if any man is in Christ, he is a new creature; the old things passed away; behold, new things have come.

–2 Corinthians 5:17

DAY 1

The Codependent's Identity

As you begin this unit, you quickly will realize that your experiences in this course and with your discovery group are changing your life. You may discard some habits on which you have depended for a long time. These learned behaviors may have kept you tangled, insecure, frantic, or frustrated, but they were familiar and comforting. Cling to the promise God made in Jeremiah 33:3: " Call to Me, and I will answer you, and I will tell you great and mighty things, which you do not know." Seek support in your group as you give up familiar, inadequate ways for the new ways God will show you.

Robert's story

Melanie approached Robert at a party. "What's new, Robert?" she asked. He replied with a smile, "If you really want to know, I'll tell you, but it will take a while to explain." Melanie was curious now. "What *is* going on with you?" Robert leaned against a wall and began, "Over the past few months I've realized how my family has affected me. My mother is an alcoholic, and I've always felt responsible for making her happy. Nothing I did seemed good enough to please her. But, now I'm becoming a new person!" "What do you mean?" Melanie was confused. "You look the same to me."

"With the encouragement of a great support group, I've been me for about a month now, and I like it!"

"I've been trying to help others so much all my life, I've been just like a puppet on a string. A couple of months ago I realized I've always tried to be the person others wanted me to be. I've never really been myself. In fact, I haven't been myself for 43 years—until lately! With the encouragement of a great support group, I've been me for about a month now, and I like it!"

Robert's insights and new sense of identity are common to people who are emerging from the darkness of codependency. The change is not instant; however, it is a process.

✎ **In Robert's story underline words and phrases that illustrate his past codependency.**

As you reviewed Robert's story, did you identify Robert's past blindness to the effects of his childhood, his people-pleasing behavior, or his loss of identity?

Components of change

Lasting and genuine change only comes when codependents experience changes in several areas of their lives. They need to experience—
. . . changes in their perception of God,
. . . changes in their perceptions of themselves,
. . . changes in their perceptions of others,
. . . and changes in their life-styles.

For these changes to take place, these four key areas are required:

cognitive–adj. based on or capable of being reduced to factual knowledge. (Webster's)

- **Cognitive.** We need to know the truth about ourselves, God, and others.
- **Relational.** Others need to model these truths for us, and we need them to encourage, affirm, and correct us; but even this is not enough.
- **Spiritual.** We need the Lord working in our lives to give us wisdom, to give us courage to take steps of faith, and to give us power to fight the uphill battle of codependency.
- **Temporal.** Finally, we need time!

✎ **Read again the descriptions of the four key areas of life required for change. In which of the four areas do you have the greatest resources and why?**

_____

_____

In which of the areas do you have the fewest resources and why?

_____

_____

You do not change in an instant years of believing certain things.

We live in a society marked by speed, automatic teller machines, drive-through banking, fast-food, microwaves, and more. You do not change in an instant years of believing certain things about yourself, about God, and about others! Change takes time. Expecting too much too soon is counterproductive. Haste usually leads people to be discouraged and even to abandon the process. Recovery may be long, and will be full of ups and downs, but hope for change exists. Now, after that warning, let's examine our identity and sense of worth.

Our Sense of Self

Sharon's story

Sharon's codependency darkened and clouded her identity, her self-concept, and her sense of worth.

I once asked a woman: "How would you describe yourself? What adjectives would you use?" Sharon thought for a minute and then she said slowly, "That's difficult for me. I guess I'd say I'm outgoing—things like that." "What else?" After a long pause, she said, "Stupid, ugly . . . I hate the way I look! I hate the way I act! I hate everything about me!" Sharon put her head in her hands and cried. Sharon's codependency darkened and clouded her identity, her self-concept, and her sense of worth.

The first three characteristics of codependency are the perceptions and behaviors which make up the condition. The second three characteristics are the emotions which result from codependency. Think again about the three perceptions and behaviors and the three emotions which result. Do you see how they affect a person's sense of worth?

The Perceptions and Behaviors of Codependency

1. Lack of Objectivity. Codependents are so busy rescuing others or withdrawing from life that they don't see the truth about their lives and circumstances. Truth is too painful to cope with, so they continue to hide behind the same ineffective and painful solutions.

2. A Warped Sense of Responsibility. Codependents play the role of "the savior"—rescuing to earn a sense of value—and/or the Judas—withdrawing to avoid the pain of rejection and failure.

3. Controlled/Controlling. Codependents act like puppets. They do whatever others want and try desperately to please them. At the same time they try to control their own lives to avoid failure and try to control others who will contribute to their success and ability to win approval.

Emotions which Result from Codependency

4. Hurt and Anger. Codependents hurt when they are condemned, manipulated, or neglected, and they become angry with the ones who hurt them. Then they repress these painful emotions, and the hurt and anger emerge as displaced anger, disproportionate anger, or depression.

5. Guilt. Codependents attempt to get their worth from being good and pleasing people. So any failure—even perceived failure—leads to intense guilt. They are ashamed of themselves and are driven to do better, to do more, and to analyze every thought, emotion, and relationship to make them better.

6. Loneliness. Codependents desperately want to be loved. They try to make people happy, make others successful, and make others feel good so other people will love them. But even when others *seem* to like the codependents, they still live in fear that they *might* do something others *might not* like.

In the margin box, write the following three introductions to help you think about your identity. First, assume you are introducing yourself to a very important person you admire and are meeting for the first time. What will you say to identify yourself? Next, assume you are reintroducing yourself to a family member you have not seen for 10 years. What will you say to identify yourself? Third, assume you are introducing yourself to yourself as if meeting for the first time. What will you say to identify yourself? That is, what do you believe deep inside about yourself?

More than likely, all your introductions are different, although you are one person. Our real identity is who we are in Christ, but our functional identity is who we believe we are. And we may be different people as our situations and relationships change. Codependent Christians pretend to be loved, forgiven, and accepted in Christ, but their actions indicate they feel and act out of guilt, fear, and bitterness. They crave to be who others are and to have what they think others have.

The remainder of this unit will help you clearly know who you are in Christ, so that your real identity and your functional identity match.

✎ **Find this unit's memory verse in your Bible. Mark it and begin to memorize it. Copy it below.**

_____

_____

Identify yourself—

to a person you admire;

_____

_____

_____

to a family member after many years;

_____

_____

_____

to yourself.

_____

_____

_____

SUMMARY STATEMENTS

- Fresh insights and new sense of identity are common to people who are emerging from the darkness of codependency.
- Emerging from the darkness of codependency is not instantaneous; it is a process.
- Recovery must involve the cognitive, relational, spiritual, and temporal areas of our lives.

<table>
<tr><td>

DAY
2

</td><td>

Your Biblical Identity

</td></tr>
</table>

The codependent identity is based on performance and on pleasing others. Thankfully, Scripture gives us a better answer to the question, "Who am I?"

 Complete the statement "I am . . ." in as many ways as you can. Write in the margin if you run out of blanks. I am . . .

_____

_____

Perhaps you just wrote: "I'm a salesman." "I'm a mother of three boys." "I'm a lawyer . . . a student . . . a secretary." "I'm an American . . . a Republican . . . a Democrat . . . a Christian." We usually think of our identity in terms of our function in society or at church or in our family.

 How many of your answers above refer to your "function"—to what you *do*? Place an *F* by those answers.

When the apostle John wanted to identify himself, he did so relationally. As he wrote the Gospel of John, he referred to himself as the disciple "whom Jesus loved" (see John 13:23; 21:7,20). John's sense of being loved and accepted by Christ was so strong that this was his identity.

 How many of your answers above refer to who you are in relationships? Place an *R* by those answers.

The apostle Paul taught first-century believers a great deal about their identity in Christ. Carefully read these verses from the first chapter of his circular letter to the believers in Ephesus.

> ³Blessed be the God and Father of our Lord Jesus Christ, who has blessed us with every spiritual blessing in the heavenly places in Christ, ⁴just as He chose us in Him before the foundation of the world, that we should be holy and blameless before Him. In love ⁵He predestined us to adoption as sons through Jesus Christ to Himself, according to the kind intention of His will, ⁶to the praise of the glory of His grace, which He freely bestowed on us in the Beloved. ⁷In Him we have redemption through His blood, the forgiveness of our trespasses, according to the riches of His grace, ⁸which He lavished upon us. ¹³You were sealed in Him with the Holy Spirit of promise, ¹⁴who is given as a pledge of our inheritance, with a view to the redemption of God's own possession, to the praise of His glory (Ephesians 1:3-8,13-14).

I am—

chosen in Him

_____

_____

_____

_____

In the margin box repeat the above "I am" exercise. This time complete the statement "I am . . ." with truths from Ephesians 1:3-8,13-14. I have given you one as an example.

Perhaps you included some of these key words to describe your identity in Christ:

• *Chosen*—Verse 4 states that believers have been chosen by God. Were we chosen because we are smart, good-looking, rich, or efficient? No, God chose us to be declared holy and blameless before Him. We are not perfect in our behavior, but we are secure in our identity.

✎ **Read John 15:15 in the margin. Jesus made a deliberate choice which answers your question, "Who am I?" Circle the word He used.**

❥ **You probably circled the word *friends*. Stop for a moment and pray; thank God for choosing you as His friend.**

> No longer do I call you slaves, for the slave does not know what his master is doing; but I have called you friends, for all things that I have heard from My Father I have made known to you.
>
> –John 15:15

• *Adopted*—Verse 5 states that God has accepted Christians as His adopted children. He didn't have to adopt us. He could have left us as helpless and hopeless people. He could have destroyed us in His righteous wrath. He could have made us His slaves. In fact, that would have been easier for most of us to accept, but He didn't. He adopted us. When Paul used the word *adoption*, he referred to the Roman practice of adopting an adult and granting full privileges as an heir. Perhaps you've seen the movie classic, *Ben Hur*. While a slave, Judah Ben Hur was adopted by the Roman admiral, Arias. Arias granted him full sonship, gave him a ring to signify his place in the family, and accepted and loved him.

Not just excused

• *Forgiven*—Paul says in verse 7 that Christians are forgiven. We are not just excused, with our sins waved off by a benevolent grandfather figure. Our sins demand payment. The price was payment of Christ's awful death on the cross. How much are we forgiven? This verse says, "according to the riches of His grace." No sin is too great, no offense is too terrible to be forgiven—except refusing to accept Christ's payment for sin. That is unforgivable.

The Holy Spirit's seal is the ultimate spiritual security.

• *Sealed*—The seal, which verse 13 mentions, signified ownership and security. Paul used the idea of a seal to explain the believer's security in Christ. The Holy Spirit's seal is the ultimate spiritual security; it cannot be broken. The Spirit's seal signifies we have been bought by the blood of Christ (see 1 Corinthians 6:19-20), so we belong to God. It means we are secure in our relationship with Him. If we have trusted in Christ as our Savior and have experienced His forgiveness, then He never will lose us or reject us.

✎ **In Romans 8 Paul stated the absolute certainty of our sealing. Read the verses in the margin. Write below all the things that can break God's seal and separate Him from one of His children.**

> For I am convinced that neither death, nor life, nor angels, nor principalities, nor things present, nor things to come, nor powers, nor height, nor depth, nor any other created thing, shall be able to separate us from the love of God, which is in Christ Jesus our Lord.
>
> –Romans 8:38-39

_____

_____

You finally found a learning activity to stump even the most compulsive perfectionist, didn't you? Absolutely no answer for the question exists, because absolutely nothing can separate a child of God from the Father.

The chart on the next page gives more insight into our identity in Christ. On the left is a list of characteristics of people who haven't trusted Christ with their lives. On the right are some traits of those who have trusted their lives to Christ. Colossians 1:13-14 clearly states the transition.

For He delivered us from the domain of darkness, and transferred us to the kingdom of His beloved Son, in whom we have redemption, the forgiveness of sins.

–Colossians 1:13-14

Colossians 1:13-14

Identity Apart from Christ	Identity as Children of God
helpless, ungodly sinners, deserving wrath, enemies of God (see Romans 5:6-10)	justified—completely forgiven (see Romans 3:21-26)
hostile, evil deeds, alienated (see Colossians 1:21)	reconciled—totally accepted (see Colossians 1:19-22)
self-righteous (see Romans 1-2; Titus 3:7-11)	propitiation provided for our sins—proof of God's deep love (see 1 John 4:9-11)
without hope (see Ephesians 2:12)	redeemed—bought by Christ's blood (see 1 Corinthians 6:19-20)
destined for eternal condemnation (2 Thessalonians 1:6-10)	no condemnation (Romans 8:1)
	near to God (1 Peter 2:10)
	chosen and precious (1 Peter 2:4-5)
	Christ's ambassador (2 Corinthians 5:20)

The scriptural truths—

of a person with the primary characteristics

_____

_____

_____

of a person with the secondary characteristics

_____

_____

_____

✎ **Review the three behaviors and perceptions (primary characteristics) of codependency by listing them.**

1. _____

2. _____

3. _____

Write in the margin box the chart's scriptural truths which reflect the attitudes, thoughts, actions, and relationships of a person with these three primary characteristics.

✎ **Review the three emotional results (secondary characteristics) of codependency by listing them.**

1. _____

2. _____

3. _____

Write in the margin box the chart's scriptural truths which reflect the attitudes, thoughts, actions, and relationships of a person with these three secondary characteristics.

Look back at day 1 of this unit and check your list of the primary and secondary characteristics. Your answers in the other blanks could have been drawn entirely from the Scriptures in the left column of the chart. Remember, everything in the right column also is true of Christian codependents, but they don't *feel* like it is. Therefore, they rarely feel the security of their identity in Christ, and it rarely shows in their attitudes, thoughts, and relationships.

All of us are "in process." None of us has "arrived." However, our past and present words influence us more than does the truth of God's Word. I don't condemn us for that! Rather, we need consistency, love, courage, and wisdom to make progress.

 In the margin attempt to write 2 Corinthians 5:17 from memory. Look up the verse and continue memorizing it.

SUMMARY STATEMENTS

- God chose believers to be declared holy and blameless before Him: not perfect in our behavior, but secure in our identity.
- Our identity is that of God's chosen, adopted, forgiven, and sealed children.
- Christian codependents rarely feel the security of their identity in Christ; therefore it rarely shows in their attitudes, thoughts, and relationships.

DAY 3

The Character of God

The work you did in unit 2 showed how your relationship with your parents shaped your view of God. Codependents seem to have a consistently inaccurate view of God. If their parents were, or are, abusive, they probably believe that God is harsh and condemning. If their parents were neglectful, they probably believe God doesn't care about them. Similarly, spouses of addicted, abusive persons develop a distorted view of God.

Codependents see God as harsh, mean, demanding, and distant.

Scripture teaches clearly that God is not like anybody or anything! He is far more loving, far more powerful, far more kind, strong, and interested in us than we can imagine. One of the painful ironies of codependency is this: God is the only consistent, loving One on whom codependents always can rely for unconditional love, acceptance, wisdom, and strength, but they see Him as harsh, mean, demanding, and distant. Codependents need to change their view of God. Perhaps you do, too. Just remember: misperceptions take years to develop; developing biblically accurate perceptions also will take time.

Applying the Truth of God's Word

After Pearl Harbor the Japanese controlled a huge area of the South Pacific. They held many heavily fortified islands. General Douglas MacArthur, commander of the Allied forces in the Pacific, decided on a bold and daring plan. He didn't attack where most military experts advised him to attack. He bypassed the fortified islands and attacked islands behind the Japanese perimeter. His forces established strong points of their own and forced the Japanese to retreat.

Codependents need to follow MacArthur's example. They need to attack the root of the condition and avoid fighting unproductive battles. Their strategy should not be to try harder, make more people happy, get more done, be more in control, or rescue more. They need to expose and attack the root of the problem: their identity and sense of worth. For many of us codependents, the truth of who we are in Christ is not new. We have known it for years. We can quote passage after passage, but the Scriptures haven't penetrated past our denial-riddled, codependent Christian facade.

Codependents need to expose and attack the root of the problem: their identity and sense of worth.

Need to experience truth

We may not need to change our beliefs about our identity. We may need to absorb these truths emotionally and to experience them in our lives. Many times such change can occur only in the company of honest people who are struggling with real issues and who are more interested in real solutions than in easy answers. That is what your discovery group and the ministry of other groups is all about.

Some passages of Scripture cause major problems for codependents. Understood through their distorted view of life, these Scriptures produce more guilt and pain instead of freedom and joyful obedience.

 Has any Scripture ever been particularly difficult for you to believe and apply in your life? Below write a summary of the passage.

_____

_____

◆→ **Pause now and pray that God will give you new understanding of this Scripture as you study this unit.**

One example of a difficult passage for codependents is one in which Jesus instructs His disciples to deny themselves. You'll find that passage printed in the margin. Take a moment now to read these verses.

Jesus made the command to deny ourselves in the context of giving up our selfish desires. This is confusing for codependents who have denied themselves and given up their own desires all their lives and who hear Jesus telling them to do more of the same! Remember, the reason codependents deny themselves and give up their desires is to earn approval and identity, not to offer true service to the Lord. Codependents need an identity based on a strong sense of being loved and accepted by God and His people. Only then will denying self make sense. We all need to be reminded often of our new identity. A friend of mine writes little notes to his codependent wife to encourage her: "You are a person who has great value and tremendous worth just by being you!"

Then Jesus said to His disciples, "If anyone wishes to come after Me, let him deny himself, and take up his cross, and follow Me."
–Matthew 16:24

In the context of this verse, Jesus has just rebuked Peter.

But He turned and said to Peter, "Get behind Me, Satan! You are a stumbling block to Me; for you are not setting your mind on God's interests, but man's."
–Matthew 16:23

In the Context of Loving Relationships

Applying these truths in a relationship of love and affirmation is like light and air to codependents. In such a context, codependents slowly learn—

Codependents have limited responsibility in the lives of others—it isn't up to them to make others happy.

- to face the truth about themselves, God, and others;
- that they have limited responsibility in the lives of others—it isn't up to them to make others happy;
- to have their own desires and dreams;
- to let other people make their own decisions;
- to be honest about their emotions, intense anger, and disappointments, as well as their love and hope;
- that it's OK to fail because failure does not threaten their sense of worth;
- to try for the right reasons;
- to love and be loved, to be honest with people, and to give and receive in relationships. Don't forget the watchword of this unit: Change takes time!

The Rest of Robert's Story

Melanie's face relaxed as she listened to Robert, who we met in day 1. She, too, had been in a recovery process but still was a bit ashamed for needing her recovery. Knowing that Robert was enthusiastic about recovery from codependency removed her lonely feelings. As she admitted these feelings to Robert, he encouraged her by saying: "Melanie, it's like peeling an onion. Each layer, each effort at change, brings new revelations, new fears, new hopes, and new change into our lives. Often, we find ourselves dealing repeatedly with the same issues, but we do it at a deeper level. If you feel discouraged by so many layers, take heart! Be glad you are in the process of healing. Your surprised recognition that God is at work in your life will make you excited that you are becoming a new person with the identity God intended for you all along!"

Does the imagery of peeling an onion encourage you or discourage you regarding changes that need to occur in your life? In the margin box explain your answer.

Perhaps you felt a bit of both—encouragement and discouragement—as you thought about this process. You may be relieved that the exposure and healing of wounds will come step by step, a bit at a time. But the fact that it does take time may be discouraging.

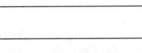 **Who will encourage you in the healing process of accepting your wonderful identity in Christ? Write this person's name in the margin.**

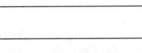 **Think of someone you feel God is directing you to encourage in the struggle to accept his or her wonderful identity in Christ. Write this person's name in the margin, too.**

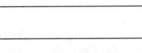 **Review the unit memory verse. Then, write it in the margin beside the name you've just written.**

The image of peeling layers of denial—

❑ Encourages me
❑ Discourages me

Because

_____

_____

_____

SUMMARY STATEMENTS

- Scripture teaches that God is far more loving, far more powerful, far more kind, strong, and interested in us than we can imagine.
- Codependents seem to have a consistently inaccurate view of God.
- Codependents need to expose and attack the root of their problem: their identity and sense of worth.

Developing Perception

Several years ago I had the opportunity to go to Thailand. On the plane, our group had a crash course in Thai culture. For example, we learned that it is extremely offensive to show the sole of your foot to anyone. We talked about greetings, etiquette, the uniqueness of the people, their religion, and the kinds of food we might be served. We thought we were prepared.

One night our group attended a special banquet. We sat on grass mats, and a local band and performers entertained us. When the first course of the meal was served, no one in the group could identify it! Yet we took the risk and ate it, and I survived to write about it! When the main course arrived, it was even more mysterious and foreign than the first course. I considered a quiet escape, but since I didn't know where I was, I had no idea where I would go! When I realized other people were carefully meeting this culinary challenge, I prayed, took a bite, and thought, "Hey, it's not bad!"

We have been studying the culture of codependency.

We have been studying the culture of codependency. We have reflected on how we relate to codependents and how our own habits and needs affect our relationships with them. Now it's time to learn to relate in new ways. Often when we relate to people in other cultures, we are the ones who learn the most. That may happen as we learn to relate to the codependents in our lives.

Recovery from codependency requires three things—perception, love, and separateness. The three are connected. Days 4 and 5 of this unit will examine *perception*. Unit 9 will interpret God's unique *love*, which even is available to Christians. As unit 10 explores the three steps to recovery—identify, detach, and decide—you'll understand the importance of *separateness*.

Looking at Perception

In the margin box write your own definition of perception before you read further.

God sent the writers of the Old and New Testament so His people clearly would perceive both *His* character and *their* needs. Perception means an accurate look at reality—seeing and believing the truth. This kind of perception is tremendously important to God. We need accurate perception because it enables us to respond more appropriately to God and to situations in our lives.

Perception means to me—

_____

_____

_____

_____

Learning to Perceive

The family bears the primary responsibility for building the skill of honest perception. The family is designed to train family members to recognize the truth of who God is and what their needs are (see Deuteronomy 6:4-12; Proverbs 3). This brings us to the central point of this unit: dysfunctional families fail, to one degree or another, in one of two areas regarding perception.

- Dysfunctional families fail to convey the truth accurately. They give the family members a warped vision of themselves, of the world, and of God.

mechanism–n. any system or means for doing something; physical or mental process or processes by which some result is produced. (Webster's)

The development of the condition—

_____

_____

_____

_____

Let your heart hold fast my words; keep my commandments and live; acquire wisdom! Acquire understanding! Do not forget, nor turn away from the words of my mouth.
–Proverbs 4:4-5

O naive ones, discern prudence; and, O fools, discern wisdom.
–Proverbs 8:5

By wisdom a house is built, and by understanding it is established.
–Proverbs 24:3

- More importantly, dysfunctional families fail to give the family members the opportunities and practice necessary to develop the skill of perception. Since family members don't see the truth in action, they cannot develop the **mechanisms** to perceive truth accurately.

When these mechanisms are damaged or undeveloped, truth becomes distorted. Adding more truth won't solve the problem until the underlying mechanisms are changed. The problem in dysfunctional families is not just one of misinformation. The ability to perceive accurately is damaged or underdeveloped. Codependents may have learned to "read" others very well in order to please them, but the codependents cannot see what's true about their own lives or the motives for their interactions with others.

Look back to the course map on the inside back cover. You now are ready to more fully describe the process pictured in the course map. Using the map and the paragraphs above, write in the margin box your own description of the development of codependency.

The warped round shapes representing the three perceptions and behaviors of codependency picture the distorted ability to perceive reality, especially a lack of objectivity and a warped sense of responsibility. Your response may have included something like: "A dysfunctional family does not teach us to see reality and our responsibilities realistically so we develop a distorted view of the world."

In the Book of Proverbs, Solomon tells us to gain truth, but he also says to develop perception (he called it _discernment_ and _wisdom_) that we may recognize and apply truth. How can persons from dysfunctional families develop a more accurate perception of reality? The task is difficult, but it is possible if they are in relationships with honest, loving, perceptive, patient people. They need—we all need—the objective input from wise friends or counselors. And we need to take "every thought captive to the obedience of Christ" (2 Corinthians 10:5). Then we are able to:

(1) _identify_ codependent traits in our lives;
(2) _detach_ ourselves from those traits to understand them better through accurate, honest perception;
(3) _decide_ to take positive, productive steps toward health.

✎ **Look again at the course map. Based on what you have just read, describe in your own words how the parts of the map work together.**

_____

_____

The steps listed above—identify, detach, and decide—are the three steps into recovery from codependency. The rest of this unit and unit 9 will give you time for further reflection on the need to change. Then you will be ready, beginning in unit 10, to explore fully the process the three steps above outline. As we identify, detach, and decide we can replace our warped codependent perceptions with a clear sense of identity, of unconditional love, and the practice of lordship resulting in a Christ-honoring life-style. I hope your response included the idea that identifying, detaching, and deciding is the way we move from codependent to healthy feelings and behavior.

♦♦ Try to say out loud and from memory the unit memory verse. Look back at the unit page and check your memory.

♦♦ Do you know people who believe the Scripture is true but who have difficulty believing the truth of this verse because of their attitudes and feelings about themselves and their worth? Pause now and pray for those persons, even if you are one of them.

SUMMARY STATEMENTS

- Recovery from codependency requires three things—perception, love, and separateness.
- Perception means an accurate look at reality—seeing and believing the truth.
- Adding more truth won't solve the problem of warped codependent perception until the underlying mechanisms are changed.

Identifying Distorted Perceptions

I once worked with a woman whose reputation as a leader varied among those she had led. Some believed her to be a wonderful, charismatic, effective influencer of others; some thought she was a manipulative power-seeker.

After a few hours in a meeting with her, I could sense people's opinions polarizing in these two different views. After several meetings, our group began to come apart at the seams! This woman's attentiveness and warmth won quite a loyal following, but several others resented her growing influence. Her response to this was to say, "They're just jealous. I'm only trying to build up people. Didn't Jesus do the same thing?" Then with obvious disgust she added, "Nobody understands me. I build good relationships. God uses me in people's lives, and others resent it!" Several of us confronted her about how she controlled the group by "serving and loving," but her ears were closed to anyone who disagreed with her.

Gary's story

Gary is a Christian from a workaholic home. He believed counseling was only one step away from the Lake of Fire. "To solve problems, all we need is the Bible," he said frequently. Gary spent several months developing a friendship with a believer named Dan. Slowly, very slowly, Gary began to listen as Dan related his struggles, hopes, and fears. The automatic defenses in Gary's heart began to take a little longer cutting Dan off, and finally Gary began to see he had a few problems to deal with, too. A crack existed in his self-sufficiency. Although it was frightening for Gary, his perceptions about himself were becoming more honest.

In the margin box describe what caused Gary to change his perception.

The most important way to help people identify their faulty perceptions is being honest about your own struggles with perception. In the margin did you note that Dan's honesty made an impact on Gary?

Gary became honest because—

_____

_____

_____

✎ **Can you remember a time when someone uncovered one of your blind spots and helped you see something positive about yourself?**
❑ Yes ❑ No
If you answered yes, describe how it felt to face that particular truth.

_____

Describe any thoughts you had or process you went through before you accepted that positive perception as truth.

_____

_____

What insight about the difficulty or ease of changing another person's perceptions of reality did you gain from recalling your experience just now ?

_____

_____

Changing perceptions

Also, seeing truth in print is a valuable help. One of the best books I have ever seen for correcting misperceptions is Robert S. McGee's, _Search for Significance_, published by Rapha and now produced in a LIFE Support edition. Consistently over the years, I have seen people's hearts warm and their spirits soar as they studied their false beliefs (perceptions), identified their painful emotions, and learned God's truths.

This chart summarizes the material taught in _Search for Significance_ LIFE Support Edition.[1]

False Beliefs	Painful Emotions	God's Truths
The Performance Trap: I must meet certain standards to feel good about myself.	**The fear of failure**	I am completely forgiven by and fully pleasing to God. I no longer have to fear failure.
Approval Addict: I must have the approval of certain others to feel good about myself.	**The fear of rejection**	I am totally accepted by God. I no longer have to fear rejection.
The Blame Game: Those who fail (including myself) are unworthy of love and deserve to be punished.	**Guilt**	I am deeply loved by God. I no longer have to fear punishment or punish others.
Shame: I am what I am. I cannot change. I am hopeless.	**Feelings of shame**	I have been made brand-new, complete in Christ. I no longer need to experience the pain of shame.

As *Search for Significance* says, you and I have a choice to make when we identify false beliefs or perceptions and find God's truth:

• Will my thinking be conformed to the pattern of this world,

or

• Will I renew my mind by accepting what God says through His Word about me?[2]

✎ **Pause now and in the margin box answer those two questions. Read each one again. Write an honest answer in the margin. Your answers may not be a definitive yes or no. The important thing is to answer honestly and without pretense.**

✎ **Review this unit. Find one statement in the text that helped you to understand better the codependent person(s) you love.**

Below rewrite that statement in your own words.

_____

_____

_____

Now, find one statement or insight you wrote that helped you to understand yourself better, whether or not you identify yourself as a codependent.

Below write it again, and describe how this new insight benefits you.

_____

_____

_____

Review the memory passage. Look it up and check your memory. Then close your Bible and write the passage below. How have you made application of this passage during your study of this unit? Below record your thoughts.

_____

_____

_____

Notes
[1] Robert S. McGee, *Search for Significance* LIFE Support Edition (Houston: Rapha Publishing, 1992), 11.
[2] Ibid., 12.

When I identify a false belief, I will—

_____

_____

_____

_____

Belonging

Case in point

STARTING TO LEARN ABOUT LOVE

Walt is a friend of mine who is in the insurance business. About two years ago, Walt started to recognize his compulsion to please and fix others. Explaining all he had learned, Walt said, "I've been a driven man all my life: driven to succeed in my business, to make money, to have a nice house. I had to make everybody happy: my parents, my wife, my children, my boss, even my dog! Everybody!

Looking back on all that, I see constant tension in my life. I was afraid somebody would find out who I really am, or wouldn't like my work, or wouldn't respect me.

"I've finally seen that a lot of my drivenness was an effort to win love. I felt some respect and had a few laughs, but I never really felt loved. When I got honest about all the anger I'd stored those many years, well, it wasn't pretty! But I'm starting to learn about love—real love. I don't think I've ever known what it was before now." (Read more about Walt on page 165.)

What you'll learn

This week you'll learn—

- how codependency creates fears about the lordship of Christ;
- how Christ's lordship applies to those in entangled relationships;
- the importance of love for emotional healing and how easily codependents confuse love with other emotions and actions;
- how everyone who seeks to recover from codependency can learn to experience and express genuine love;
- four key traits needed by those who support a codependent's recovery.

What you'll study

Lordship and Belonging	The Bible and Lordship	Love: Required for Emotional Healing	Experiencing and Expressing Love	Find a Friend
DAY 1	DAY 2	DAY 3	DAY 4	DAY 5

Memory verse

This week's passage of Scripture to memorize

"You shall love the LORD your GOD with all your heart, and with all your soul, and with all your mind." This is the great and foremost commandment. The second is like it, "You shall love your neighbor as yourself."

–Matthew 22:37-39

Lordship and Belonging

After a seminar I could tell that a young man named James was troubled. He approached me, and wanted to ask a question. We walked a while, talked a bit. Suddenly James blurted out, "I can't buy your talk about Christ being the Lord of our lives, giving us direction about what we should and shouldn't do. I don't want Him to be the Lord of my life! I can handle Him being my Savior but not my Lord." I asked him why he felt that way. He replied. "Life is difficult enough now! Look at all the commands in the Bible! How can I do all of those when I'm already having a difficult time keeping my life together?"

As we continued to talk, I learned that James had a lifelong investment in rescuing and fixing people. The demands of Christ's lordship brought him feelings of confusion, anger, and guilt.

Lordship is an intimate relationship with Christ. It is meant to be beautiful and fulfilling.

The lordship of Christ frightens codependents like James. Lordship is an intimate relationship with Christ. It is meant to be beautiful and fulfilling, but seen through the codependent lenses of overresponsibility, perfectionism, repressed emotions, and guilt motivation, lordship looks distorted and demanding. Instead of viewing it as a sense of belonging, trust, and affirmation, codependents see the Christian message as one of more demands, more condemnation, and more guilt. Consequently, Christian codependents feel driven by this relationship and feel lonely in spite of this relationship.

Codependent Fears About the Lordship of Christ

This week we will study lordship in detail. Today we will begin by looking at several assumptions codependent believers may have about Christ and the Christian life. Codependents may believe that—

1. God is mean. Many codependents do not believe God has their best interests at heart. They think He chooses us only to use us. They serve Him through an increasing number of activities out of fear that He will punish them if they don't please Him.

Fear rather than trust

✎ **What about you? Do you ever have this fear? Who or what convinced you that God wants to use and abuse you?**

_____

_____

2. God demands too much. Overly responsible codependents fear they'll never measure up to the extremely high expectations of the Christian life. They are motivated by a double-edged sword: fear of failure to meet every Christian standard and guilt for having failed. Codependent Christians may give lip service to grace and forgiveness, but they feel only demands and expectations.

Never measure up

✎ **What about you? Do you ever have this fear? Who or what convinced you that God demands too much?**

_____

_____

Anger turned sideways

3. I'm already trying as hard as I can; what more can I do? When codependents feel guilt for inadequately meeting the demands of their harsh, strict concept of God, they soon find themselves also feeling anger. Unfortunately, this anger likely is turned against a friend, a family member, or against the church. Why? Because they believe that *no one* can express anger toward God or admit feeling anger toward God.

✎ **What about you? Do you ever have this fear? Who or what convinced you that God cannot tolerate your anger?**

_____

_____

Need to be in control

4. I don't want to lose control of my life. Codependents live their lives attempting to control every detail, activity, and emotion. Codependent believers encounter great internal difficulty when they try to turn control of their lives over to another person—even to the Lord.

✎ **What about you? Do you ever have this fear? Who or what convinced you that you must never "lose control" of your life?**

_____

_____

Unable to risk ridicule

5. God will make me into something "weird." Codependents are already lonely people. They feel distant and alienated from others who are supposed to be close family or friends. When they hear stories of those who stand for Christ and who suffer ridicule or rejection, it does not draw them to the Christian life. They feel neither safety nor assurance in such a choice.

✎ **What about you? Do you ever have this fear? Who or what convinced you that God will make you into something weird?**

_____

_____

Rather than back away from radical kinds of commitment, they plunge head first into Christian activities.

6. I only earn worth by serving God. You've been reading about the fears that push codependents away from God and the Christian life. This is the other side of that coin. Some Christian codependents see serving God as a means of earning security and worth. Rather than backing away from radical kinds of commitment, they plunge headfirst into Christian activities. They hope God and others will give them recognition of their value and worth as persons. They feel the same fears as those listed above, but their thirst for approval drives them to take risks others won't take. They do this to become acceptable to others and to God.

✎ **What about you? Do you ever have this fear? Who or what convinced you that you only earn worth by serving God?**

_____

_____

7. If God loves me, He won't ask me to do anything difficult. Codependents sometimes read the Scriptures selectively. They pick out passages that soothe, and they overlook passages that prompt guilt feelings. They may focus entirely on one aspect of God's character such as His love and never hear the balance or see the larger perspective of biblical teachings.

✎ **What about you? Do you ever have this fear? Who or what convinced you that God won't ask you to do anything hard because He loves you?**

_____

_____

✎ **Reread your responses to the seven fears you've studied today. Use those thoughts to write a prayer to God about how you feel and what you need to share with God about your fears.**

_____

_____

_____

_____

➡ **Find the unit memory verse in your Bible and mark it. Begin now to memorize it.**

SUMMARY STATEMENTS

- Lordship is an intimate relationship with Christ. It is meant to be beautiful and fulfilling.
- Seen through the codependent lenses of overresponsibility, perfectionism, repressed emotions, and guilt motivation, lordship looks distorted and demanding.
- Many codependents do not believe God has their best interests at heart.

DAY 2

The Bible and Lordship

✎ **Begin your study today by reading the five verses printed in the margin of this and the next page. What one word do these writers use to describe their relationship to Jesus Christ?**

_____

✎ **Describe the mood or attitude you sense in these writers.**

_____

_____

Paul, a bond-servant of Christ Jesus, called as an apostle, set apart for the gospel of God.
–Romans 1:1

Paul, Timothy, James, and Peter—very important leaders of the first-century church—all called themselves Christ's "bond-servant." Some translations say "servant" or even "slave." Yet their attitudes seem to be confident, joyful, and focused on others' good. How can one have such an attitude when being a slave?

Paul and Timothy, bond-servants of Christ Jesus, to all the saints in Christ Jesus who are in Philippi, . . . Grace to you and peace from God our Father and the Lord Jesus Christ.
                    –Philippians 1:1-2

Paul, a bond-servant of God, and an apostle of Jesus Christ, for the faith of those chosen of God and the knowledge of the truth which is according to godliness.
                    –Titus 1:1

James, a bond-servant of God and of the Lord Jesus Christ, to the twelve tribes who are dispersed abroad, greetings.
                    –James 1:1

Simon Peter, a bond-servant and apostle of Jesus Christ, to those who have received a faith of the same kind as ours, by the righteousness of our God and Savior, Jesus Christ.
                    –2 Peter 1:1

These Christian leaders chose to describe their relationship of lordship by using the term *bond-servant*. If we understand the picture the term *bond-servant* represents, we'll better understand as positive and freeing Christ and His lordship in our lives.

In Exodus 21:1-6 Moses first described the process of becoming a bond-servant. Perhaps you would like to pause a moment and read those verses from your Bible. According to this passage, becoming a bond-servant involved two issues:

- The character of the master, and
- The new identity of the slave.

When slaves earned their freedom after six years of service, they faced an important choice. They could choose to become a free person; many chose this when the master had been harsh. Or they could choose to become a bond-servant; many chose this when the master had provided love, protection, and provision for needs. Instead of being a slave forced to serve a master, the slave became a bond-servant. The slave willingly chose to serve a master.

An entirely new relationship began. The master pierced the bond-servant's ear. This showed that the servant had freely chosen to remain with the master. The love of the master compelled the slave to remain and to serve with love and respect as a bond-servant. The "have-to" life of the slave was replaced with the "want-to" life of the bond-servant.

✎ **Summarize the change from slave to bond-servant by describing . . .**

. . . the change in identity: _____

_____

. . . the change in relationship: _____

_____

. . . the change in motivation: _____

_____

✎ **Choose whether you are more like a slave or a bond-servant, and then below explain why. Finish this statement, "I am more like a slave (or a bond-servant) because . . .**

_____."

The change in identity is from slave to a bond-servant. The change in relationship is from owner to loved master. The change in motivation is from have-to to want-to, from motivation by fear to motivation out of love and respect.

To codependents the terms love and respect usually mean fear and guilt.

The twin motivations of love and respect too often are foreign to codependents. We may use these words, but we usually mean fear and guilt instead. As usual, we lean toward one of two extremes in our response to God and our perception of Him. We tend to respond either in fear without love or to love without respect. The chart on the top of the next page shows these extreme responses, and the balance the Bible teaches.

Fear Without Love Leads to . . .	Love and Respect (Biblical "Fear")	Love Without Respect Leads to . . .
Condemnation, guilt, loneliness, withdrawal, or drivenness as we relate to God.	The love of God and the awesome character of God motivate us to know, love, obey, and serve Him.	It doesn't matter what we do; God still loves us so we can do whatever we want.

 On the dashed line in the box above, place an *X* on the point which best represents how you relate to the lordship of Christ in your life.

Are you somewhere in the middle, balancing love and respect? Do you tend toward one of the extreme ends, fearing God without loving Him or loving God without respecting Him? If you had done this activity before you began this discovery group, where would you have placed the *X*? In the margin box write a description of the difference, if any, in your two answers.

A Major Roadblock

Codependent Christians stall behind a roadblock which prevents them from experiencing the love and power of God. Jesus observed the same roadblock during His ministry.

 Read the verse in the margin. In 20th-century words, what would you call the roadblock?

_____

Many times in this study we've noted how persons with a compulsion to fix try to gain feelings of worth by rescuing, controlling, and serving others. People-pleasing is one modern term for the roadblock. We value the approval and respect of certain other people. We feel their approval and respect gives us security and worth.

Perhaps this sounds harsh, but I'm firmly convinced that any time people try to find their security and worth from someone or something other than God, their efforts are *idolatry*. Attempting to control their own lives and the lives of others ultimately puts themselves in God's place. *Replacing God is idolatry.*[1]

During this study have you found yourself wondering, "What about Jesus? He came to earth to serve. Could *He* be codependent? Surely *He* was not idolatrous." Yes, Jesus came to serve, more than anyone ever has or ever will. But His service *definitely* was not codependent! He offered His help and God's truth and allowed people to make their own decisions about how to respond. Even on the cross, abandoned by all but a few women and one disciple, He continued to do His Father's will. He did not seek to control other people, and other people's attitudes and actions did not control Him.

How I have changed—

_____

_____

_____

_____

They loved the approval of men rather than the approval of God.
—John 12:43

Jesus offered God's truth and allowed people to make their own decisions about how to respond.

Codependents have a choice to make between idolatry and biblical service.

Like Jesus, we have a choice to make. We can serve to earn worth and others' affection or serve to control others so that others will meet our needs. That is *idolatry*. It produces fear, guilt, withdrawal, and a drivenness to your life. Or we can serve out of gratitude for God's grace and forgiveness. That is *biblical* service. It produces love, trust, and joyful obedience to God.

 The illustrations below picture the two types of service you've just been studying. Write on the arrows words to describe idolatrous service and biblical service. You may choose words from the last four paragraphs, or you may use your own descriptions.

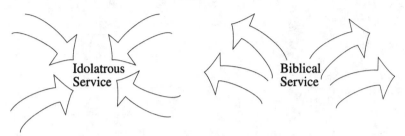

You may have noted that the arrows point inward toward idolatrous service because it is *selfish* service—motivated by personal needs to succeed, or to feel loved, or to receive affection. You may have written on the arrows which point outward from biblical service that it is *unselfish* service—motivated by a love for God and a desire to serve Him by serving others.

Individuals with a compulsion to control have followed the wrong master. They serve a compulsive spouse, a nagging parent, a critical friend, an abusive employer—vainly hoping to win affection and approval. They learn to live with fear and guilt and call it normal. They believe they are bad people who deserve to be treated badly.

You and the Roadblock

Today as you've studied the roadblock of misguided service, perhaps you've recognized your own tendency to earn love and worth by serving others. This awareness and all the personal insights you've gained in this discovery group experience may overwhelm you with the depth of your need to change. *Please don't give up!* The Lord knows your past, and He knows your pain.

As you once trusted Him for your salvation, trust Him today to be the kind and gentle Father who waits to give you the encouragement, strength, and time you need to change. Overcoming a lifetime of idolatry and codependency is difficult work, but it is the best difficult work you'll ever do. As the Lord frees you from these taskmasters, your identity and your view of God will change. You will increasingly feel God's deep care for you, experience Him as trustworthy, and learn the purposes He has for your life. To remind you of these truths, review all your memory verses to this point.

Steps to joyful service—

_____

_____

_____

_____

_____

 Consider all that you have read and done thus far in *Untangling Relationships*. In the margin box write some specific choices we can make to move from serving others compulsively (idolatry) to choosing joyfully to be a bond-servant.

Perhaps your answers are similar to these: recognize the drive to rescue and control others; remember the deep wounds that produced these compulsions; repent of actions and attitudes that do not honor God; replace codependent misconceptions with God's truth; or find resources and people who reinforce biblical living and encourage recovery.

✎ **Recovery from the effects of tangled relationships is a process. On the lines below list the roadblocks you have already overcome in your recovery.**

_____

_____

List the obstacles to your growth which you still need to overcome.

_____

_____

1. **Recognize the drive**
2. **Remember the wounds**
3. **Repent of actions and attitudes**
4. **Replace misconceptions**
5. **Recruit people who will reinforce healthy behaviors**

Each of the suggested answers at the top of this page represent a stage on the road to recovery. Possibly you wrote some of them on your list of obstacles you have overcome or need to overcome. Review the five actions in the margin. Consider if each is an obstacle you are overcoming.

✎ **Recall how the disciples in the Scriptures described themselves. The passages are written in the margin on pages 158 and 159. In the style of those verses, write your own identifying statement of who you are.**

I, _____, a _____ of
   (your name)   (a slave/bond-servant)

_____, to _____,
(codependency/Jesus Christ)   (a person you choose)

_____.
(an unselfish blessing you wish for them)

✎ **Practice your Scripture memory verse for this unit by writing it below from memory if possible.**

_____

_____

SUMMARY STATEMENTS

- Being a bond-servant of Christ is intended to be a positive and freeing experience.
- The lordship of Christ is based on love and healthy respect for the master.
- Individuals with a compulsion to serve others substitute fear and guilt for love and respect in their relationship with God.
- The love of God and the awesome character of God motivate us to know, love, obey, and serve Him.

Substitutes for love

Love: Required for Emotional Healing

Love is both the major requirement for emotional healing and the by-product of emotional healing. As codependents reflect on why they feel hurt, fear, or anger, they learn that they are both *victims* and *victimizers*. They are victims of others' neglect, abuse, or manipulation, and they are victimizers when they treat others in harmful ways.

Sometimes codependents reenact in the present the past ways they were treated. On other occasions they choose some opposite extreme. In either case they continue a harmful relationship pattern, and they confuse other emotions and actions in place of love.

Codependents tend to . . .

. . . **confuse pity with love.** Wanting to express love, they communicate pity:

- "I'm so sorry for you."
- "I wish that hadn't happened."
- "That's just awful—you poor thing!"

Codependents fear failure and label it unacceptable.

Failing is a vitally important part of living. Humans learn and grow by failing, but codependents fear failure and label it unacceptable. They say, "What a tragedy! That never should have happened!"—rather than offer encouragement or provide perspective to the one experiencing failure.

. . . **confuse worry with love.** This is a bit more aggressive than pity:

- "I have been so worried about you."
- "I didn't know what in the world had happened to you."
- "You must take better care of yourself; I've been up all night worrying about you!"

Codependents personalize everything as a reflection on themselves.

Notice how self-centered the comments are. Codependents personalize everything as a reflection on themselves. Faced with their own or others' failure, codependents exclaim: "I just *knew* it! My worst nightmare has happened!"

. . . **confuse domination with love.**

- "I know what's best for you. I am 45 years old, and I have handled that situation many times before."
- "You'd better do it like I tell you, or you'll be sorry!"
- "After all, no one knows what's best for you better than I do."

If the one they dominate fails, they say, "You should have listened to me! Didn't I tell you . . ."

. . . **confuse correction with love.**

- "Get your arm off the table!"
- "Don't forget your wallet!"

- "Be sure and remember . . . ."
- "Do this and this and this and . . . ."
- "Don't forget, like you always do . . . ."

When they notice failure, they communicate judgment: "I can't believe it! You did it again!"

Use the information from the paragraphs above to answer the questions in the margin box about the following four people.

Al has just driven all night to spend Christmas with his parents. His mother doesn't even take time to greet him before she launches into a tirade about how upset she is about his late arrival.

Paul only feels attracted to broken and hurting people whom he thinks he can help.

Elaine's daughter brings home a perfect score on the history test, but Elaine points out three misspelled words.

Terry says, "I love you and you *will* do what I say."

In the margin you identified the substitutes for love. They were worry, pity, correction, and control. As you read the next two substitutes which codependents confuse with love, think of your own examples of each.

. . . confuse need with love.

- "I need you so much; you just don't know how much you help me."
- "You're the *only one* who really understands me and cares about me."

When failure touches the relationship, codependents respond either with denial: such as "Oh, it doesn't matter; I'm fine," or with condemnation: such as "You let me down!"

. . . confuse rescuing with love.

- "I'll be glad to help you. Here, let me do that for you."
- "I don't mind working so hard on your project—you really need help!"
- "You're lucky I came along!"

If the project fails, they respond with either more rescuing: "That's OK; I'll fix it," or again, with condemnation: "This all could have been avoided if you'd only listened to me and done what I said."

> You are the writer for your own "soap opera." From your family life, write an example of confusing need with love and an example of confusing rescuing with love.

_____

_____

_____

_____

Substitutes for love—

What has Al's mother substituted for love?

_____

What has Paul substituted for love?

_____

What has Elaine substituted for love?

_____

What has Terry substituted for love?

_____

Everyone needs occasional helpful advice and sympathy. The test of whether such statements are helpful or harmful depends on the *tone* and *frequency* of the statements, the motivation of the speaker, and on the receptors of the hearer. I recommend this rule of thumb: Twenty positive statements counterbalance one negative one. We need to communicate better than a 20-to-1 ratio of affirmation, trust, and love to remain balanced on this scale!

Many of the seemingly positive communications in dysfunctional families are actually manipulative.

As you've seen repeatedly, many of the seemingly positive communications in dysfunctional families actually are manipulative. That means they can't be counted as positive. I do not say this to belittle or condemn but to increase our understanding. Remember: those who communicate using condemnation or manipulation, or are passive or neglectful, have deep wounds hurting them. They need our objectivity and compassion. They do not need more condemnation in return.

 Try to say the memory verse. Look at it and check your memory. What truth in the verse would you most want the persons in the examples in today's lesson to understand?

SUMMARY STATEMENTS

- Love is both the major requirement for emotional healing and the by-product of emotional healing.
- Codependents confuse other emotions and actions in place of love.
- Many of the seemingly positive communications in dysfunctional families are actually manipulative.

Experiencing and Expressing Love

DAY 4

Walt's story

Walt is a friend of mine who is in the insurance business. About two years ago, Walt started to recognize his compulsion to please and fix others. Explaining all he had learned, Walt said, "I've been a driven man all my life: driven to succeed in my business, to make money, to have a nice house. I had to make everybody happy: my parents, my wife, my children, my boss, even my dog! Everybody! Looking back on all that, I see constant tension in my life. I was afraid somebody would find out who I really was, or wouldn't like my work, or would not respect me.

"I finally have seen that a lot of my drivenness was an effort to win love. I felt some respect and had a few laughs, but I never really felt loved. When I became honest about all the anger I'd stored those many years, well, it wasn't pretty! But I'm starting to learn about love—real love. I don't think I've ever known what it was before now."

Walt's father and mother divorced when he was four years old, and his mother never regained her emotional stability. Although Walt was just a child, he began to try to rescue his mother from her emotional needs. Growing up in a dysfunctional family, he rarely experienced or expressed genuine love. As an adult, he did not recognize it or know how to give it. His wife genuinely had loved him, but he had great difficulty recognizing and accepting it. It was as if his receptors for receiving and transmitting love were damaged and inoperable.

Walt had great difficulty recognizing and accepting love.

Damaged Receptors

Every member of a dysfunctional family fails to some degree to develop these receptors adequately. Their ability to recognize, receive, and give love are limited.

Laura's story

The story of Laura, a six-year-old girl, illustrates this. Her parents believed she was having problems. She wasn't rebellious, yet she was unresponsive to them. Her father was an angry man who seldom communicated warmth and tenderness to Laura. He explained, "The other day I told Laura to come give me a hug, but she didn't move. I walked over to hug her, but when I did, her arms hung down at her sides. I asked her why she didn't hug me back, and she said, 'I don't have any arms.' "

 Suppose you are a friend of Laura's family and have just heard this conversation. Laura's father turns to you, angry again, and asks: "What on earth does she mean, 'I don't have any arms'?" What would you say?

_____

_____

How does the father's anger toward Laura affect you? Would the fact that he was angry make a difference in your response to him?

_____

Laura's receptors were so damaged by her angry father that even when he tried to communicate love, she couldn't receive it or express it back to him. You may have wanted to say to Laura's father that his anger has hurt his daughter so that she is no longer able to give or receive love. If the father's anger would intimidate you and make a difference in your response, think for a moment how it must be to a six-year-old.

Think for a moment how it must be to a six-year-old.

Your study today focuses on codependents' need—actually, everybody's need—to experience and express love. Individuals from tangled relationships experience repressed pain and broken receptors. These are realities we cannot simply overlook, but genuine recovery is also possible. In the face of these realities, let's affirm these facts:

Openness and honesty

• As we become increasingly honest about our lives, we increase the genuineness and openness of our relationships. In spite of the hurt and anger we have felt and still feel, we also discover some people who won't give up on us just because we aren't perfect. We begin to sense, "Somebody cares!"

• As we experience the new sensation of people asking caring questions instead of making manipulative statements, we begin to feel valued.

Who can separate us from the love of Christ? Shall tribulation, or distress, or persecution, or famine, or nakedness, or peril, or sword? . . . But in all these things we overwhelmingly conquer through Him who loved us. For I am convinced that neither death, nor life, nor angels, nor principalities, nor things present, nor things to come, nor powers, nor height, nor depth, nor any other created thing, shall be able to separate us from the love of God, which is in Christ Jesus our Lord.
–Romans 8:35, 37-39

• As we risk being honest about our weaknesses and sins, we experience the forgiveness and acceptance of others. Write in the margin a recent example of being honest about a weakness or sin in your life. Mention anyone who offered you forgiveness or acceptance in that situation.

• As people listen to us without correcting us, we gain confidence.

• As others let us make our own decisions, feel our own feelings, and think our own thoughts, we gain new strength.

• As we begin to believe God isn't harsh or aloof, we genuinely experience His tender, strong, consistent love. And we learn to express that love—His love—to others.

God has gone to the greatest lengths communicating His love to us and showing us how to love one another.

1. Through the _covenants_ in the Old Testament, God communicated His lovingkindness and proved His commitment to loving His people.

2. The _prophets_ repeatedly admonished wayward people to return to God who is both just and forgiving.

3. The _incarnation_ and the _crucifixion_ occurred because "God so loved the world" (John 3:16).

4. _Our relationship_ with God is designed for warmth and intimacy (Romans 8:15). Nothing can separate us from His perfect love, His affection, or His unconditional acceptance. Read carefully the verses in the margin.

5. We will spend _Eternity_ attempting to discover the depths of His love.

Perhaps one of the most compelling stories of the change God can bring into broken lives is told in Luke 7. Simon, a Pharisee, invited Jesus home for a meal but treated him rudely, according the customs of that day. A sinful woman in town risked rejection and punishment for entering this religious leader's home.

"She brought an alabaster vial of perfume, and standing behind Him at His feet, weeping, she began to wet His feet with her tears, and kept wiping them with the hair of her head, and kissing His feet, and anointing them with the perfume" (Luke 7:37-38).

On the surface, her actions fulfilled the social customs by providing greeting, cleansing, and anointing that honored guests normally received. But deep within, her desperate needs for love and forgiveness drew her to Jesus who provided what she needed.

To Simon, Jesus remarked: "Her sins, which are many, have been forgiven, for she loved much; but he who is forgiven little, loves little" (Luke 7:47).

Remember your work in unit 6? Only when we confess our sins do we experience in our lives the forgiveness God has given. How much have you experienced God's forgiveness? For how much has He forgiven you? How aware are you of His forgiveness?

✎ **Describe how you have experienced God's forgiveness in the past few weeks.**

_____

_____

How will it affect you as you learn to experience God's forgiveness even more?

_____

_____

Note that the question at the top of the page was not "For what has God forgiven you." If you are His child you are *already* completely forgiven. Confession does not cause God to forgive you. The issue is whether or not you are *experiencing* God's forgiveness. Lack of confession keeps us from experiencing the forgiveness God for which Christ died and which God has freely given. Trying to show love is difficult when our own emotional tanks are empty. Learning to accept God's forgiveness will help us to receive His love and forgiveness, and it will enable us to give and receive love and forgiveness.

◆▸ **Perhaps it's been a long time since you knew you had been "forgiven much" and "loved much" by God. Spend an extended time in prayer. Thank God for providing His love for you by daily forgiving your sins. Then, ask Him for memory and courage to bring your confessions up-to-date! When your confession concludes, sit still and silent in His presence and surrounded by His love.**

> **SUMMARY STATEMENTS**
>
> - Every member of a dysfunctional family fails to some degree to develop the ability to recognize, receive, and give love.
> - Nothing can separate us from God's perfect love, His affection, or His unconditional acceptance.
> - Only when we confess our sins do we experience in our lives the forgiveness God has given.

DAY 5

Find a Friend

Codependents do not loosen the grip of codependency alone. They need living, breathing persons who model the joy of finding self-worth in Christ. Such persons help to convince them that they can have the same joy. Codependents need the security of friendship of such people. Such friends are rare, but God never has called "Lone Ranger Christians!" More than 40 times the New Testament tells Christians to live out their faith, to prove their faith with "one another."

Which of the words or phrases below do you suppose appear in the New Testament followed by the words *one another*? Circle those words.

Love	Bear burdens of	Encourage	Forgive
Be kind to	Don't bite and devour	Speak to	Greet
Pray for	Spur on to love and good deeds		Exhort

All these commands appear in the New Testament. Convincingly the Scriptures teach Christians to be involved in the lives of other believers because all are part of Christ's body (see Ephesians 4:15-16).

In fact, Paul said to the Galatians, "When we have the opportunity to help anyone, we should do it. But we should give *special attention* to those who are in the family of believers" (Galatians 6:10, ICB, author's italics).

Codependents committed to recovery and healing need friends who will provide four key ingredients to their recovery process.

1. Affirmation of who they are

God's love and acceptance of us flows out of His good grace, not from our good deeds. The Scriptures explain our identity in terms of who we are, not what we do. For example, Peter assured his Christian friends:

"You are a chosen people, a royal priesthood, a holy nation, a people belonging to God . . ."

He did this *before* describing what that identity empowered them to do:

". . . that you may declare the praises of Him who called you out of darkness into his wonderful light" (1 Peter 2:9, NIV).

Does affirmation work when people fail? I've certainly seen it work. My dear friend Melanie rejoices sincerely with people when they do well. And when they fail, Melanie says gently and convincingly to them: "It's OK. This doesn't change how I feel about you at all. I care about you, and nothing you do will keep me from caring about you!"

The pain of failure and the fear of rejection seem to dissolve before that kind of affirmation.

2. Encouragement of what they do

Encouragement is closely linked to affirmation. Encouragement is like a coach on the sidelines—cheering the players, calling out directions they are capable of following, and communicating confidence in them.

Lisa's story

Lisa was married to an alcoholic for 12 years before they divorced. This left her with two small sons to raise alone. The accumulated pain of her codependency compounded the difficulties of working and single parenting.

Lisa tried coping alone, but on a friend's recommendation began visiting a Christian counselor at her church. Her counselor told her about a weekly support group at the church. Lisa hesitated to attend. She was afraid people would see her there and would think she was weird or crazy.

Speaking the truth in love, we are to grow up in all aspects into Him, who is the head, even Christ, from whom the whole body, being fitted and held together by that which every joint supplies, according to the proper working of each individual part, causes the growth of the body for the building up of itself in love.

–Ephesians 4:15-16

God's acceptance flows out of His good grace, not from our good deeds.

Lisa did go to the group. That evening, and for the next several months in the circle of loving relationships, Lisa finally felt understood and encouraged. She began to experience healing as she allowed herself to form friendships with other group members who encouraged her recovery.

3. Honesty in the relationship

Most codependents have for years repressed deep hurts and anger. They feel depressed for long periods. Then they explode in anger over relatively small issues. They need friends who will allow them to express their emotions and thoughts, friends who will not feel threatened by the heat or intensity of those expressions. Just as important, they need people who are not committed to simple answers like "Just pray about it," "Confess it and move past it," or the oh-so-understanding, "Get a grip!" Those bits of advice may be well-meaning, but they only encourage codependents to continue the dishonesty of repressing their thoughts and feelings.

Exposing accumulated hurt and anger usually is a messy process. Once codependents begin their recovery, challenges and difficulties will continue to surface as they relate to their abusers and addicted loved ones. A patient, listening friend can say, "Be careful about responding that way again to your husband. That is rescuing him, and you need to let him be responsible for his own choices and consequences."

This honesty flows both ways. Codependents need someone to talk to honestly without fear of ridicule or gossip about their lives. They also need someone who will be honest—even painfully honest—with them.

4. Modeling emotional and spiritual health

Gathering new insights and information about codependency is an important part of recovery, but nothing prompts greater growth than does time spent with a good example. Like most aspects of life, emotional and spiritual health often is "caught, not taught." Rescuers need to spend time with healthy people in healthy situations where people express real emotions and where they seek real solutions to real problems. Codependents heal as they see healthy people succeed and fail and as they observe them in jobs, families, play, church, and neighborhood. Simple solutions and glib answers just won't do!

Christ used this method with His disciples. For three years they observed His ministry. They discussed difficult questions with Him, listened to His encounters with hard-hearted legalists, and watched Him deal with ridicule, grief, agony, and death. Finally, they saw Him risen from the tomb and His ascension into heaven. They saw it all! No human ever can duplicate the completeness of Christ's modeling for His disciples. Yet Paul said, "Follow my example, as I follow the example of Christ" (1 Corinthians 11:1, NIV: see also Philippians 3:17 and 2 Thessalonians 3:7). People who are honest about the struggles of life and are faithful to God in the midst of those struggles are worthy models to know and follow.

Review the four sections you have just read. Read the four "I need people who will" statements in the margin box. From the subheadings of the four sections, choose one word which best summarizes each of the "I need" statements in the margin box. For example, the first statement in the margin box corresponds to the second section in the text. I would choose the word *encouragement* from the second subheading to describe someone who cheers me on in my struggles and achievements.

I need people who—

1. will cheer me on in my struggles and achievements.

_____

2. will demonstrate health in their speech and action.

_____

3. will accept me for who I am

_____

4. will both let me talk without judging me and yet will tell me the truth

_____

But who?

All believers, whether or not they identify with the label of codependency, need affirmers, encouragers, honest friends, and healthy models. But where do you find them?

You already may have a precious friend who provides these ingredients in your life. Some find that their spouses are a major part of their codependency problems, but others (myself included) are married to persons who provide the patient understanding they need to heal and grow.

Warmth and affirmation

You may benefit from time with a professional, Christian counselor. Despite the stigma many attach to counseling—"Counselors are quacks!" and "Only really messed up people go to counselors!"—the warmth, affirmation, and objectivity of a good counselor can be a tremendous help to recovery.

✎ **What are some dangers in trying to recover from codependency alone?**

_____

_____

First, codependents struggling with a lack of objectivity cannot on their own effectively process the information and insights they gather. Secondly, the Lord created us to live in healthy, redeemed relationships—first with Him, and then with others.

✎ **Before your next discovery-group meeting, take a walk through your neighborhood or building, through your work place (home qualifies!), and through your church building. Three walks! On each walk, jot in the boxes below names of persons which fit the categories. Remember, you need people supplying the four key ingredients we've studied today in your life; but you also may be able to supply one or more of those ingredients in others' lives as well.**

	Provided for me by	I can provide to
Affirmation		
Encouragement		
Honesty		
Modeling emotional and spiritual health		

✎ **Review this unit. Find one statement in the text that helped you to understand better the codependent person(s) you love. Rewrite that statement below in your own words.**

_____

_____

_____

Now find one statement or insight you wrote that helped you to understand yourself better, whether or not you identify yourself as a codependent. Write it again below, and describe how this new insight benefits you.

_____

_____

_____

Review the memory passage. Look it up and check your memory. Then close your Bible and write the passage in this margin. How have you made application of this passage during your study of this unit? Record your thoughts below.

_____

_____

_____

Notes

_____

[1]For a discussion of manipulative control as idolatry, see John N. Oswalt, _The Book of Isaiah_ (Grand Rapids: Eerdmans, 1986), 82-89.

Three-Step Process to a Healthy Life

Case in point

FROM VICTIM TO VICTOR

Jay recalls, "I was a victim for thirteen years. Many things happened that weren't fair or right, but I had absolutely no control over them. My dad was drowning himself in alcohol, and he took us with him. It wasn't my fault. I wasn't the only one to ever experience this type of pain or abuse, and I didn't know how to cope. In response, I exchanged the role of victim for that of villain. I knew what was right, but I couldn't seem to put it together for myself. Since every villain needs a victim, I continued the cycle by making victims of those around me.

"Now I am a victor. I had to stop viewing those who hurt me through the blurred vision of my tears and begin to see them with the clarity of God's perspective. I had to decide that I was not going to allow toxic parents or personalities to poison the well that I had to drink from for the rest of my life and which I would leave as a heritage for my children to drink from. I realized that I was crucifying my today between the thief of yesterday and thief of 'I'll get help tomorrow.' "[1]

What you'll learn

This week you will explore the three-step process to healing from codependency and to untangling codependent relationships. You'll learn—

- the first step—IDENTIFY—is the crucial beginning of the process; identifying what "normal" means helps you take the first step;
- to identify four specific situations where you dealt with codependent feelings, thoughts, words, and actions;
- the second step—DETACH—is the critical step left out of most problem solving; asking good, key questions helps us to detach;
- nine perspectives for better understanding the work of detachment;
- the four components of the third step—DECIDE—and how they work in the recovery process.

What you'll study

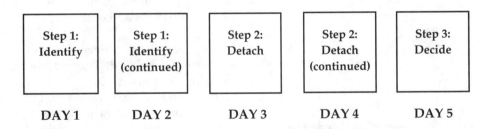

Step 1: Identify	Step 1: Identify (continued)	Step 2: Detach	Step 2: Detach (continued)	Step 3: Decide
DAY 1	DAY 2	DAY 3	DAY 4	DAY 5

Memory verse

This week's passage of Scripture to memorize

Acquire wisdom! Acquire understanding! Do not forsake her, and she will guard you; love her, and she will watch over you.

–Proverbs 4:5-6

Step 1: Identify

As codependents learn more about how dysfunctional relationships have affected their lives, they also learn how to respond in new and more positive ways. These new responses come through a three-step process. The steps are identify, detach, and decide.

First, *identify* the feelings, thoughts, words, and actions that are the learned behaviors of codependency.

A three-step process

Second, *detach* from these habits and reflect on positive, healthy ways to respond.

Finally, *decide* on a course of action based on objective reality, not on codependent reflexes.

IDENTIFY . . . SEE IT.
DETACH . . . .ANALYZE IT AND DISCONNECT FROM IT.
DECIDE . . . . CHOOSE YOUR RESPONSE.

For some, this is fairly easy: "Oh yeah! I've done that for years!" they say. Others have a more difficult time. They will see isolated actions or words but miss the lifelong patterns of codependency. And others, still stuck in their lack of objectivity, don't recognize any codependent characteristics at all. No healing begins until the Holy Spirit overcomes our denial. One barrier keeps most codependents from honestly identifying their codependency—they continue to think of their lives and their relationships as "normal."

Continuing to think of their lives and relationships as normal is one barrier that keeps most codependents from identifying their condition.

What Is "Normal?"

Dysfunctional behavior destroys objectivity. As a result, codependents believe their lives are fairly normal. Compared to the alcoholic, drug addict, perfectionist, workaholic, bulimic, sexual abuser, or whoever in the family is "really messed up," they look pretty good! They fail to recognize that the exaggeration, guilt, loneliness, susceptibility to manipulation, manipulation of others, and outbursts of anger in their lives are *not* normal.

Codependents do not face the reality of their lives objectively. In your study, you've seen this over and over.

• Many codependents believe that they are terrible people—though they try so hard to be helpful. These codependents generally believe that the offending persons in their lives are wonderful—though those persons manipulate the codependents through guilt, self-pity, anger, and fear.

Powerful deception

• Other codependents rationalize that they have no hidden motives or appreciable faults. The power of this deception is great. One man, frequently overcome by guilt and morbid introspection, told me he didn't think he ever had sinned!

• Codependents typically are produced in families which are dysfunctional to some degree. Codependents have defended and rescued the people in their lives so much that they cannot understand the impact of addiction or abuse on the family. Accepting the truth is very difficult.

A woman I knew always defended her alcoholic mother. As the woman learned about her codependency, she said of her mother: "I always thought she was normal, but I'm starting to see how she manipulated me so I would please her and rescue her. She isn't normal. She's sick!"

Codependents feel lonely when they want intimacy.

Codependent responses are not normal either. Codependents feel guilty even when they've tried to help. They feel lonely when they really want intimacy. They have controlled, been controlled, and rescued others from the consequences of their destructive choices. When others have condemned, used, and ignored them they haven't allowed themselves to feel normal hurt and anger. They haven't known a "normal" day in their lives!

No basis for comparison

Most people, whatever their family story, believe their families are normal because they've never had another family experience. No basis for comparison exists. As you share with your discovery-group members, don't try to decide whose situation is worse. Every person's pain is legitimate; every person needs to experience love and care in the present and hope for the future.

A Place to Start: Identify Feelings

Cannot identify feelings

If codependents haven't experienced or expressed authentic love, what have they experienced? Most could not tell you, because they cannot identify their feelings. The instability of a dysfunctional family creates threatening situations—people out of control, angry explosions, no one and nothing on which to rely. Codependents want dysfunctional family members to get their anger, addictions, and abusive acts under control, but codependents cannot make this happen. So without really thinking about it, they deny their hurt and anger.

Codependents try to keep themselves under control and hope everyone else in the family will do the same. They cope by practicing dishonesty about painful emotions. They clamp down on these feelings before the feelings bubble to the surface. Do this for years, and eventually you'll never know about the hurt and anger stored inside.

• One woman who was abused as a child said, "I wasn't really affected. I don't feel angry at all."
• A man explained, "It's amazing that my father's alcoholism and my mother's steady supply of boyfriends didn't bother me!"

Often, it takes weeks in an atmosphere of support and care for codependents finally to admit their true feelings. When they do, those feelings invariably include hurt, bitterness, emptiness, fear, and loneliness.

My prayer as I've written this material is that you've been facing your true feelings gradually and honestly during the time you've already invested in your discovery group. I've prayed you would find support and unconditional love from your group members and from God through times of prayer and Scripture memory. In other words, you've been doing step one—identify—for weeks now.

Identifying what you feel is the hardest part of this step of recovery.

Identifying what you feel is the hardest part of this step of recovery for many persons. Use the list of feelings words atop the next page to help identify your emotions.

Circle every word in the list of feeling words that expresses a feeling you can recall feeling in the past several months.

Then, check every word that expresses how you usually feel when you encounter difficult people or difficult situations. If you usually are out of touch with your feelings, you may not realize what you've felt until you read these words. Go slowly, and ask God to guide you to circle and check what you feel honestly.

I can remember a time when I felt—

Angry feelings	Fearful feelings	Sad feelings
mad	scared	depressed
furious	unnerved	bored
hurt	anxious	ashamed
hostile	weak	bad
alarmed	concerned	down
irritated	foolish	disheartened
frustrated	embarrassed	lonely
angry	helpless	sleepy
rage	jittery	inferior
jealous	despairing	miserable
selfish	confused	guilty
aggravated	rejected	bored
hateful	pessimistic	inadequate
displeased	submissive	lost
dismayed	insecure	confused
critical	discouraged	apathetic

Joyful feelings	Peaceful feelings	Capable feelings
loving	serene	confident
jubilant	relaxed	powerful
excited	thoughtful	proud
energetic	calm	satisfied
daring	intimate	important
inspired	trusting	faithful
playful	nurturing	committed
free	comfortable	high
optimistic	glad	strong
creative	pleased	intelligent
delightful	relieved	worthwhile
alert	sentimental	valuable
invigorated	mellow	respected
stimulating	confident	enlightened
interested	responsive	pleased
amused	steady	happy
contented	strong	hopeful

This list of feeling words includes a lot of words. You may not have realized how many ways exist to describe what you feel! Look back over your circles and checks and write in the margin box the answers to the questions you find there.

Regarding your feelings—

What words did you mark that you never before have used to describe your feelings?

_____

_____

_____

_____

What did you learn about yourself that you never before have acknowledged?

_____

_____

_____

_____

How do you feel about yourself after completing this exercise with the list of feelings words? Choose at least three words from the list.

_____

_____

_____

✎ The course map pictures the development of and recovery from codependency. On the partial map below, draw in the missing element which represents the path from the dysfunctional life-style of codependency to the Christ-honoring life-style of recovery.

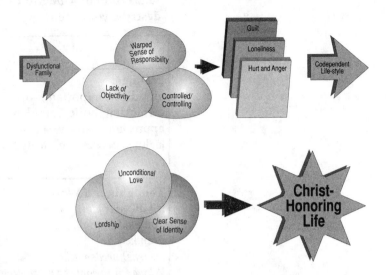

On the arrow you have drawn, write in the three steps of this unit. You may refer to the inside back cover to check your work.

◆▸ Find the unit memory verse in your Bible and mark it. God has the wisdom you need to understand your feelings. He created you and your emotions. Thank Him for that gift. Ask for the wisdom to enrich your life through helping you understand your feelings.

◆▸ Begin now to memorize the unit memory verse by copying it on a card to carry with you.

SUMMARY STATEMENTS

- New healthier responses come through a three-step process. The steps are identify, detach, and decide.
- Most codependents cannot identify their feelings.

Step 1: Identify (continued)

Today you will continue to identify codependent patterns and specific examples of those patterns. The chart which follows lists some of the more common codependent feelings and behaviors. I have divided them into the "savior" and "Judas" categories again because these two images are so powerful and so effectively describe the black-and-white extremes of codependency. This chart may seem redundant; after all, we've studied all these ideas earlier in the course. Remember, you're now ready to do the difficult work necessary to break the grip of codependency in your life (or to understand better the difficult work someone you love must do). This is application, the nitty gritty, the water hitting the wheel!

✎ **In the chart below read through the savior column first; then read the Judas column. Underline the feelings, thoughts, words, and actions that describe your life.**

Savior	Judas
Feelings: grandiose, important, superior, certain, euphoric, confident, appreciated, angry, self-righteous, jealous, possessive, easily hurt	**Feelings:** depressed, lonely, angry, helpless, confused, afraid, hurt, inferior, hopeless, guilty, numb, trapped, martyred, persecuted, lethargic, worthless, ashamed, tired
Thoughts and Words: *It's all your fault.* *You made me fail.* *I can help.* *He (she) needs me.* *Why aren't people as perceptive as I am?* *I deserve their respect and love.* *I can make life good.*	**Thoughts and Words:** *It's all my fault.* *I'm a failure.* *I can't do anything right.* *Everything I do is wrong.* *Yes, but I mean no.* *No, but I mean yes.* *I don't deserve their respect and love.* *Life never will be good for me.*
Black-and-White: *People really need me.* *I am indispensable to the kingdom of God.* *People won't be helped and the Great Commission can't be fulfilled without me.*	**Black-and-White:** *People really need me, but I'll only let them down.* *Good Christians wouldn't think or act this way.* *God must be mad at me. He'll punish me.*
Actions: positive exaggeration, self-promotion, overcommitment, workaholism, susceptibility to manipulation, control of others through praise and condemnation, rescue of people without being asked, denial of reality, compulsion to avoid failure, giving, helping, trying to please people, defensiveness, overly responsible, prone to outbursts of anger, rationalizing, trusts self and others	**Actions:** negative exaggeration, self-denigration, withdrawal, avoidance of people and risks, susceptibility to manipulation, control of others through self-pity, denial of reality, passive-aggressive behavior, fear of failure leading to passive behavior, defensive, irresponsible, prone to outbursts of anger, rationalizing, doesn't trust self but may trust others

Now read through each column again, and circle the feelings, thoughts, words, and actions that described your life before you began this discovery group.

Look at the underlined words. Do you find a pattern, or do these words picture for you an important insight about yourself today? In the margin box, describe what you see.

> **From the underlined words, I see—**
>
> _____
>
> _____
>
> _____
>
> _____

From the circled words I see—

_____

_____

_____

My responses are alike/different—

_____

_____

_____

_____

No temptation has overtaken you but such as is common to man; and God is faithful, who will not allow you to be tempted beyond what you are able, but with the temptation will provide the way of escape also, that you may be able to endure it.

–1 Corinthians 10:13

2. Look at the circled words. Do you find a pattern, or do these words picture for you an important insight about yourself as you were before you began this course? In the margin box, describe what you see.

3. In the margin box, complete this statement: Comparing my two sets of answers, my feelings, thoughts, words, and actions today are alike/different from those I had before I began this course. Now, what additional insight about yourself do you have? Explain.

Only in Your Mind?

Before you worked with the chart today and the list of feelings words yesterday, you may have thought that step one—identify—was a purely mental exercise. I suspect that working with the chart and list, you felt many emotions as you realized how deeply life's events and relationships affect you. This realization is good news and bad news. The good news is that hope is ours in the Lord. For the difficult work of recovery He gives us wisdom, strength, and godly friends who encourage us. The bad news is that you may have seen only the outer layers of your hurt, fear, anger, and the patterns in your life. Most likely, more lies beneath the surface. That's a discouraging bit of reality to face, but we must face even the most difficult truths.

Remember: you are not alone! Paul encouraged the strugglers in Corinth when he used the words that appear in the margin.

✎ **At this point in your study, what is your temptation? In the list below, check any that apply, or add your own.**

❑ Not taking time to do the exercises in this unit
❑ Failing to attend this week's discovery group
❑ Not believing God is "faithful" to love me when I'm honest about my anger and pain
❑ Unwillingness to identify codependent patterns in my life
❑ Desire to continue blaming others—being the victim
❑ Desire to continue controlling and manipulating others—being the victimizer
❑ Neglecting the Scripture memory for this unit
❑ Other: _____
❑ Other: _____

➜ **Be honest in God's presence about any temptation you checked or wrote. In prayer admit to Him that without Him, you are unable to endure or to escape this temptation. Ask for what you need in order for you to continue the healing process during the final units in this study.**

Identify Situations

You'll finish today's study by describing situations from your life in which you now can identify codependent feelings, thoughts, words, or actions. Remember, you may not be a codependent, but you undoubtedly can find examples of codependent-like thinking or acting in your life. That's the effect of sin we've studied previously. You may not want to do all the writing this requires. My encouragement to you is to persevere! If you can take time now

Feeling check

Feeling: _____

A recent time I felt this: ___

_____

What I said or thought about myself at the time:

_____

_____

What I did because of how I was feeling at the time:

_____

_____

You will find that writing brings a clarity which you cannot receive in any other way.

to identify these situations effectively and honestly, you'll be building a habit of honesty which will work for your health and recovery in the future. You've come this far—keep on!

The chart on page 178 has four sections with different headings. Choose a word you underlined or circled from either the savior or Judas column of the "feelings" portion of the chart. In the margin box, write that word on the first line. Then describe a recent situation where you've felt that feeling. To explain your feeling identify a specific way you thought or acted or what you said in that situation.

 Repeat the last activity on the lines below. This time choose from the chart on page 178 a thought or word you underlined or starred in the section of the chart labeled "Thoughts and Words." Write an example and complete the activity below as you did in the margin box.

Thought/Word: _____

A recent time I thought/said this: _____

_____

What I said about myself at the time: _____

_____

What I did because of how I was thinking at the time: _____

_____

Thinking carefully about our feelings, thoughts, and actions is difficult work. Congratulate yourself for doing the activities. You will find that writing about life situations brings a clarity and understanding which you cannot receive in any other way.

Choose a phrase from both of the two remaining sections of the chart on page 178. On a separate sheet of paper write about those phrases. Use the same four-part method you have used above to write about an instance of black-and-white thinking and about an action.

❖ **Review the unit memory verse. God gives the wisdom to identify codependent behaviors in our lives. He created you, He knows you best, and He has the best to give you. Thank Him for that gift, and ask for the wisdom to identify honestly and objectively in your life any codependent habits of thought, feeling, or action.**

SUMMARY STATEMENTS

- You generally must feel many emotions to realize how deeply life's events and relationships affect you.
- Because of the universal damage done by sin you undoubtedly can find examples of compulsive thinking or acting in your life even though you may not be a blue-chip, card-carrying, bona fide codependent.
- Thinking carefully about our feelings, thoughts and actions is hard work.

Step 2: Detach

"I know what's wrong; I just don't know what to do about it!" Have you ever made such a statement? We all have! And why is it so true? Because we've taken the first step—identification ("I know what's wrong") and tried to skip to the third step—decision (". . . what to do about it"). But an intermediate step exists—a crucial step called detachment. For codependents detachment is very important in the process of healing.

What Is Detachment?

A positive, healthy term

Some psychologists use *detach* to mean a defensive reaction to block pain and avoid reality by isolating self from others in a negative, harmful way. But the literature of recovery uses *detach* to describe a positive, healthy action— stepping back to obtain objectivity about a person or situation. So we're not equating detaching with withdrawing. The goal of detachment is opposite of withdrawing. We detach to become objective, to deal with reality, to feel real emotions, and to determine the best actions.

Detaching requires time, objectivity, and distance—both physical and emotional distance. No simple formula for detaching exists because situations are so different for each person. Ask yourself one key question, "What do I need—time, space, objectivity, or something else—so that I can reflect on this situation?"

Some people can identify, detach, and decide quickly, especially when they've practiced this process over time. Most people, however, need distance from difficult persons or situations to be objective and to reach decisions. They need to take deliberate action to detach.

What helps you to detach in order to become objective and make decisions? In the margin box you will find some ways others have used to detach. Check all of the methods you have found helpful.

Notice that some strategies for detaching actually are distractions. As long as you get back to doing the important work—reflecting on the person or situation—no harm is done!

Strategies to detach—

- ☐ take a brisk walk
- ☐ read a book or magazine
- ☐ listen to favorite music
- ☐ whip up something in the kitchen
- ☐ plan a weekend away
- ☐ take a drive
- ☐ call a trusted friend
- ☐ go to another room
- ☐ other: _____

Help from the Word

The Scriptures have a lot to say about reflecting on reality and truth so that our responses are wise. According to the Scriptures, the time needed to acquire this kind of wisdom is worth taking.

◆◆ The Scripture memory verse for this unit certainly affirms this truth. Pause now for 10 minutes of concentrated effort to memorize it.

Proverbs 24:3-5, printed in the margin, also offers hope for individuals and their families. Proverbs 26:4-5, printed in the margin on the next page, gives practical advice on how to respond to abusive, manipulative, and condemning people.

By wisdom a house is built, and by understanding it is established; and by knowledge the rooms are filled with all precious and pleasant riches. A wise man is strong, and a man of knowledge increases power.
–Proverbs 24:3-5

Do not answer a fool according to his folly, lest you also will be like him. Answer a fool as his folly deserves, lest he be wise in his own eyes.

–Proverbs 26:4-5

Doing the Work of Detaching

Once you've recognized your need for time and distance to detach and gain objectivity, questions like the ones below will help you.

- Why did he/she say that to me?
- What did he/she actually mean by those words?
- How am I feeling right now?
- How would a healthy, objective person feel right now?
- Why do I feel guilty? driven? afraid? lonely?
- Am I feeling the need to rescue in this situation?
- Am I acting like a savior or a Judas?

 What questions of your own can you add to this list to help you feel and think clearly when you detach? Write them beside the list above.

Begin to program your thinking with key statements that will help you think objectively about codependency. Use statements such as:

Truths for life

- I'm not responsible for making this person happy.
- I'm not responsible for fixing his/her problems.
- This person needs to be responsible for himself/herself.
- I can respond calmly.
- I can say no. I can say yes.
- I can make my own decisions.
- I feel angry (or lonely, guilty, driven, afraid).
- I am loved and accepted by God through Jesus Christ.

Since starting this discovery group, what statements have you learned to say about yourself that remind you of your identity in Christ and of your value as a person? Add those statements to the list above.

The Gift of Having Choices

Changing responses makes us feel awkward and guilty.

Codependents are accustomed to limited options, to instinctively repeating the same reactions to difficult people or situations. Changing responses makes them feel awkward and guilty. This precisely is the reason detaching is so important. Only by detaching can we distinguish between codependent reactions and healthy responses.

Growing confidence

Persons trying to recover from codependency are like small boats cut loose from an ocean liner. Being tied to the giant boat created safety even if it took them where they didn't want to go. Cutting the lines and being suddenly on their own feels awkward and overwhelming. They make wrong moves before they make right moves. But with time and practice they can determine the right direction. Their confidence and independence grows. Soon codependents can anticipate their need to detach before they are confronted with the difficult situation or person. Just as people do preventive maintenance on their cars, codependents learn to think through situations before they occur. They learn to think, reflect, ask questions, and be prepared ahead of time.

This preventive detachment releases codependents from the trap of assuming they have only two ways of responding—the same way, or not at all. That's just more black-and-white thinking! Preventive detaching means pausing to ask questions such as:

Building options

- What are realistic expectations in this situation?
- How does this person typically respond to me?
- What do I want from this conversation (visit, situation)?
- What if I do (brainstorm several responses)? What will happen?
- How can I respond if these things happen?

✎ Reflect once more on the situations you described on page 180. Choose one of the preventive questions above, or others you add, which would have helped you reflect honestly and with objectivity about each situation. In the margins write those questions in the appropriate places.

➥ Review your memory verse and attempt to quote it out loud. Realize that God has wisdom which you need so you can detach from old habits in your life. Thank Him for that gift and ask for the wisdom to take the time needed to do the work of detaching.

SUMMARY STATEMENTS

- For codependents detachment is very important in the process of healing.
- The goal of detachment is to become objective, deal with reality, feel real emotions, and determine the best actions.
- Detaching requires time, objectivity, and distance—both physical and emotional distance.
- Pausing to ask questions is the key to detaching.

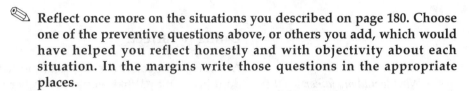

Step 2: Detach (continued)

DAY 4

I hope you finished day 3's material feeling both the confidence and the competence you need to detach. However, I know that simply asking a series of questions is not like uttering magic words and POOF! You detach. Today you'll consider some important principles about how detaching works. This is crucial material, so don't rush through it. Consider each of these principles carefully. Pray for wisdom to understand them and for courage to make the applications you need for your own recovery and healing.

Love or Anger?

When it's possible, and when you have a choice, detach calmly and with a loving attitude. But by all means, do the work of detaching. One writer noted:

If you can't detach in love, then detach in anger.

"I think it is better to do everything in an attitude of love. However, for a variety of reasons, we can't always do that. If you can't detach in love, it's my opinion that it is better to detach in anger rather than stay attached. If we are detached, we are in a better position to work on (or through) our resentful emotions. If we're attached, we probably won't do anything other than stay upset."[2]

Anger actually can be used constructively in detaching. Anger strongly motivates you to develop your independence and to clarify your identity. It gives us the courage to say: "I refuse to be manipulated again," or "I'm not going to take this anymore. I'm detaching from this person or situation to develop my own identity and to make my own decisions."

Doing it perfectly!

"What would my father say if I made a mistake?"

A woman once told me she was afraid to try detaching because she might not do it just right. "What would my father say if I made a mistake?" she asked. She finally realized her fear and her perfectionism were the very reasons she needed to detach! If you believe everything must be said and done perfectly while you detach, then you still carry the oppressive weight of over-responsibility. Have the courage to admit that detaching requires a major change in your feelings, thoughts, words, and actions. You cannot be reprogrammed instantly like a robot or computer. You are a person, and people need time, practice, and patience to change deeply ingrained habits.

What would "normal" people do?

From this day on, define "normal" people as sinners who are prone to selfishness and pride at times but who are not codependent. Healthy, independent persons sometimes may seem selfish because the whims of others do not control them. But labeling them terrible, selfish, or awful because they can make their own decisions is codependent thinking at work again.

Expect conflict.

Your family and friends will not stand and applaud when you stop playing the codependent role. They are as caught in the pattern as you have been. When they realize you are acting independently, outside those patterns, they may apply more guilt, more manipulation, and more accusations like "You are so selfish!" Expect this resistance of others to your changes. Expect to feel isolated from your family. Realize that this fear of being left on the outside of family or relationship boundaries is why many codependents continue to be used, neglected, and controlled. Courage and honesty are needed to work through this process of healing.

Review the first four principles of detachment. In the margin box write the principle that corresponds with each of the four summary statements. You'll find the answers on the next page.

The price of change.

Identifying, detaching, deciding—this process will bring you wonderful freedom and independence. But with the freedom will be the pain of realizing how codependency has damaged your life and the insecurity of acting in ways you've never chosen before. The fear and awkwardness are normal; they are the price you pay to change, so accept them. Welcome them, in fact, as proof you're on the right track! They gradually will end as your recovery and

---

Match the principles—

A. The other people in my life will not immediately appreciate having to do their own work and be responsible for themselves.

_____

B. What would someone who was not codependent do in this circumstance?

_____

C. Even if you have to detach in anger, detach!

_____

D. Don't wait until you can do it just right; just do it.

_____

healing continue, and you'll enjoy your independence and freedom from codependency. (The answers to the last exercise were A. 4, B. 3, C. 1, D. 2).

What about final solutions?

What about divorce?

The pain and bitterness of relating to an abusive, addicted person makes completely severing such relationships very attractive. Particularly in a marriage relationship of codependency, finality in detaching—divorce—seems very viable.

My counsel is to proceed very carefully. A temporary separation may be needed for the two spouses to look honestly at their marriage, seek competent, Christian counseling, and commit to God's plan for marriage.

Do not make major decisions without good Christian counsel.

Tragically, many hurting codependents dump one abusive spouse only to marry another, and the codependent cycle perpetuates. We'll not resolve this sticky, emotionally-charged issue here. Do not make major decisions about relationships—especially about divorce—without good Christian counsel.

How do I know when I'm detached?

If you've removed yourself from difficult situations or people long enough to think, feel, and reflect, you are detaching. If you're aware of a growing objectivity, you are detaching. If you're distinguishing between codependent and healthy responses, you are detaching. If you're thinking for yourself and not for others, you are doing the work of detaching.

Notice no guarantees exist that detachment will arrive with calm feelings, that you always feel loving, that guilt never crops up, or that the desire to control and rescue magically vanishes!

Become attached to the Lord!

When detaching begins, you give up others' approval, and you gain independence from their manipulation and control. As detaching matures, you accept the paradox that the strength you need for this independence comes through a growing dependence on God. He is loving, kind, strong, and wise. He never takes advantage of our dependence or violates our freedom to choose. We learn to celebrate life joyfully in His perfect love.

Easy

_____

because _____

_____

_____

Difficult

_____

because _____

_____

_____

The objectivity of an affirming friend

Detaching is almost impossible to do alone. As you studied in unit 9, a friend who helps you be objective, encourages you, and models a healthy life-style is essential. Such friends won't change the way they feel and act toward you as you go through the difficult, time-consuming process of change.

Review the nine principles on detaching which you have studied in today's material. In the margin box identify which one of these nine principles on detaching will be easiest for you and which will be most difficult for you. In the margin box explain why these will be difficult or easy for you.

DAY 5

Step Three: Decide

✎ **Begin your study by today reviewing the unit Scripture. Then in the margin write the Scripture from memory. Pause and pray for wisdom about deciding—a major step from codependency to recovery.**

A person may complete steps one and two—identify and detach—without doing step three. Step three is **deciding** to act in positive, healthy ways. Today you'll better understand four important parts to deciding: making healthy choices, setting limits, surrendering control of others, and enjoying life.

Making Healthy Choices

Able to make choices

Detaching and becoming objective enables us to admit our feelings, consider our options, and make the best choices. Only then do we choose and act confidently instead of codependently. When we aren't sure what to do or when we feel pressured to react to outside expectations, we'll often avoid choices. Here is a perfect example. One day a person invited me to a party I really didn't want to attend. But I wanted to be polite (meaning, I didn't want to offend the person and risk his rejection!), so I said, "We'll see." One of my friends who heard the conversation piped up, "When Pat says, 'We'll see,' he really means 'no!' " Ouch! But how true!

Making healthy choices means speaking honestly.

Making healthy choices means speaking honestly without evasive language or double-talk. It means saying what we mean and meaning what we say. It means doing helpful things for people by honestly choosing to do so, not because we feel guilty if we don't. In a nutshell, making healthy choices means doing the right things for the right reasons!

The crucial question

The crucial question Christians must ask is: "Lord, what do You want me to do?" Once we've identified codependent feelings, thoughts, words, and actions in our lives, and detached from them long enough to understand them better, we can be confident decision-makers. With the Lord's wisdom and direction, codependents finally can take responsibility for their own lives.

- If they've been passive, they'll learn to take positive steps of action.
- If they've been driven, they'll learn to say *no* to some things, even in the face of others' misunderstanding and disapproval.
- If they've acted like saviors, they'll let others experience the consequences of their behavior without rushing in to rescue them.

- If they've acted like Judases, they build their confidence by focusing on the unconditional love and acceptance of Christ.
- If they've continued to act like children into their adulthood, they'll begin to act like responsible adults.

Setting Limits

I have a friend who uses the following analogy to describe the importance of limits.

Codependents encourage others to take advantage of them because they hope to win others' approval.

Every person is given a piece of land at birth. Codependents allow other people to take water from their property, cut down their trees, and trample their pastures. In fact, they encourage others to take advantage of their land because they hope to win others' approval by their generous acts. When their houses are gutted, their crops and pastures trampled, and their possessions all stolen, codependents finally get angry and decide to set limits. Initially, they allow no one to set foot on their property because they are guarding carefully against ever being taken advantage of again. They proceed to renovate their homes, plant new crops, and gather new possessions. When they do allow people onto their land again, it is only within limits so that they are not taken advantage of again.

Few limits

Codependents enforce few limits because they feel responsible for everybody and feel guilty about everything. But as independence and identity grow, they learn life cannot continue without limits. Limits sound like:

I will not respond to this kind of behavior anymore.

- This is what I will do. This is what I won't do.
- I will not respond to this kind of behavior anymore.
- I'm not responsible for another's happiness.
- I refuse to be manipulated.
- I'm sorry. I wish I could help you, but I don't have the time/money/energy/interest to help this time.
- I'm wondering why you said that to me. I feel angry/sad/confused/judged when you use such words.
- Now is not the best time for me to talk about this.
- I need to talk about this. When are you available to discuss it with me?

Incredible benefits

What incredible benefits come from setting limits! Instead of anticipating others' needs and jumping to rescue, codependents learn they can listen with patience, wait for others to request help, and only then make a decision regarding the request. Remember: if others want help, respect them enough to leave with them the initiative of asking for help. Then, your decision will be an objective one, not a selfish, rescuing, make-it-all-right one.

Regarding setting limits, you may be feeling: "This seems selfish! What about being a servant and going the extra mile?" Inherent in the compulsive codependent's mind is the idea, "It's all up to me. If I don't help, who will?" Here's a better question with which to struggle: Is the almighty, omnipotent, sovereign Lord able to take care of those persons you are determined to rescue? Are you so indispensable that you take God's place in their lives? The truth is, you may be hindering their own responsibility and independence by rescuing them continually. Or, you may be blocking their dependence on God to provide and protect, not to mention the possibility that you are blocking your own dependence on Him.

My sheep listen to my voice; I know them, and they follow me. I give them eternal life, and they shall never perish; no one can snatch them out of my hand. My Father, who has given them to me, is greater than all; no one can snatch them out of my Father's hand.

–John 10:27-29, NIV

 The Lord can take care of them and He can take care of you! Read the verses in the margin, and paraphrase them below.

_____

_____

_____

Setting limits means limiting ourselves! We limit ourselves to being friend, parent, spouse, and neighbor, and do not cross the line into the Savior's area!

Surrendering Control of Others

Codependents too often try to control the attitudes and actions of others by praising or condemning them. Since most people need and want acceptance, such manipulation produces results. But manipulation, even for all the right reasons, does not respect or honor others. Your "declaration of independence" should provide independence for those you love, too. Surrendering control of others means letting others know and experience the consequences of their own decisions. Rather than yelling or withdrawing to express disapproval of another's choice, say: "Your choice of words hurts me" or "This certain behavior is hurting our relationship" or "I will not trust you in this particular situation until you prove your responsibility."

Manipulation, even for all the right reasons, does not respect or honor others.

Patterns of control through praise, condemnation, anger, withdrawal, or certain expressions or gestures are used extensively against children. These patterns work for a while, but children get used to a level of manipulation, test its limits, and resist. Then adults must use more powerful measures in an attempt to control the children. And in adulthood, the children will perpetuate the cycle they know best and will treat their children in the same way.

Calm, loving discipline

Calm, loving discipline is so different from such codependent manipulation. It allows children to develop much-needed responsibility and to learn the consequences of their behavior.

 Take an extra sheet of paper. At the top, list the people you've tended to control or manipulate in your life. Then answer the question, "What would it look like if I surrendered my control of their lives back to them?" Draw a picture of this. Insert it here, and consider sharing it with your discovery group. For example, one person drew herself giving her loved ones back the keys to their lives.

Enjoying Life

You may choke here in the decision-making process. You are capable of, or learning to, make healthy choices, with appropriate limits and without controlling others in the process. But can you enjoy the results? Does it still seem too good to be true?

What do you withhold from yourself because you believe you are unworthy to have or enjoy it?

_____

What goals could you pursue if you put them in the place of the driven, compulsive desires of codependency?

_____

_____

_____

Southern California lawns can illustrate periods of emotional barrenness followed by new growth. Summer heat and drought bake people's yards and turn them brown. By midwinter, they look utterly barren and lifeless. But spring brings rain and a couple of weeks of mud! And finally, almost overnight, grass sprouts again and spreads. Life!

Many codependents are like those mid-winter yards; they're emotionally, spiritually, and relationally dry. They've seen no signs of life for such a long time. Then the refreshment of objectivity and independence begins to grow, but the grip of codependency lingers long. Substantive change seems forever out of reach. But growth is occurring, and what was barren blooms again!

The refreshment of objectivity and independence begins to grow.

Recovering codependents learn that after identifying, detaching, and deciding, they find hope, life, depth, intimacy, reality, and love! These flow from God's unconditional love and from the encouragement of healthy, loving friends.

✎ **Let's say you really enjoyed life today. What would that mean? What would you be doing just for the fun of it? Circle all that apply.**

- Go out for dinner
- Play a game
- Go to a movie
- Buy a canoe

- Take a vacation
- Laugh out loud
- Tell a joke
- Help somebody just because I want to

- Dream new dreams
- Make a friend
- Relax
- Hug my family

Who would be most surprised to catch you enjoying life today? Why?

_____

Does this sound selfish? Encouraging a guilt-riddled, overly responsible codependent to relax and have fun only brings balance and health to life. It is not selfish. Remember the wonderful advice Nehemiah gave to the newly-returned exiles? "Do not grieve, for the joy of the LORD is your strength" (Nehemiah 8:10, NIV).

✎ **Reread Jay's story on page 173 (the first page of unit 10). He describes three roles he played in recovering from codependency. As you end this unit, write below the role that best describes you today—victim, villain, or victor.**

_____

Explain why you chose that description by completing this sentence: "I feel this way because . . .

_____

_____

_____

_____

_____

**Evidences of
detachment were—**

_____

_____

_____

In the margin box write the codependent feelings, thoughts, words, or actions Jay identified in his recovery process. In the margin box, describe the evidence of detachment you find in his story.

Explain why the decisions he finally made were healthy ones.

_____

_____

Did you write that Jay identified the fact that his situation was out of control and that he had gone from being victim to victimizer? The fact that he now sees both his family's problems and his own wrong behavior is evidence that he now is practicing detachment. From Jay's identification and detachment he seems to have decided—he will go on to do the work necessary to recover.

✎ **Review this week's lessons. Find one statement in the text that helped you to understand better the codependent person(s) you love.**

Below rewrite that statement in your own words.

_____

_____

Now, find one statement or insight you wrote that helped you to understand yourself better, whether or not you identify yourself as codependent .

Below write it again, and describe how this new insight benefits you.

_____

_____

Review the memory passage. Look it up and check your memory. Then close your Bible and write the passage in this margin. What application have you made of this passage during your study of this unit? Below record your thoughts.

_____

_____

_____

_____

Notes

[1]Jay Strack, *Good Kids Who Do Bad Things* (Dallas: Word Publishing, 1993), 122.
[2]Melody Beattie, *Codependent No More* (New York: Hazelden Foundation, 1987), 58.

Learning to Grieve

> ### FEELING THE PAIN OF HEALING
>
> Mary grew up with a workaholic father and a chemically addicted mother. In her 20s she became a Christian. She seemed to grow quickly in her faith, but some things plagued her relationship with the Lord. A friend in her Bible study remarked that Mary seemed to be a driven, overly intense person. Mary's defensive response was, "The Lord wants excellence. He doesn't appreciate us being sloppy or lazy!" Later, Mary read a book on codependency. She told her friend, "Maybe a couple of things related to me."
>
> Two years later in a Bible study, one woman was very open about the hurts and fears she had struggled to overcome. Mary began to realize she had experienced the same struggles but had considered them a normal part of life. Slowly, Mary began to see her life more objectively.
>
> Today Mary is in the middle of the healing process. Sometimes she wishes she never had met that open, vulnerable woman in her Bible study because then she wouldn't have started the painful process. But she sees progress. It's slow, but it's there. (Read more about Mary on page 193.)

What you'll learn

This week you will learn—

- more about your need to heal and how to grieve over your past;
- how bargaining may begin once we replace denial with objectivity;
- healthy ways to think about anger and to act when you are angry;
- how we must grieve before we attempt to accept life again and continue to grow;
- the nature of spiritual conflict and its effects on recovery and healing.

What you'll study

Moving Through Denial	Bargaining	Anger	Grief and Acceptance	Spiritual Conflict
DAY 1	DAY 2	DAY 3	DAY 4	DAY 5

Memory verse

This week's passage of Scripture to memorize

Blessed be the God and Father of our Lord Jesus Christ, the Father of mercies and God of all comfort; For just as the sufferings of Christ are ours in abundance, so also our comfort is abundant through Christ.

–2 Corinthians 1:3,5

Moving Through Denial

For the past 10 weeks you've been dealing with the traumatic, emotional condition called codependency and its effects on the thoughts, feelings, words, and actions of yourself or those of someone you love. Recovering from a difficult past and changing a difficult present is more than a push-button, 1-2-3 process. You probably recognized this after studying the three-part process of recovery in unit 10.

As you work to implement the three parts in your life, you will deal with five very predictable stages: denial, anger, bargaining, grief, and acceptance.[1] You may move quickly through one stage and slowly through others. You may go back and forth, re-entering a stage you've already gone through as you become aware of other layers of pain. The following diagram may be helpful.

Objectivity is the door which opens to begin the grief process. *Acceptance* is the door leading out of the stages of grief and into health. In the middle of the diagram are three containers representing *anger*, *bargaining*, and *grief*. Persons don't progress to constructive anger until bargaining is finished and don't experience genuine grief until anger is spent. (This does not mean that the person does not experience anger or grief except in that phase. It only means that these emotions will be dominant during that time.)

Denial

In unit 2 you devoted a lot of study to denial. Denial prevents compulsive fixers and rescuers from developing the objectivity they need to identify and detach. Let's recap briefly some reasons why this happens.

Review unit 2 for a few minutes. What do you remember about codependents and denial? In the margin box, jot down as many reasons as you can why codependents lack objectivity and why they deny their need to see more clearly.

Perhaps your list included some of the following reasons:

1. Codependents think their families, circumstances, thoughts, emotions, and actions are normal; they do not believe that what they know as normal life actually is dysfunctional.
2. Some codependents stay so busy they don't feel their pain. Consequently, they are driven to achieve and do more but do not regard their wounds or their feelings.
3. A lifetime of blocking pain leaves codependents numb and passive. They avoid decisions and relationships where risk and rejection seem high.

Why we lack objectivity—

_____

_____

_____

_____

_____

_____

_____

4. Some codependents have decided that nothing good ever will happen, and so they withdraw from relationships. They have a very fatalistic view of life.

5. The pain of neglect or condemnation is so great for some that they deny the existence of love. They say, "Affirmation hurts, and love is painful. I can't take that."

How to Overcome Denial

Sooner or later, codependents realize they will face risks in life, whether or not they ever begin the healing process! The two lists below show the risks of either experiencing or avoiding the healing process.

Risks of the Healing Process	Risks of Avoiding the Healing Process
Dealing with buried hurt Experiencing stored-up anger Feeling deep-seated fears Learning new ways to make decisions Clearly identifying feelings Being a different person Friends and family not supporting independent thinking and healthy living	Distorted self-concept Distorted image of who God is Dysfunctional relationships with parents, siblings, spouse, children, friends, co-workers Never have a satisfactory answer to "Who am I?" question Unable to experience or express love

The level of change required to recover from codependency is not easily achieved. Among codependents, the experience below is typical.

Mary's story Mary grew up with a workaholic father and a chemically addicted mother. In her 20s she became a Christian. She seemed to grow quickly in her faith, but some things plagued her relationship with the Lord. A friend in a Bible study remarked that Mary seemed to be a driven, overly intense person. Mary's defensive response was, "The Lord wants excellence. He doesn't appreciate us being sloppy or lazy!" Later, Mary read a book on codependency. She told her friend, "Maybe a couple of things related to me." Her friend replied enthusiastically, "I've learned so much from this book, Mary. I knew you would too." Her friend's high enthusiasm made Mary wonder if the problem of compulsive rescuing had affected her more than she realized.

Two years later in a Bible study, one woman was very open about the hurts and fears she had struggled to overcome. Mary began to realize she had experienced the same struggles but had considered them a normal part of life. Slowly, Mary began to see her life more objectively. Today she is in the middle of the healing process. Sometimes Mary wishes she had never had met that open, vulnerable woman in her Bible study because then she wouldn't have started the painful process of recovery. But she sees progress. It's slow, but it's there.

The first part of the story tells how Mary avoided the healing process. In the margin box list the risks she brought on herself because she avoided that process. Look at the right column of the chart above for your answers and add additional ones of your own.

The risks Mary brought on herself—

_____

_____

_____

_____

_____

_____

Mary's risks in the healing process—

_____

_____

_____

_____

_____

There was a man who had two sons. He went to the first and said, "Son, go and work today in the vineyard." "I will not," he answered, but later he changed his mind and went. Then the father went to the other son and said the same thing. He answered, "I will, sir," but he did not go. Which of the two did what his father wanted?

–Matthew 21:28-31, NIV

The last part of the story tells about her beginning the healing process, which also is "risky business." In the margin box list the risks she took in recovering. Look at the left column of the chart on the previous page for your answers, and add additional ones of your own.

Some people seem to jump into the healing process full-steam ahead, ready and willing to do the difficult work needed to recover from codependency. But in most people's lives, the Lord uses a combination of events and people over time. The "lights come on" slowly. For years some persons hear important truth about recovery and still never see their need. That's denial! Only objectivity begins to overcome the power of denial.

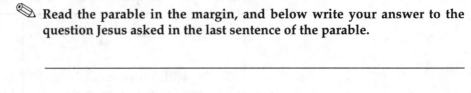 **Read the parable in the margin, and below write your answer to the question Jesus asked in the last sentence of the parable.**

_____

_____

You, or the codependent person you love, may have made a thousand promises to change without following through with any new behaviors. The second son in the parable was like that. You may have talked yourself out of even trying new thoughts or behaviors because (1) you don't need to change, or (2) you don't believe you can change. Better to do what you know to do than to talk about doing it.

How does Jesus' teaching from this parable and your answer above apply to you and to beginning the healing process?

_____

_____

Whether or not you believe you're capable or worthy or strong enough to change, _act_ like you're capable enough, worthy enough, strong enough. Seeing _is_ believing, and you may not believe in your possibilities for growth and change until you see them in your own life. Don't talk yourself out of your own healing and recovery before you've given the Lord a chance to make them real in your life!

➦ **Find the unit memory verses in your Bible and mark them. Begin now to memorize them.**

SUMMARY STATEMENTS

- Denial, bargaining, anger, grief, and acceptance are the five predictable stages of the grief process.
- We will face risks in life, whether or not we ever begin the healing process.
- The level of change required to recover from codependency is not easily achieved.
- Don't talk yourself out of your own healing and recovery before you've given the Lord a chance to make them real in your life.

Bargaining

From a close friend Christy learned about dysfunctional families. She realized that those painful effects were at work in her own life. Desperate for relief and healing, she blurted out, "Then how can I get my father to love me?" Her friend explained, "That's the wrong question, Christy. It's not up to you to make your father love you. He's responsible for that. It's up to you to become a healthy, growing independent adult who depends on the Lord for love and acceptance, whether or not your father ever loves you."

Bargaining means offering some change in ourselves in order to get other people to change.

When those in entangled relationships begin to identify their compulsive feelings, thoughts, words, or actions, they often try to solve the problem by bargaining. Here, bargaining means offering some change in ourselves in order to get other people to change. We make such statements as:

- I'll be a better husband to her so she'll trust me more.
- I'll spend more time with him so he'll understand my thoughts.
- I won't nag him anymore, and then he'll love me the way I want to be loved.
- I'll keep the house clean, and our family will be happier.
- I'll get a job, and then she won't think I'm dependent on her alone.
- I'll be more affectionate, and he'll love me more.

Bargaining does show the beginnings of responsibility. If you read the first part of each sentence above, you saw that the intentions stated there were good ones. But these statements still lack objectivity because they indicate the codependent still is believing the best about the other person. What's wrong with that? Believing the best about others usually is good. But when months and years of irresponsible, manipulative behavior prove that someone is dysfunctional, then believing the best is naive and foolish. It is denial.

Living in reality

Codependents need to abandon the vain hope that people who have hurt and abused them will change and will begin giving them what they need. Doesn't sound very spiritual, does it? But it is. Giving up means admitting what is true now, not what *might* be true if circumstances and people eventually change. Giving up is abandoning the idol of pleasing others to win acceptance, love, and self-worth. Giving up all these notions is the beginning of an act of worship to God.

When you give up, when you stop bargaining and look truth in the face, you may become very angry with the ones who lied to you, used you, and hurt you so deeply.

Moving Past Bargaining

Persons in the bargaining stage of recovery cling to the hope of being loved by the ones who have hurt them deeply even though they are very angry at these same individuals for not loving them. This stage feels terribly confusing. One day the bargainer is bitterly angry; the next day the bargainer feels ashamed and guilty for being angry.

You can learn to deal with anger—and possibly advance past the bargaining stage—by assigning appropriate responsibility for offenses. A man once told me that for three-and-a-half years he had clung to the hope that his alcoholic parents would meet his deepest needs. Then he realized that they probably never would love him the way he wanted to be loved. He finally gave up on his unrealistic hope. He's healthier and happier now—free from the pressure of the bargain he wanted to make.

Affix the right responsibilities to the right persons for the right reasons.

Assigning appropriate responsibility means you affix the right responsibilities to the right persons for the right reasons. Instead of taking all the blame, guilt, and anger on yourself, you can begin to feel appropriate hurt and anger which leads to appropriate forgiveness and healing.

Watch for Wide Swings

You've seen the sign on large truck trailers, "Caution! This truck swings wide when turning." Recovering codependents need to carry a card saying, "Caution! This person swings wide while healing."

It's true. These early stages of overcoming codependency bring wide swings in feelings and behavior. As the cap is taken off their emotions, codependents may feel more hurt, anger, and fear than they ever thought possible. They may become afraid of the intensity of those emotions and put the cap back on until their courage returns to try again. Conversely, they may feel more joy, freedom, and love than ever before. They may cry for the first time in years and feel loved and comforted for the first time ever. They may ask hundreds of questions and may be vulnerable to bad advice because so much is so new.

Imagine I'm your friend, and we've been talking about these wide swings in feelings and behaviors. I say to you:

"These wide swings are inevitable and understandable. Don't try to clamp down on them. Such surges of emotion will happen after a lifetime of repressing and denying them. New behaviors will seem mechanical, even frightening, until they fit you better. No, you won't swing wide the rest of your life! After a while, your emotions and actions won't be as extreme. You'll know you are controlling them instead of feeling they are controlling you. This hard work you're doing is vital! And each step brings spiritual, emotional, and relational healing."

In the margin box write how you would respond to me after you hear these words.

I would say to you—

_____

_____

_____

_____

Take a Chance on Forgiveness

The ability to forgive others often shows how honestly and at what depth we've experienced reality. Perhaps Cindy's story will help illustrate.

After a conference, Cindy asked me, "When you talked about forgiveness tonight, I was confused. I've forgiven my father for all he did to me. I know I have. And I've worked through all of my feelings about his abuse and neglect, but I still hate him. What's wrong with me?" We talked a bit more, and I replied, "Cindy, you've forgiven your father, but you haven't yet felt all the pain you repressed. Your forgiveness goes only as deep as the pain you've allowed yourself to feel." I explained the two things necessary to forgive other people genuinely.

O Jerusalem, Jerusalem, who kills the prophets and stones those sent to her! How often I wanted to gather your children together, the way a hen gathers her chicks under her wing, and you were unwilling.

–Matthew 23:37

Woe to you, scribes and Pharisees, hypocrites! For you clean the outside of the cup and of the disk, but inside they are full of robbery and self-indulgence.

–Matthew 23:25

My soul is deeply grieved, to the point of death; remain here and keep watch with Me.

–Matthew 26:38

He came to the disciples and found them sleeping and said to Peter, "So you men could not keep watch with me for one hour?"

–Matthew 26:40

1. **You need to feel the pain of the offense.** Repressing those feelings to lessen their power to hurt you will only keep you from forgiving. You'll believe you've forgiven the offender, but the resentment is safely harbored inside. On the other hand, if you are open and honest about the pain, you will know exactly why you're forgiving the other person. The old saying goes, "Forgive and forget!" But "Remember and still choose to forgive" is much more powerful and cleansing.

Jesus was very honest about His feelings, yet He continued to offer salvation and forgiveness. Read the four Scriptures in the margin. All were spoken by Jesus. Jesus felt and expressed the four basic emotions of anger, fear, hurt, and sorrow. Under the four Scriptures write the basic emotion Jesus was expressing in the verse.

Jesus felt anger and sorrow at those who rejected Him, fear at the imminent crucifixion, and hurt that His followers abandoned Him. We need the same levels of honesty and the same commitment to forgive which He modeled.

2. **You need to feel deep, daily appreciation that Christ has forgiven you.** Your forgiveness of others reflects the grasp of your own forgiveness. The more you realize you've been completely forgiven of all bitterness, pride, malice, and neglect of others, the more you will be able to forgive others.

➥ **Read the following Scripture from Ephesians. Read it out loud several times in this way: Preface it with your name; replace the two "one another" phrases with an individual's name you have forgiven or need to forgive. Continue this activity until you feel you've finished what God would have you do right now. Finish this time of forgiveness with a prayer of confession and praise to God.**

Be kind to one another, tender-hearted, forgiving one other, even as God in Christ also forgave you (Ephesians 4:32, NKJV).

SUMMARY STATEMENTS

- Bargaining means getting other people to change by offering some change in ourselves.
- When you stop bargaining and look truth in the face, you may become very angry.
- Repressing feelings to lessen their power to hurt you will only keep you from forgiving.

DAY 3

Anger

Anger—what a difficult issue about which to write! But understanding anger is essential to grieving and recovering. Here's a brief summary of what we Christians know about anger.

- All anger is not wrong, nor is all of it right. Some expressions of anger are good and wholesome, but many expressions of it are sinful.

- Feeling angry and acting angry are two different issues entirely. Feeling anger as a natural response to pain and threat in our lives is not wrong. But some people see such anger as sinful. They'll either deny it exists or express it indirectly and inappropriately (such as passive-aggressive behavior mentioned in unit 4).
- The active expression of anger can be either righteous or unrighteous. It can either hurt or heal. If anger prompts a person to stop being manipulated, to be independent of others, to state his or her case clearly and calmly instead of withdrawing or attaching, then the response to that feeling is good and healthy. If, however, anger prompts revenge and/or withdrawal, then the response is destructive.

Two classic passages about anger appear in the margin. We are taught to feel anger but not to express that anger unrighteously. James warns us not to let our expression of anger hurt others. Evidently, then, anger can be destructive or constructive.

Destructive anger seeks to harm another person through angry outbursts, seething rages, and revenge. *Constructive anger* results either from being harmed by another, like the harm done in tangled relationships, or becoming aware of injustice, as when Jesus threw moneychangers out of the temple.

Too many Christians believe anger is wrong. In the process of healing they try to skip from anger to grief because grief seems more acceptable. Just know this—you'll never thoroughly do your grieving until you come to grips with your anger. Codependents have difficulty with anger because the backlog of repressed anger from past offenses compound and complicate the process of forgiving present offenses.

> **Be angry, and yet do not sin; do not let the sun go down on your anger, and do not give the devil an opportunity.**
> –Ephesians 4:26-27
>
> **Let everyone be quick to hear, slow to speak and slow to anger; for the anger of man does not achieve the righteousness of God.**
> –James 1:19-20

Study the drawings above. In the margin box write your own summary of the truths the drawing teaches about dealing with anger.

Codependents struggle to cope with current anger effectively because they carry such a backlog of repressed anger. Only after a long period of honest reflection (detaching) and expression of repressed anger are they able to stay current with anger—dealing with each offense as it occurs. I hope your

---

The secrets to dealing with anger are—

_____

_____

_____

_____

_____

summary included the importance of removing old repressed anger and of quickly and appropriately expressing and disposing of current anger.

✏️ **Listed below are many reasons codependents stop their healing process at the phase of expressing anger. As you read through the list, check any that apply to you and how you feel about acknowledging hurts or anger in your life.**

❑ 1. "All anger is wrong and sinful, and being angry makes me a bad person."

❑ 2. "If any problem exists in this relationship, it must be my fault!" Codependents often feel a misguided loyalty to people who abuse or hurt them; they feel guilty for feeling anger toward their abusers.

❑ 3. "Oh, that's OK, I don't mind. It doesn't hurt me. I'm used to it. She couldn't help herself." Such statements excuse the offender.

❑ 4. "If I express anger, I fear the other person's anger, rejection, ridicule, withdrawal, and wrath."

❑ 5. "Now that healing has begun and I am finding a measure of warmth and closeness in formerly tangled relationships, the risk of losing it again seems too great. Being angry is not worth it!"

❑ 6. "Patterns of denial still are so strong. I struggle just to admit to problems; certainly anger doesn't seem an acceptable response to problems."

❑ 7. "Without objectivity, I find only good in others and never see their harmful, selfish, negative, or abusive acts for what they are. Or if I do, I rationalize them away."

❑ 8. "I have been taught that my parents or spouse have authority over me and that I must submit to them unconditionally." In some families, submission offered by one member becomes a weapon of manipulation and condemnation used by others.

Now that you've identified some of your responses to anger, detach a moment and reflect on those responses. In the margin box describe how you feel about your attitudes toward anger.

You even may have felt anger at yourself for not allowing yourself to be angry about the hurts and wounds in your life. Tread carefully through this part of your healing process. It's important to find a safe environment of unconditional love and acceptance while you learn to be honest about the effects of repressed anger in your life.

Exposing hurts and anger is awkward, difficult, and time-consuming. Your discovery group, or some other recovery group, may be your safe place. Be sure you are surrounded by support as you deal with your anger; you'll never believe relationships can be untangled until you spend time in relationship with people who accept you, correct you in love, and grow with you.

✏️ **Close today's study by writing a prayer. Ask God to help you find your repressed anger and be free of it so that you may be honest about today's anger.**

_____

_____

_____

About anger I feel—

_____

_____

_____

_____

_____

DAY 4

Grief and Acceptance

- "I feel like a little girl who never was loved by her father, and I feel I never will be."
- "I had such hopes and dreams for our marriage, but now it never will be what I hoped it would be. I feel so empty."
- "Our darling little girl was so cute and so loving. Drugs have ruined her life and almost ruined ours, too. We'll just have to make the best of it now."

Such words are spoken when anger is spent and grief has begun. When the container of anger drains to a trickle, a sense of loss begins to take over. We grieve as if death has touched us—because it has. We had something—innocence—and it was taken away. Or we realize we needed something from a certain person very badly—love and acceptance—but we'll never have it. Intimacy, warmth, and laughter die, and we feel loss, hurt, and emptiness.

Janice's story

Janice was progressing through this process of healing and grieving. She described her grief to me like this. "I was sitting in church one day when I had the strangest feeling. I felt like I was going to cry and throw up at the same time. I thought, 'I'm losing it! I'm really going crazy!' After the service, I realized I was grieving. I guess I'd bottled up my emotions for so long that when they came out, it was in a strange way."

Janice grieved for several months. She felt sad and lonely but knew that she was moving through normal grief. She wasn't going crazy. She was becoming healthy!

Doing the Work of Grief

Have you ever lost close friends or family members to death? Do you remember feeling shocked that they were gone, angry that they were taken, and filled with sorrow for days or weeks? Do you remember a kind of numbness settling in while the hurt eased away? Do you remember finally accepting the finality of their death and discovering, to your surprise, that life still could reach you with its wonder and moments of joy? If you remember anything like this, then you are remembering the work of grieving.

How long does grief last? For every person and every situation, it's different. Grief does not follow rigid formulas. But it must include the stages you're studying in this unit.

✎ **Remind yourself of the stages of grief. On day 1 you examined a chart similar to the one below. Rely on your memory to name the doors and the stages of the grief process. Look back at day 1 to check your work.**

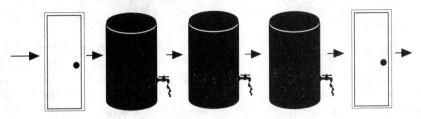

When recovery is under way, grieving must be done.

- Give yourself the freedom to feel loss as long as it takes.
- As with every step of recovery, stay close and feel the support of someone who'll affirm the hard work you're doing and provide the perspective of where you're going.

catharsis–n. (to cleanse) a purification that brings about spiritual renewal or release from tension. (Webster's)

Months may go by. Your emotions will vary. Sometimes you'll feel the **catharsis**—the release of past hurts—through grieving. The relief inside will feel wonderful and freeing. Some days you'll be incredibly sad. You'll feel emotional over things that never affected you before—a kind act toward you, a crying child, a new disappointment in your tangled relationship.

All of this is normal and healthy. It is part of being a real person with real feelings in real relationships. If the question "Why?" continues to plague your time of grief, I encourage you to say the unit memory verse over and over until the Lord Himself is speaking to you those words of grace and comfort.

✎ **Pause now to review the memory verses. Write them out on a piece of paper, and place it an an envelope. Take a break from your studying; during your break reflect on God's comfort. Try to determine at least three reasons to praise Him for His comfort. When you return to your study, record your thoughts here.**

1. _____

2. _____

3. _____

An old Greek proverb says, "To learn is to suffer." When I read it, I thought of a movie in which a very shy but very brilliant medical researcher finds himself caring for chronically ill mental patients. Over time, he discovers a group of them apparently frozen in non-responsive bodies and is plagued by the thought that they are alive and aware inside. He experiments with new drugs until first one man, Leonard, and then the entire group is "awakened." After 30 or more years of exile in an unexplained illness, these people finally are free.

They revel in their freedom. They rediscover the joys, as Leonard puts it, of the simple things: work, play, family, life. But the drugs begin to fail, and the bodies of these apparently normal people begin to tremble, have seizures, and eventually go rigid again. The doctor is stricken with guilt for opening them up to life but having it slip away again. And he is stricken with grief because Leonard is his friend. During a terrible seizure, with body control and coherent speech almost gone, Leonard's last words to the doctor are, "Learn! Learn! Learn!" "Make sense of it; help someone else by it; continue your life and your learning because of it," he seems to say.

How that kind doctor suffered! He never solved the puzzle of these patients' terrible illness or of their brief awakening. But the peace to continue seeking and working returned. No wonder the best news in grieving comes from God's Word. God gives us the reassurance that His peace will protect our hearts and minds in Christ Jesus.

In the margin read the Amplified version of Philippians 4:7.

Healing Through Acceptance

Finally, peace and calm will come to you, even if understanding lags behind. The bargaining, anger, and grief—each in time and in turn—will be exposed and expressed. You will be able to be objective about life—its good and bad, its righteousness and wickedness. And you'll find you're uncomfortable with simple, easy answers, knowing they just don't work. More important than clear-cut answers is the new depth in your relationship with the Lord and with people. You'll discover new perspectives on life, new values, and new life-styles.

You won't feel driven to accomplish every goal because you'll have a new set of priorities based on—

- a healthy blend of independence from others; and
- a new dependence on the Lord.

 Are these currently your priorities, or would they represent a new set of priorities for you? Circle your answer: Current   New

In the margin box list the benefits in your life of these priorities, whether they already are at work in your life or whether they will be a new growth experience for you.

Throughout this study, you may have been a student of, not a sufferer from, codependency. But balancing independence among others with dependence on the Lord is every Christian's task!

The $64,000 Question

Mark once asked me, "When I get through grief and find acceptance, will I experience total freedom from the effects of my codependency, or will I always be scarred by it?"

I thought for a minute, then told Mark about an incident in my life years ago. One New Year's Eve, when I was a boy, my father bought and shot off beautiful fireworks for my family. I was safely parked under my mother's arm on the front porch, but the fireworks were so exciting. My father lit a Roman candle, and I ran down the steps, grabbed that cylinder, held it straight up, and waited for the colors to blast into the sky! Instead, it backfired and burned

And God's peace (be yours, that tranquil state of a soul assured of its salvation through Christ, and so fearing nothing from God and content with its early lot of whatever sort that is, that peace) which transcends all understanding, shall garrison and mount guard over your hearts and minds in Christ Jesus.
    –Philippians 4:7, Amplified

Benefits of these priorities—

_____

_____

_____

_____

_____

me inside the sleeve of my winter jacket. Like it was yesterday, I remember crying buckets of tears as my parents quickly checked my injury. It was much worse than they expected. I was rushed to the hospital, and they learned my forearm was covered in third-degree burns.

For months after, the burns required constant medical attention. I remember wrapping and unwrapping dressings, applying medicine, visiting the doctor, crying at night. My exuberant sprint to join in the fireworks fun brought agony to my whole family.

Finally, scar tissue formed, and the burns needed less and less attention. I still have a sizable scar on my arm, but I rarely think about it until I catch someone staring at it when I'm wearing short-sleeved shirts.

The moral to my story: Though the scar remains, the pain has been gone for years, and the consuming attention I gave the injury is just a memory.

What I wanted Mark to know is this: codependency is a deep wound requiring lots of attention for a while. The emotional bandaging and medication hurt, but if the treatment is a good one, scar tissue will form gradually as the healing continues. A scar probably will remain, but the pain gradually will be replaced by healing and health. It's not pleasant, but it's essential if the wounds of codependency are to heal.

Pause now to pray about any grieving or acceptance you need to start or finish in your life. Commit these processes, as you've committed your life, to the Lord.

Practice your memory verses by writing them in the margin from memory.

SUMMARY STATEMENTS

- When the container of anger drains to a trickle, a sense of loss begins to take over.
- Many persons going through grief have thought they were losing their minds.
- Give yourself the freedom to feel loss as long as it takes.
- Finally, peace and calm will come to you.

DAY 5

Spiritual Conflict

The stage of acceptance requires you to accept one more thing—part of your struggle to recover will be a spiritual struggle. You've been reminded throughout this study of your spiritual resources to conquer codependency and of spiritual truths to guide your personal and relationship growth. But Satan, the deceiver and enemy of our souls, violently opposes God's will and God's love for you. Satan will fight you every step of the way, primarily through deception and distraction.

All Christians experience spiritual conflict; all are under attack from Satan's lies and schemes against them. But people who have been hurt in dysfunctional families particularly are susceptible to deception and must be alert and aware during this conflict. The apostle Peter spoke powerful truth when he said: "Your adversary, the devil, prowls about like a roaring lion, seeking someone to devour" (1 Peter 5:8). For this reason, in every unit I've asked you to pray about what you are learning and how you are applying it in your life. I have asked you to pray and reflect so that Satan cannot snatch new truths from you and use them against you.

Today, you'll review five principles about spiritual conflict. You need to accept these for your recovery and for the good of your life with Christ.

Principle 1: Acknowledge Spiritual Conflict as a Reality

Jesus didn't mince words when He rebuked the religious leaders who opposed Him. Read His words in the margin. He recognized the source of the opposition they were posing to Him.

> **You are of your father the devil, and you want to do the desires of your father. He was a murderer from the beginning, and does not stand in the truth, because there is no truth in him. Whenever he speaks a lie, he speaks from his own nature; for he is a liar, and the father of lies.**
>
> **–John 8:44**

The Book of Daniel in the Old Testament and Ephesians in the New Testament document the reality of spiritual conflict. Jesus Himself made many references to Satan's purposes. He did this in the verse you just read and in other verses like John 10:10: "The thief comes only to steal, and kill, and destroy."

Satan frequently accomplishes his destructive purposes through the neglect, abuse, and manipulation which takes place in many families. The hurtful relationships in such families effectively steal any sense of self-worth. The behaviors there kill the ability to experience healthy separateness and intimacy and destroy the joy of life Christ desires for us. The evil present in such families is not limited to the destructive acts and absence of nurturing in the families. The greatest damage comes in the family members' thoughts and beliefs. Those thoughts and beliefs distort their perception, blind them to truth, and perpetuate the cycle of tangled relationships.

The damage done in families today is an extension of the conflict Satan orchestrated in the garden of Eden. He promised happiness and God-likeness to Adam and Eve. What he delivered to them was chaos; God's judgment and their sorrow followed. The spiritual battle is real.

Principle 2: Acknowledge Christ's Ultimate Power and Authority

Though demonic forces are strong, Christ is much more powerful. I cannot offer any explanation more compelling than the Bible's own. Read in the margin the apostle Paul's words about Jesus.

> **[He is] far above all rule and authority and power and dominion, and every name that is not only in this age, but also in the one to come. And He [God] put all things in subjection under His feet, and gave Him as head over all things to the church, which is His body, the fulness of Him who fills all in all.**
>
> **–Ephesians 1:21-23**

Paul also assured the believers in Philippi of Christ's supreme authority:

Therefore also God highly exalted Him, and bestowed on Him the name which is above every name, that at the name of Jesus every knee should bow, of those who are in heaven, and on earth, and under the earth, and that every tongue should confess that Jesus Christ is Lord, to the glory of God the Father (Philippians 2:9-11).

Christ's death conquered both sin and the power of the enemy:

When He had disarmed the rulers and authorities, He made a public display of them, having triumphed over them through Him (Colossians 2:15).

 What difference does it make in your life knowing Christ is all-powerful and has been given God's own authority?

_____

_____

In the margin box describe a time or times when during these past 10 weeks you have seen evidence of Christ's power.

> **I have seen Christ's power through—**
>
> _____
>
> _____
>
> _____

For our struggle is not against flesh and blood, but against the rulers, against the powers, against the world forces of this darkness, against the spiritual forces of wickedness in the heavenly places.
—Ephesians 6:12

Principle 3: Learn the Schemes of the Enemy

A soldier knows he must discover as much as he can about the strategies of his enemy. This is crucial preparation for battle. Read in the margin how Paul by describing Satan's strategies prepares us for this battle.

Satan and his troops know they lack the power to capture men and women by direct and honest warfare, so they use deception and schemes:

- They lie to us.
- They try to fill our minds with confusion and destructive thoughts.
- They use the hurts in dysfunctional families to twist, distort, and crush the hearts of children.
- They continue to build blockages to our growth.

 We are helpless until we become aware of their plots. If you can think of examples from your life of these schemes of Satan, jot them beside the appropriate statement above. Pause to pray after each example you write. Ask the Lord to be your strength.

Principle 4: Fortify Yourself with Truth and Love

Applying this principle takes more than knowing it; it takes your time and commitment to study the Scriptures. Growing Christians will tell you about experiences when they have read familiar verses in the Bible and gained new insights and applications from it they'd never considered before. That's because God's Word comes alive in the lives of those who love God. So when you find powerful truths in Scripture, know they will make you strong with God's strength.

Satan uses common deceptions based on shame, fear, confusion, hate, blame, introspection, and denial, but the Bible speaks clearly and powerfully to them all. Lack of forgiveness is a major strategy the enemy uses to prevent our growth. But consistently finding love, honesty, and knowledge in Scripture equips us to find forgiveness for ourselves and to offer it to others.

 Read again all the Scriptures used in this unit. When you find one which deals with the "common deceptions" listed above, write beside it which of the deceptions it addresses. Take all the time necessary to do a thorough review. Then celebrate the truth and love of God's Word!

Principle 5: Pray for Wisdom, Insight, and Strength

Ask, and it shall be given to you; seek, and you shall find; knock, and it shall be opened to you. If you then, being evil, know how to give good gifts to your children, how much more shall your Father who is in heaven give what is good to those who ask Him!

–Matthew 7:7,11

In the verses printed in the margin Jesus taught us about prayer. A wise pastor once said that these verses do not promise certain answers to our prayers. They promise that where there is asking, there is answering; when there is seeking, there is finding; when there is knocking, doors are opened.

We would not always have chosen for ourselves the answers or openings God gives, but His gifts are good and perfect. They are based upon His wisdom and love. Prayer enables us to tap into the resources of God. We need His wisdom and power to help us fight our battles.

When you battle codependency, you feel very earthbound, and life weighs on you every moment. Sometimes we need His wisdom and power even to know how to pray. Paul reminded us:

For though we live in the world, we do not wage war as the world does. The weapons we fight with are not the weapons of the world. On the contrary, they have divine power to demolish strongholds. We demolish arguments and every pretension that sets itself up against the knowledge of God, and we take captive every thought to make it obedient to Christ (2 Corinthians 10:3-5, NIV).

✎ **Prayer is your primary weapon in your battle with Satan! Describe:**

your purposes in prayer: _____

_____

your expectations in prayer: _____

_____

persons you regularly pray for: _____

_____

persons you have difficulty praying for: _____

_____

your most meaningful experience with prayer: _____

_____

As codependents continue to grow in their independence, self-esteem, and healthy relationships, the characteristics of codependency gradually will subside. Eventually, much of their lives will be characterized by new freedom and authentic love in their families and friendships. And they no longer will consider themselves codependent!

Recovering persons will remember what they've been through. They will be understanding and compassionate toward those who are in the healing process.

The greatest sign of recovering persons growth and new life is that they can help others conquer their codependency—without becoming entangled with the other persons problems. Helping a friend or a relative continue the process of gaining health can be an exciting adventure. Both probably will gain greater insights into the love of God, the freedom and new motivation we have in Christ, and the perception, love, and separateness we experience as we grow.

✎ **Review this unit. Find one statement in the text that helped you to understand better the codependent person(s) you love.**

Below rewrite that statement in your own words.

_____

_____

_____

Now, find one statement or insight you wrote that helped you to understand yourself better, whether or not you identify yourself as codependent.

Below write it again, and describe how this new insight benefits you.

_____

_____

_____

Review the memory passage. Look it up and check your memory. Then close your Bible and write the passage below. How have you made application of this passage during your study of this unit? Below record your thoughts.

_____

_____

_____

Notes

[1]Many books describe this process, or a process very similar to it, for recovering from such things as divorce, grief, addiction, or codependency, or for learning to live with such things as chronic pain, terminal illness, or irrevocably broken relationships. Most acknowledge the pioneering work of Elizabeth Kubler-Ross as the beginning point for understanding this process. See her book *On Death and Dying* (New York: MacMillan Publishing, 1969).

New Ways of Relating

Case in point

FROM EXCUSING TO FORGIVING

Beth and Tim had been married four years before she finally admitted to herself that Tim was a workaholic. Tim worked 60-hour weeks and still brought work home. Beth had accepted it, even encouraged it, because he was doing so well at work. But four years was enough, and the Christmas visit back home was what opened her eyes.

Beth had noticed before how Tim's father stayed busy with projects around the house, even when they visited. Looking objectively at her father-in-law, she thought, "He's a workaholic, too! No wonder Tim's the way he is. And his dad neglects his mom the same way Tim neglects me." That flash of insight helped Beth make sense of Tim's work habits; she felt better, and she understood him better.

In the months that followed, she tried to excuse Tim's preoccupation with work, but finally realized that excusing him and forgiving him were not the same. Excusing him meant doing nothing. Tim was the same and Beth's reactions to him were the same. Forgiving him freed Beth to love him enough to confront him with the effects of his workaholism on their relationship. (Read more about Beth on page 217.)

What you'll learn

This week you will learn—

- how to begin redeeming your relationships with the people who have hurt you;
- how to review the importance of healthy independence, healthy identity, and healthy responsibility;
- four important suggestions for relating to the person who has hurt you;
- the parallel between recovery from codependency and authentic Christianity;
- patience for the Lord's timing, and the certainty of the Lord's healing in your recovery.

What you'll study

Redeeming a Hurtful Relation-ship	Balanced Respon-sibility	Respon-ding in a Healthy Way	Authentic Christian-ity	Waiting on the Lord
DAY 1	DAY 2	DAY 3	DAY 4	DAY 5

Memory verse

This week's passage of Scripture to memorize

For I am confident of this very thing, that He who began a good work in you will perfect it until the day of Christ Jesus.

–Philippians 1:6

Redeeming a Hurtful Relationship

Other units already have dealt with most of the issues we'll examine in this final unit. In fact, before unit 12 is complete you'll review the entire process of discovery in *Untangling Relationships*.

The course map also will help you review and remember the many ideas and insights about codependency you've been discovering. Turn to the back cover and review it now. You will fill in the details of the course map as you review the recovery process.

✎ **DISCOVERY REVIEW—UNIT ONE. Recall the roots of codependency by filling in the left arrow on the course map below.**

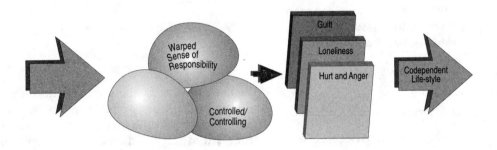

"How do I relate to the one who has hurt, neglected, used, and condemned me?"

Since codependency begins in dysfunctional families, one of the most pressing issues for the person emerging from it is: "How do I relate to the one who has hurt, neglected, used, or condemned me?" Admitting that a problem exists often is the most difficult part of the healing process.

The key choices you must make include: Will you continue to let another person determine your behavior—in effect, be your lord—or will you be responsible and make your own decisions? Whether you'll love that person unconditionally is a key decision you must make for yourself.

Idolatry and bondage

The desire for acceptance and intimacy is so strong, you've done everything you could to make that person happy. You've called those efforts to please and to control other people's responses love. But it's not. It's idolatry—allowing another person to be your lord. And it's bondage—allowing another person to determine your thoughts, feelings, words, and actions.

✎ **DISCOVERY REVIEW—UNIT TWO. What is the first characteristic of codependency we studied? Add it to the first misshapen circle on the course map above.**

The first evidence is a lack of objectivity. People who finally are being objective reveal the deep-rootedness of their lack of objectivity. They make statements like the following:

- "I've lived to please my father all my life. He said, 'Jump!' and I didn't even ask, 'How high?' I just jumped as high as I could as often as I could. He praised some of what I did—just enough to keep me jumping—but not enough to give me a sense of security."

- "My mother always could get me to do anything she wanted. She rarely yelled, but she could get a powerful message across with the expressions on her face."
- "I did everything I could to get my daughter to stop eating. I begged, I threatened, I hid food, I sent her to classes, I screamed at her, I avoided her. I can't tell you how many nights I lay awake trying to think of ways to get her to stop. I thought she was the one who was hooked, but I was an addict, too. I was an addict to her performance and happiness."

✎ **Read the verses in the margin. Reprinted below are the questions posed in the verses. To evaluate your own healing process answer the questions. Give examples to support your answers.**

Am I seeking the favor of others? _____

_____

Am I seeking God's favor? _____

_____

We need objectivity about our relationship with that other person, regardless of how difficult or painful it might be. Don't bargain with that person any more to give you the love and acceptance you've tried so hard to get. Turn from that idolatry and accept your significance and worth from Christ alone. Give Him your devotion and allegiance. Then, and only then, will you be able to respond in the way the Lord wants to the one who's hurt you. You can do this in objectivity, healthy independence, forgiveness, and unconditional love. You'll either be a slave to others or a slave of Christ, but you cannot be both.

✎ **Finish this statement from unit 9, day 2: ". . . any time people try to find their security and worth from someone or something other than God, their efforts are . . .**

_____."

Did you answer "idolatry?" Scripture severely condemns idolatry because it harms people and dishonors the Lord. The idolatry of codependents—striving to please, rescue, fix, or control others—is rooted in deep wounds from their relationships with "other people." Persons with a compulsion to fix, control, and manipulate need comfort, compassion, and insight, as well as repentance. They don't need condemnation; they usually heap plenty of that on themselves.

Practice your objectivity once again. Decide who is the most difficult, yet closest, person in your life. In the margin box write that person's name. Then based on that relationship, respond to the questions and statements in the margin box.

✎ **What cues does this person give you when he or she likes something you've said or done?**

_____

_____

Therefore also we have as our ambition, whether at home or absent, to be pleasing to Him.
–2 Corinthians 5:9

For am I now seeking the favor of men, or of God? Or am I striving to please men? If I were still trying to please men, I would not be a bond-servant of Christ.
–Galatians 1:10

Objectivity practice—

My most difficult person

_____

How do I feel when he/she disagrees with me?

_____

_____

When disagreements occur, I change my feelings or behavior to suit him/her.
❏ Yes ❏ No   Why?

_____

_____

How do I change for him or her?

_____

_____

How do you respond when you detect these cues of approval?

_____

In the margin box mark your typical response to his or her criticism of things you've said or done.

 When this person tries to manipulate your feelings, thoughts, words, or actions, how do you respond? What effect does this manipulation have on your relationship?

_____

_____

List specific choices or actions you still need to make to be independent from the hurt and manipulation imposed by this person.

_____

_____

Remember, only One is worthy of our ultimate affection and obedience. If we put others in His place, if we try to please others to gain love and worth, then we are idolatrous people.

➡ **Find the unit memory verse in your Bible and mark it. Begin now to memorize it.**

SUMMARY STATEMENTS

- "How do I relate to the one who has hurt, neglected, used, and condemned me?" is a pressing question for those who seek recovery.
- Allowing another person to control your life is idolatry.
- God desires for you to experience objectivity, healthy independence, forgiveness, and unconditional love.

When he/she criticizes I respond with—

- ❏ sarcasm
- ❏ abusive words or actions
- ❏ withdrawal
- ❏ feeling of being needed
- ❏ silence
- ❏ appreciation for feedback
- ❏ acceptance of the criticism as truth
- ❏ depression
- ❏ other _____

_____

DAY 2

Balanced Responsibility

I once explained how personal responsibility was a key part of healing from codependency, and I heard a woman exclaim: "But that seems so selfish, like telling people to look out for number one instead of loving and serving others!" The very thought of taking responsibility for one's own life can seem selfish, especially for someone who always has defined life in terms of rescuing others, fixing others, and controlling others.

 DISCOVERY REVIEW—UNIT 3. On the course map at the top of the next page fill in the middle misshapen circle with the second of the perceptions and behaviors characteristics we studied.

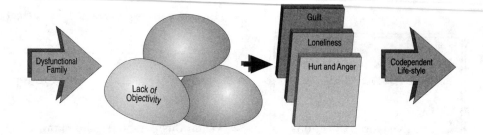

Find a codependent, and you'll always find an overly responsible person who looks out for the needs of other people but neglects his or her own responsibilities. The circle represents a warped sense of responsibility.

Let each one examine his own work, and then he will have reason for boasting in regard to himself alone, and not in regard to another. For each one shall bear his own load.

–Galatians 6:4-5

Notice in the margin how Galatians 6:4-5 speaks of a warped sense of responsibility. Dysfunctional families practice just the opposite of the healthy separateness the Scripture passage describes. Rather than taking responsibility for their own actions, family members allow the anger and manipulation in the family to become the excuse for their own behavior. Instead of independence, the family members are at others' mercy because they attempt to win acceptance. Instead of healthy identity, family members evaluate life based on their performance and on others' respect for what they achieve. Instead of healthy responsibility for themselves, they slavishly care for others and expect others to care for them in the same manner.

 DISCOVERY REVIEW—UNIT 3. Reread "One Family's Story" in day 1 on page 53. Determine at least one action Susan and Rob could take to achieve the three healthy characteristics listed above. Use the chart below to record your answers.

	Susan	Rob
Healthy Independence		
Healthy Identity		
Healthy Responsibility		

Extreme responses

The problem with Susan and Rob—as with all codependents—is that they were living and responding in the extremes. They began with no independence at all. Their father reared them as if they were robots. Then Susan responded in the opposite extreme. She became rebellious rather than independent. Rob filled her spot by continuing to be a slave to his father's whims. Both Susan and Rob need to decide what they need to do, what they need to be, and for what they need to be responsible. They need to make those choices for themselves, rather than reacting to their controlling father.

One woman, learning about the dysfunctional past of her family, suddenly realized she was practically indistinguishable from her mother. "We both like the same kind of houses, the same kind of furniture, the same kind of clothes. I vote like she does. We have the same hobbies. People say we laugh alike; come to think of it, we even married the same kind of man!"

I asked how she felt when she and her mother disagreed. She reacted quickly: "That doesn't happen very often. I feel guilty and usually change my mind because she's almost always right. She respects my opinion—well, she respects my opinion if I agree with her."

The Bible and Control

 Which verse in the margin teaches that Christians are to have self-control? Draw an arrow from here to that verse.

Which verse in the margin teaches that Christians are to be controlled by God? Draw an arrow from here to that verse.

> Walk by the Spirit, and you will not carry out the desires of the flesh.
> –Galatians 5:16
>
> The fruit of the Spirit is . . . self-control.
> –Galatians 5:22-23

The Bible instructs us to submit to government and authority, to employers, and to each other (see Romans 13:1; Colossians 3:22-23, and Ephesians 5:21). But submission is very different from control. Submission is a *voluntary act* motivated by a desire to please God in our relationships with others. Control, on the other hand, is demanding, manipulative, and self-seeking. It usually crushes another's spirit—in the case of Rob—or sparks another's rebellion—as it did with Susan. True submission is winsome and reasonable and is based on what is best for others according to God's plan.

Submission is a choice, and in Christian relationships of all kinds, it should be evident. The Bible says "Honor Christ by submitting to each other" (Ephesians 5:21, TLB).

✎ DISCOVERY REVIEW—UNIT 4. Fill in the final misshapen circle on the course map on page 212 with the third primary characteristic of codependency.

Being controlled or manipulated by "the other person" has deeply wounded you; so has trying and failing to control that person's abusive or addictive behavior. Moving beyond the control issues of codependency keeps you on the path to healing and recovery.

✎ In day 1, you identified a person with whom you have (or had) a difficult relationship. Pause now and pray for that person. Ask God to love him or her unconditionally through you. Then, answer the two questions in the margin box.

Responsibility—

What is your responsibility in your relationship to this one who has hurt you?

_____

_____

_____

What is his/her responsibility to you?

_____

_____

_____

Basically, your responsibility is to claim or to own your own feelings, thoughts, words, and behaviors, and to stop blaming that other person for your problems. You are responsible before the Lord to act appropriately toward that other person. Continuing to behave in a rescuing or controlling manner is not treating the other person in a healthy or godly manner. If you are treated badly, responsibility means legitimately feeling the hurt and anger, choosing to forgive that person, and taking appropriate steps to insure that you are not hurt again.

I would prefer to respond—

to being manipulated by guilt by . . .

____

____

____

to being manipulated by comparison . . .

____

____

____

This difficult person in your life is responsible for his or her own feelings, thoughts, words, and behaviors. Your job is not to force responsibility on this person. You can model responsibility, but you cannot make another person act responsibly.

✎ **DISCOVERY REVIEW—UNIT 4. In a chart on page 72 you described your response to two situations in which you were manipulated. Review the chart. In the margin box describe how you would prefer to respond today to two similar situations.**

➧ **Practice memorizing the unit memory verse. Thank God for the healing He has begun in your life. Praise Him for His promise to complete what He has begun.**

SUMMARY STATEMENTS

- A warped sense of responsibility is a key part of codependency. Assuming personal responsibility is a key part of recovery.
- The very thought of taking responsibility for one's own life can seem selfish for someone who has always defined life in terms of rescuing, fixing, and controlling others.
- Healthy independence, healthy identity, and healthy responsibility are three Christ-honoring characteristics we develop in recovery.

DAY 3

Responding in a Healthy Way

Your relationship with your difficult other person probably has been characterized by some or all of the following: rescuing, outbursts of anger, displaced anger, compliance, withdrawal, guilt, hurt, loneliness, pity for him or her, and pity for yourself.

A sense of loyalty probably contributed to your inability to see the relationship objectively. You may have decided that negative thoughts or emotions are signs something is dreadfully wrong with you.

✎ **DISCOVERY REVIEW—UNIT 5. On the course map atop the next page fill in the lower box with the missing emotional result of codependency. Read the unit title on page 87 if you need to check the answer.**

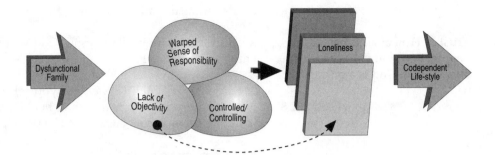

Perceptions lead to more pain

Lack of objectivity can lead to more hurt and anger by—

_____

_____

_____

_____

On this version of the map we have connected the lack of objectivity to the "hurt and anger" box. Think for a moment about the possible sources of hurt and anger. In the margin box describe how a person's compulsion to fix, rescue, and control could cause him or her to experience hurt and anger.

Now your objectivity is growing. You've learned about repressed emotions and begun the difficult task of exploring those feelings. Your source of security is changing. You're learning to make your own decisions. All of these are good things.

You may have described any of many situations in the margin box. For example, lack of objectivity leads many of us to experience pain and anger needlessly because we believe others are rejecting us when they don't bow to our unrealistic expectations or when they simply are caring for themselves.

 DISCOVERY REVIEW—UNIT 6. If you stop this healing process, you'll be stuck in the top box of the course map. Label that box now in the map above.

Remember what you learned in day 2 of unit 6? Guilt motivates! But for your recovery to succeed, healing must motivate. Read carefully the following suggestions for how to relate to the other person. As you study these four suggestions, be thinking, as you have the past two days, of the same difficult person and of your relationship with him or her.

1. Set Limits. Decide how much communication and contact you need to have with that person. Determine which issues you will discuss and which ones you won't. Decide these before you see or talk with this other person, and you'll be much less likely to succumb to his or her pressures of manipulation or condemnation. This relationship has been on the other person's terms, perhaps for your whole lifetime, but you can now define your side of it in your own terms. This isn't selfish. Remember, you're the one trying to live in reality. You are making your decision. Setting limits means choosing to please God according to His definition of real life.

Live in reality

 What limits do you need to set in your relationship with this person?

_____

_____

_____

Perhaps you listed such items as amount of time to spend together, topics of conversation, or limits on the way he or she can talk to, or treat you.

Read the Scripture in the margin. God will be your refuge as you seek to set limits which honor Him.

2. Know How Much to Say. Do you tell that person about your difficult, disturbing relationship with him or her? Do you elaborate your dark thoughts, your bitterness, hatred, and fear? The principle is:

- Express yourself fully to God.
- Express yourself appropriately to the other person.

Your relationship with God is secure. He can bear the force of your questions, your agony, your anger, and whatever else wells up within you. That is why the psalmist calls Him a "refuge."

But carefully weigh your words with others. Don't determine what you say by what the other person wants to hear. You may tell the other person a little or a lot. The other person may or may not notice changes in your life or ask you about those changes. The verse in the margin from Ephesians reminds us that the words God will honor are: (1) spoken according to another's need; (2) to help others become stronger; and (3) to benefit those who listen to you. Quite a checklist! Using it before speaking will force you to choose your words carefully and to speak unselfishly out of godly motives.

Reread this section until your heart believes it. Then, write in the margin box a prayer asking God for the courage to express yourself fully to Him. Ask for the strength to speak only messages to others according to the teaching in Ephesians 4:29.

You need to be aware of something many newcomers experience in recovery. They begin to experience some healing and become overly anxious to share their insights. Sometimes they realize how sick their relationships are and get in a hurry to fix them. One woman in a group wanted badly to fix her relationship with her mother. She told her mother all that she was learning about how dysfunctional their family had been. Rather than respond as this woman had expected, her mother was severely offended and hurt by her daughter's comments. The result was further alienation from her mother.

As you progress in your recovery you will learn to set better limits in your relationships with your "difficult others." One young man said he had developed a list of "safe" topics for when he goes home to his family. He has learned to limit his discussion to those topics because he knows he will be attacked otherwise. He is protecting himself by his caution and preparation.

Some counselors suggest that—in cases where maintaining some distance is possible—persons work on their own recovery for one year before seeking to tell their family about issues involved in recovery. Beware of expecting too much too fast. You may have taken years to come to the awareness you now have. Allow others the time they need.

3. Expectations. Don't expect to set limits perfectly. Don't expect to always know how much to say. Be kind to yourself. You're living a new life compared to the past. Don't expect the other person to say, "Well, now I completely

---

Trust in Him at all times, O people; Pour out your heart before Him; God is a refuge for us.

–Psalm 62:8

When you talk, do not say harmful things. But say what people need—words that will help others become stronger. Then what you say will help those who listen to you.

–Ephesians 4:29, ICB

Dear Lord,—

_____

_____

_____

_____

_____

_____

understand. Thank you so much for explaining codependency to me. I'll change today and never treat you the same way again. And I'll also understand why you're not treating me the same way." You realize how impossible that sounds as you read it here. But don't be surprised when part of you really expects to hear these words and becomes angry or grieves when you don't hear them.

Realistically, you can expect to hear:

- "I'll change this time." Just remember, he or she has said those words hundreds of times.
- "Let's talk about this." This talk isn't about understanding your new insights and commitments to recovery; it's about convincing you that you're wrong, misguided, or confused so you'll return to being the docile, compliant puppet you've always been.
- "It's all your fault!" Denial of personal responsibility is a common characteristic of manipulative people. Remember, you struggle with it, too, when codependency has you in its grip.
- "I'm so sorry." If this is said, it means: "I'm sorry you feel that way. I've never done anything to hurt you, but you are certainly hurting me." He/she will seek quick, superficial forgiveness from you so the relationship can revert back to its dysfunctional status quo.
- Or, you may hear nothing. The other person may withdraw from you—an old weapon from the dysfunctional arsenal—to shake your recovery.

Look again at the list of responses above. In the margin box describe which of these responses you are expecting to hear or already have heard.

Initially, you may expect your other person to say "I'm so sorry," to repent, and to comfort you. Realistically that probably won't happen. Offenders often redouble their assaults when codependents begin to change the way they relate to the offender.

Realistic expectations are vital to your recovery and your continued relationship with this person. Don't expect resolution and reconciliation soon, if ever. Let your identity in Christ and His lordship fill your thoughts. The other person may never change, but you can. Do it, and be independent, healthy, and realistic.

4. Excusing or Forgiving? Read the unit story again on page 208. Here is the rest of the story. When Beth finally forgave Tim, she was able to confront him about the effects of his workaholism. Tim responded with anger and defensiveness but agreed to read a book and to talk with their pastor. He gradually recognized his addiction to work and performance. Together, he and Beth experienced healing of their relationship and a greater intimacy. It all began with objectivity, forgiveness, love, and courage.

Beth discovered that understanding the background of Tim's workaholism was not the same as forgiving Tim for the hurt his workaholism inflicted on her and their marriage. When a person first learns about codependency, a giant flip-flop often occurs regarding the one who has hurt or abused. The other person goes from being all-good—she can do no wrong—to being all-bad—she can do no right. As time goes by, however, a growing objectivity allows the codependent to see the other person between those extreme poles of good and bad.

Of these responses—

I expect to hear . . .

_____

_____

_____

_____

I have already heard . . .

_____

_____

_____

_____

Tim and Beth experienced healing of their relationship.

Out of unconditional love for you and me, Jesus willingly died on the cross for sins He did not commit. Forgiveness acknowledges the reality of the offense, the full weight of the wrong, and the consequence of that wrong, and then chooses not to hold that offense against the other person. That's not excusing hurtful behavior; it's forgiving it. Perhaps this summary of forgiveness will help:[1]

Forgiveness is not

Forgiveness does not mean . . .
. . . just forgetting.
. . . the other person was right.
. . . you give the other person permission to continue hurting you.
. . . the other person can do it again without any consequences.
. . . pain vanishes instantly.
. . . the other person controls you.
. . . you are weak.

Forgiveness is

Forgiveness means . . .
. . . you are more interested in understanding the dynamics of the past than in blaming someone for what happened.
. . . you no longer regard the offending person as indebted to you.
. . . you are more interested in moving ahead than in being controlled by the past.
. . . you can deal with today's feelings of hurt and anger honestly and openly.

 Take a separate sheet of paper. Rewrite the two paragraphs above, "Forgiveness does not mean . . ." and "Forgiveness means . . .." Insert specific names and details about your relationship with the other person. After those two paragraphs, list any insights you've gained about yourself, the other person, your relationship, and your future. Insert it here in your book and consider sharing with your discovery group.

SUMMARY STATEMENTS

- Recovery brings a growing objectivity, an expression of repressed emotions, a changing source of security, and the ability to make your own decisions.
- Setting limits means choosing to please God rather than another person.
- Express yourself fully to God, and express yourself appropriately to the other person.

DAY 4

Authentic Christianity

A person who becomes aware of accumulated hurts is self-absorbed for a while, like someone with a broken leg. The person goes to the doctor, gets X-rays, considers surgery, acquires a cast, lives with pain for days, and walks with difficulty for weeks. Finally, the cast is removed, but the weak leg muscles still need special attention. Is all this time and attention narcissistic and selfish? No, it is required for recovery. The choice is not between pain or no pain. The choice is between the endless pain of continuing bondage and the pain of recovery, leading to Christ-honoring life and joy.

Time is required for recovery just like—

_____

_____

_____

_____

 What other analogies can you make to the time needed for healing? In the margin box describe what the healing time of recovery is like.

Unless we are honest about the hurts and wounds of our past and our relationships, we'll never really know God. We'll never really know His love, forgiveness, and strength. We'll never have those essentials to propel our growth and healing. The reason Jesus attracted people was His honesty about the real issues of their lives. He never minced words or offered superficial, quick-fix solutions.

 DISCOVERY REVIEW—UNIT 7 (Days 1 and 2). Fill in the middle box on the course map with the missing emotional result of tangled relationships.

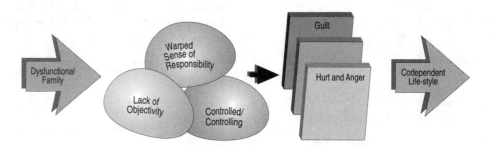

Many active codependents are too busy managing other peoples' lives to feel lonely.

We experience the loneliness of codependency in different ways. Some of us drive others away with our controlling behaviors. Others only have relationships with dysfunctional people who cannot meet our need for love. But many active codependents are too busy managing other peoples' lives to feel lonely. In fact, many find that when we enter recovery we experience great loneliness. We begin to see that we have been wearing masks to gain approval. We realize that our relationships have been based upon projections of who we wanted others to be rather than on reality. Remember, real relationships occur when we have the courage to walk through the loneliness of recovery. Codependency is a lonely, isolated, joyless life. Recovery from it often feels even more lonely—for a while.

I've watched many people at this turning point in recovery. I've seen them mustering the courage to take the next scary steps. I've also watched those so frightened, bitter, or blind that they refuse to go on.

Love your enemies, and do good, and lend, expecting nothing in return; and your reward will be great, and you will be sons of the Most High; for He Himself is kind to ungrateful and evil men.
–Luke 6:35

Through the past 11 units, you've grasped, I'm sure, how slowly and painfully codependents begin the process of addressing their deep wounds. Healing affects their most fundamental motivations. Instead of rescuing, giving, and serving in order to be appreciated and valued, they learn to love and give without demanding an appreciative response. They learn to practice the authentic Christianity about which Christ spoke. In the verse in the margin, read His words.

Here are some changes that mark the move from codependency to authentic Christianity. You'll quickly recognize that each statement begins with one of the primary or secondary characteristics of codependency.

• Instead of a *lack of objectivity*, codependents develop a clearer perception of God, themselves, and others.

- Instead of a *warped sense of responsibility*, they understand the limits of their accountability; they give because they want to, not because they feel they "ought" to.
- Instead of being easily *controlled* by others, they sense the strength of a clear identity in Christ. Instead of *controlling* others, they value them enough to let them make their own decisions.
- Instead of repressing *hurt and anger*, they are honest about their feelings and deal with these feelings appropriately.
- Instead of feeling recurring *guilt* and shame, they experience more forgiveness, peace, and contentment.
- Instead of *loneliness*, they develop authentic relationships based on honesty, respect, and love.

The changes of healing

✎ DISCOVERY REVIEW—UNIT 8. Review the four components of change you studied in day 1 on page 141. Describe the changes that have occurred in your life since beginning your discovery group. What changes have occurred in . . .

. . . your perception of God? _____

_____

. . . your perception of self? _____

_____

. . . your perception of others? _____

_____

. . . your perception of your life-style? _____

_____

In the margin box describe one new insight about yourself and about the healing process you gained from the exercise above.

Does this unit's memory verse apply to these new insights? Explain your answer.

_____

_____

New insights—

A new insight about myself

_____

_____

_____

A new insight about the healing process

_____

_____

_____

_____

Though no one can go back
and make a new start,
anyone can start from now
and make a brand new end.[2]

✦ Pause now and thank God for the gift of change and the hope and healing it brings. Ask Him to give you a "new start" and the desire for "a brand new end."

DAY 5

Waiting on the Lord

Have you ever been filled with such anticipation for what a new day would bring that you were unable to sleep? No matter how wonderful a new day is, the turning of the earth and the coming of dawn are fixed and cannot be hurried. The sky doesn't instantly turn from pitch black to noon. First, glimmers of light nudge the dark—light so faint you question whether it is light at all. Then, the sky lightens slowly before the actual sunrise makes its stately, glorious appearance over the horizon. Several hours pass before the chill leaves the air and you feel warmth from the sun.

Spiritual and emotional growth are very much like the dawn—slow and gradual, but certain!

 DISCOVERY REVIEW—UNIT 9. Fill in the course map below. Indicate the three healthy characteristics which replace the characteristics of codependency. Record them in the perfect circles at the bottom of the course map.

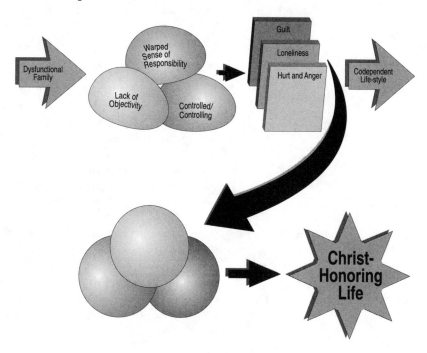

**My soul waits for the Lord,
More than the watchmen for the
morning.**

–Psalm 130:6

Many codependents who become convinced recovery is possible want complete relief from their pain and want it immediately. Their cry is the same the prophet heard and recorded: "Watchman, how far gone is the night?" (Isaiah 21:11). The endurance necessary for healing and real change is difficult enough to test the strongest faith. We need to express the psalmist's prayer printed in the margin.

Remember, the dark has its purpose in God's hands, just as does the light. The light of recovery reveals those things hidden in the darkness, and many of those things are deep wounds and hurts. Increased light (objectivity) eventually brings healing, but pain paves the way for the healing. This pain is not regressing or losing the battle. As the light shows new insights and new pain, hope for more healing occurs. That is progress.

 DISCOVERY REVIEW—UNIT 10. From the course map on the previous page label the pathway toward healthy characteristics and a Christ-honoring life with the three-step process for healing from codependency.

Requires vigilance

The ancient watchman who waited on the city's walls for dawn was not passive. His job was vigilance—to warn of attack or the approach of an enemy. He had to be prepared, active, sharply observant, and ready to act.

Your wait on the Lord's timing for your healing is not passive, either. You are responsible for being prepared, observant, and actively defending your life against the attack of the enemy.

DISCOVERY REVIEW—UNIT 11. Lest you forget the reality of the enemy's attack, find the principles for engaging in spiritual conflict you studied in day 5. List them to the right of the pathway you just labeled on the course map.

Take heart

The night of codependency may seem even longer once hope begins to grow in front of you. You may feel that you now know the way but can't seem to get on the way. And you're discouraged. Please take heart! You are not alone. You've come to this point in your journey surrounded by fellow pilgrims in your discovery group.

Pause here and list in the margin the names of your discovery group members and leader. Pray for each one by name; celebrate the recoveries you've observed. Thank God for the gift of your discovery group experience.

And you've come to this point in the Lord's real and powerful compassion for you. He is acting to change your heart and mind, and He will take all the time necessary to do a thorough job of it!

**Let us press on to know the
LORD. His going forth is as
certain as the dawn; and He will
come to us like the rain, like the
spring rain watering the earth.**

–Hosea 6:3

So don't expect too much too soon, but do expect what Paul described when he said: "It is God who is at work in you, both to will and to work for His good pleasure" (Philippians 2:13). You can be sure He is at work, slowly, patiently, and certainly. His care for you took Him to Calvary, and He has not changed His mind about your worth. You can be sure His light will outshine the darkness of your codependency and that He will bring you healing, hope, and health.

✎ **Review this week's lessons. Find one statement in the text that helped you to understand yourself better or the codependent person(s) you love.**

Below rewrite that statement in your own words, and describe how this new insight benefits you.

_____

_____

_____

Review the memory passage. Look it up and check your memory. Then close your Bible and write the passage below. How have you made application of this passage during your study of this unit? Below record your thoughts.

_____

_____

_____

Congratulations for completing *Untangling Relationships*. You deserve a big pat on the back. By now you realize that overcoming the life-long habits of codependency is a long-term task, but you have done important work in this process. You will use again and again the principles you have learned in your study.

All of us who have worked to bring you *Untangling Relationships* pray for you. Our prayer is that this study will help you develop a life of wisdom and strength in the service of our Lord Jesus.

Perhaps you have come to this point in your recovery journey and you are asking "What do I do now? I've seen some of the problems but I need to do more." *Conquering Codependency: A Christ-Centered 12-Step Process* is the companion volume to *Untangling Relationships*. *Conquering Codependency* will guide you in applying the 12-Step process to your recovery. (Send orders or inquiries for *Conquering Codependency* to Customer Service Center; 127 Ninth Avenue, North; Nashville, TN 37234; call 1-800-458-2772; or visit your local book store. Ask for item 7203-73.)

_____

Notes

[1]From Tim Sledge, "Forgiving the People Who Have Hurt You," unit 10 in *Making Peace With Your Past* (Nashville: LifeWay Press, 1992), 177-183.
[2]Carl Brand, quoted in Barbara Johnson, *Pack Up Your Gloomees in a Great Big Box, then sit on the lid and laugh!* (Dallas: Word Publishing, 1993), 26.